APPLIQUÉ
BASICS

FLOWER
WREATHS

Located in Paducah, Kentucky, the American Quilter's Society (AQS) is dedicated to promoting the accomplishments of today's quilters. Through its publications and events, AQS strives to honor today's quiltmakers and their work and to inspire future creativity and innovation in quiltmaking.

EDITOR: HELEN SQUIRE
BOOK DESIGN/ILLUSTRATIONS: CASSIE ENGLISH AND MICHAEL BUCKINGHAM
COVER DESIGN: MICHAEL BUCKINGHAM
PHOTOGRAPHY: CHARLES R. LYNCH AND JOSEPH BUCKLEY

Library of Congress Cataloging-in-Publication Data
Buckley, Karen Kay
      Appliqué basics: flower wreaths / Karen Kay Buckley
                 p.   cm.
      Includes bibliographical references.
      ISBN 1-57432-730-5
      1. Appliqué--Patterns. 2. Quilting--Patterns 3. Flowers in art. 4. Wreaths in art.
      I. Title: Flower wreaths. II. Title
TT779.B77   1999
746.46'041--dc21   99-048652
                                                CIP

Additional copies of this book may be ordered from the American Quilter's Society, PO Box 3290, Paducah, KY 42002-3290 @ $21.95. Add $2.00 for postage and handling.

2nd Printing

APPLIQUÉ BASICS

FLOWER WREATHS

Karen Kay Buckley

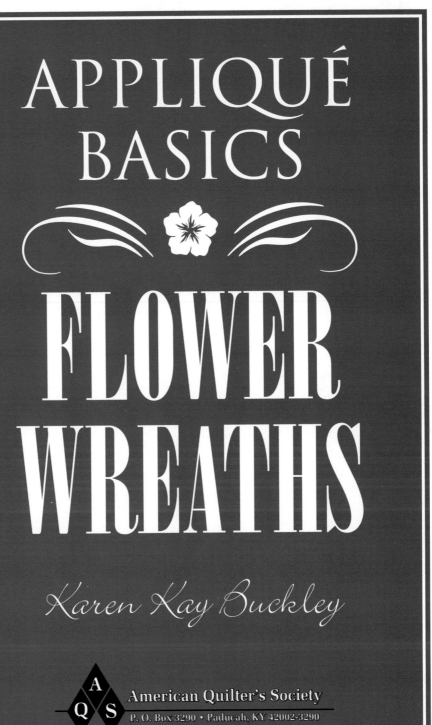

American Quilter's Society

P. O. Box 3290 • Paducah, KY 42002-3290

Contents

FLOWERS & FRIENDS, by Annie P. Johnson, Littlestown, PA
(details shown here and throughout the book)

Introduction

After making a Baltimore Album quilt and teaching Baltimore Album classes for eight years, I wanted to challenge myself and my students to do something beyond Baltimore. I began designing blocks to teach different techniques and different appliqué methods. I wanted each block to have several different types of dimensional leaves or flowers. A student of mine, Peg Myers, is a photographer and quilter with an interest in insects. We lovingly call her the "Bug Lady." She started me thinking about the possibility of putting an insect on each block. It was a challenge, but it sure was fun. When I was designing the Orchids & Bluebells block, my husband Joe and I went to the Internet to search for an orchid. We found an amazing website with about 30 color pages of orchids. Toward the end of the site, there was a photograph of a moth along with an explanation that the moth pollinates the flowers. So, I decided to put a moth on the orchid block. Everything just seemed to fall into place. The more blocks I designed, the more challenging and fun it became to find just the right bug for each block.

There are many ways you can set the blocks from this book. Before you decide on layout and design, ask yourself the following questions: *Does the finished size matter? Does it have to fit a bed or a specific area on a wall? Do you like a horizontal or vertical layout? Do you prefer a diagonal layout? Do you like sashing between the blocks? Do you like the blocks set side by side? Is the idea of a center medallion appealing?*

One of the first decisions you must make is whether the blocks will be set horizontally, vertically, or diagonally. This decision may determine how you trace the pattern onto your background fabric. In some cases you may just need to position the bug or insect in a different direction, but doing that will have no effect on the wreath.

Study the quilts in the gallery for some ideas. It is easy to get caught in a rut, so I encourage you to try something new. If you always place your blocks on a horizontal layout, try a diagonal layout. If you always use sashing between your blocks, try it without sashing. I have made numerous quilts with a diagonal setting, but had never placed the blocks side-by-side. I usually like sashing between my blocks. When I designed FLOWERS AND FRIENDS TWO, I decided to try a diagonal setting with no sashing. I loved it and will do it again. With each new quilt I attempt something I have not done before. It makes life, and my quilts, much more interesting. Trying new things can be frustrating, but it is always worth it.

Karen Kay Buckley

SECTION
1

Basics

Supplies

Choosing Fabrics

I am often asked how I make fabric selections. I have taken art classes and read several books on color and color theory, which have been helpful. But when choosing fabric for a quilt, I often start with a multicolored theme fabric which is rarely used in the quilt but gets me started and helps me focus. I first choose a background fabric, then look for fabrics that match the theme fabric and contrast well with the background fabric. That does not mean they have to be the same colors as the theme fabric. The use of various tints, shades, and tones of the colors in the theme fabric will make your quilt more interesting.

Selecting a Fabric

The fabric you choose to appliqué should contrast with the background fabric. Consider beige prints, black, navy blue, plaid, light green, sky fabrics, gray prints, and soft large prints for your background. You may also choose a background of pieced blocks which can dramatically affect the look of the quilt. You might get some ideas by looking at the Gallery starting on page 135.

Caring for Your Fabrics

Pre-wash all your fabrics to remove the sizing and make sure the fabric is colorfast. Once the sizing is removed, the fabric is softer and easier to handle when turning under seam allowances. When washing medium and dark fabrics, place a scrap of muslin in the washer with the fabrics. If the muslin is discolored after washing, treat the fabric with Retayne® to set the color. There are other products and methods that can be used for setting the color in fabrics, but I have found that Retayne® provides the most consistent results.

If the fabric in your stash has been washed but not tested for colorfastness, there is a quick and easy way to test it. Cut a small scrap from each fabric you plan to use. Place each scrap on a piece of muslin and spray with water. After the fabric has dried, remove one piece at a time from the muslin. If there is discoloration on the muslin, that fabric should be treated before using it in a quilt.

The makers of Retayne® also offer Synthrapol®, a product that can sometimes remove excess dye when a dark color migrates into a lighter color on a completed quilt. I have saved a couple of quilts with this product. The people at Pro Chemical, where Synthrapol® is made, recommend you keep the quilt wet and follow directions on the bottle. Even though they cannot guarantee individual results, I have been pleased with the product's performance.

Sewing Supplies

Needles

You will need several types of needles for the projects in this book. For the appliqué stitch, John James Sharps, size 10 or 11, are recommended. Since there are embroidery stitches on each block, you may also need an embroidery needle. To stuff the stems with yarn on the Heard It Through the Grapevine block, you will need a tapestry needle because of its blunt point. Size 18 usually works well, but the size you need depends on the thickness of the yarn.

The only parts of the blocks sewn on the machine are the bumblebee and dragonfly wings. Metallic thread and iridescent thread are good choices for the wings. If metallic or iridescent thread breaks while machine stitching, try using a metallic needle or Metafil® needle. Try your regular sewing machine needle before purchasing a specialty needle, since there is such a small area to be stitched with special thread.

Scissors

You will need good fabric scissors, paper scissors, and embroidery scissors. A pair of good fabric scissors is a wise investment. My favorites have serrated edges that grip the fabric and make cutting easier and more accurate.

Sandpaper or Sandpaper Board

Sandpaper or a sandpaper board helps hold fabric in place while you trace patterns. Place the sandpaper or sandpaper board grain side up on a table. Place your fabric on the sandpaper. When you trace around a template, the sandpaper grips and secures the fabric, making the template easier to trace. Sandpaper boards are available on the market, but you can also make one by removing the clip from an inexpensive clipboard and gluing a piece of sandpaper to the board. The board keeps the paper flat and secure, making it easier to use.

Batting

In addition to the batting needed for the middle of your quilt, you will need some very small pieces for stuffing some flowers, leaves, and grapes. Cotton batting is recommended because polyester batting can beard through to the surface of your fabric. Cotton batting will not beard.

Pins

Silk pins are great for securing appliqué shapes to background fabric. They are thin and sharp and secure the fabric so that it does not shift as you work. Place pins in from the back of the piece you are appliquéing. This keeps the thread from catching on the pins as you stitch; I learned this little tip from Nancy Pearson.

Template Plastic

You may want to make some of your appliqué patterns from template plastic. There are several kinds on the market that work well and are usually sold in sheets or by the roll.

Freezer Paper

Freezer paper may also be used to make appliqué templates. Refer to page 16 for more information. Some brands of freezer paper adhere to the fabric better than others. Reynolds Wrap® freezer paper, which can be found in most any supermarket, always gives good results.

Templar®

My favorite method of turning under seam allowances on appliqué is to use Templar, a heat-resistant plastic, and spray starch. You can read about this method on page 14.

Thicker heat-resistant plastic is available, but can be difficult to cut. Accurate templates are essential to the success of this method, and that is why I recommend Templar.

Starch

Apply spray starch to the seams prior to pressing over heat-resistant plastic templates. You may need to experiment with different brands of starch. Magic Sizing works great! The starch will add some stiffness to the seams, but does not leave any thick residue, which can make stitching difficult.

Stencil Brush or Cotton Swabs

Cotton swabs and stencil brushes are great tools for applying spray starch to seam allowances. You will find more information about this technique on page 14.

Permanent Markers

Permanent markers will be used to add embellishments to your blocks. Some markers look like they have thin tips, but when the tips touch fabric, the pigment bleeds out and creates large, fat lines. Test the marker on a scrap of fabric before marking the actual block. I prefer Pigma™ brand markers. There are several colors available, but black and brown are the ones used here.

The pens come in a variety of thicknesses: 01 (finest), 03 (medium), and 05 (thickest). The size you choose depends on the width of the line you need. You may want to have one of each thickness on hand to achieve just the right look.

Rotary Cutter, Board, and Ruler

Rotary cutting tools are used very little in the appliqué portion of the blocks, but they are great for trimming blocks to the desired size after the appliqué is complete.

Supplies

Ruler Squares

These can be used for cutting the background squares and for squaring up the completed block.

Plexiglas Square

I cut a lot of 16" squares for background blocks, but my largest ruler square was 15" x 15". I went to the local hardware store and had them cut a Plexiglas square 16" x 16". It was inexpensive and saves time during the cutting process since re-measuring is no longer necessary.

"Window Template" from Plexiglas or Matte Board Squares

When working with dimensional appliqué, the background square can become distorted. Allow for this distortion by cutting your background fabric larger than the finished block size. When the appliqué is completed, trim the block to size.

A window template cut from Plexiglas or matte board is the perfect tool for squaring up dimensional blocks. I tried using a ruler square to trim the blocks, but the ruler did not lie flat because of the dimensional shapes on the blocks.

Hardware stores, glass-cutting shops, or framing studios can cut a window template from Plexiglas or matte board. Plexiglas is harder to cut and is more expensive. A framer can cut a piece of matte board for a few dollars. The window template should have a center opening of 14½" x 14½". This includes the seam allowance. The outside edge can be cut to 16" x 16" for cutting the background fabric into squares so one tool can be used for two jobs.

After the appliqué is complete, center the window template over the block. Measure and mark around the 14½" square opening. Remove the template and cut on the lines with a rotary cutter, ruler, and board, or scissors. With ¼" seams, the finished block size will be 14" x 14".

Fabric Markers

To mark the right side of fabric, use white or gray chalk pencils, silver pencils, white pencils, Saral® paper, or washout markers. The marker you choose depends on the fabric you are marking.

Any marker that will be used on the right side of fabric should be tested to be sure it washes out. Heat from ironing can set a mark in the fabric permanently so if you plan to iron over any mark prior to washing, you need to test for heat setting. To test, mark a corner of fabric, iron over the marked line, then wash the fabric. If the mark does not wash out, try another type of marker and test again.

A mechanical pencil can be used to mark the back of your fabric when tracing around a template because it has a fine, sharp point.

Transfer Paper

Drawing a pattern on background fabric is easy to do with transfer paper. Saral® brand paper comes in packages of five sheets, each a different color. It can also be purchased on a roll. A package of five color sheets is a good choice because no matter what background fabric you select, one of the colors will show clearly. Saral® paper on the roll works well for marking borders.

You can find Saral® paper in some quilt shops, in the wood-working section of some craft stores, or by mail order from suppliers advertising in quilting magazines and catalogs.

Appliqué Thread

For appliqué, my favorite thread is Mettler® fine embroidery 100% cotton 60/2. Mettler® makes many different kinds and thicknesses of thread. Look for the spool with the green printing on the ends. Be sure to test threads for colorfastness before using.

Mettler® 60/2 comes in a wide variety of colors and is so fine it gets lost on your fabric. To determine the best color match, take a small section of thread and place it over your fabric. Never place the entire spool of thread

over the fabric to make this decision because it can be deceiving. If you cannot find a good match, try gray. There are several shades of gray that work well on many fabric colors including blue, green, mauve, and brown.

Because the thread is fine, work with about 18" of thread on the needle. If the thread is too long, it will fray and break.

Piecing and Gathering Thread

There are several dimensional appliqué methods that require gathering. Use 100% cotton 50/3 sewing thread for gathering and piecing. It holds a pieced seam and is strong enough to take the pressure of gathering. Quilting thread also works for gathering.

Metallic or Iridescent Thread

Metallic and iridescent threads are used to create the veins of the bumblebee and dragonfly wings. I prefer Sulky®, because it is smooth and seems to break less often in my sewing machine. Some metallic thread has nubbies and breaks easily when machine sewing.

Perle Cotton Thread

The daisy stitches in the forget-me-not flowers in Pansies and Other Posies were sewn with perle cotton, size 8. Two strands of embroidery thread could be substituted if you do not have perle cotton.

Thread Bag

I use and love a thread bag designed by Pat Campbell. Its clear plastic windows make it easy to see the thread colors. There are small holes in the area above the thread that allow you to pull one strand of thread through from each spool. The thread stays in the bag, and you just pull on the tail to remove the length you need.

As I began using the Mettler® 60/2 thread and collecting all of the colors, I started filling my thread bag. I now have all the colors, and my bag is full!

Yarn

Yarn is used to stuff stems and for some insect bodies. Try working with a four-ply yarn. However, if you have a thinner weight, like baby yarn, double it, and it will work just as well.

Wool yarn comes in eight-yard skeins and is frequently found in the same department as embroidery thread. It is used the same as embroidery thread, but because of its thickness, it creates a different texture. You can substitute regular embroidery thread if you cannot find wool yarn.

Fusible Web

Fusible webs bond two pieces of fabric together. Always use press cloths with fusible web. If the web melts onto your ironing surface or iron, they could be ruined. Place a press cloth on the ironing surface and another on the fabric. If the web melts, it will melt into the press cloth, not onto the iron or ironing surface.

Glue Stick

Glue may be necessary to temporarily hold things in place. A water soluble glue stick is recommended since you want the glue to wash out.

Beads

Beads are used to embellish some of the flowers. In all but one block, size 11 seed beads are used. On the Tulips, Thistles & Tobacco Flowers block, size 6 seed beads are used. French knots can be substituted for beads.

Ribbons

Some flowers are made with ribbon. The type and width of ribbon needed for each block is listed in the pattern's supply section. Wire-edged ribbon is listed for some blocks, but regular ribbon can usually be used.

Soutache

Soutache is a trim used for the stems of the thistle flowers and other flowers. It adds another dimension and texture to the block.

Supplies

Soutache can be found in many fabric stores, but is often available only in white, navy blue, and black. Since none of those colors looks great as stems, I dyed some soutache in moss green dye. Using a small container, follow the instructions on the package of dye. After the dye and water are mixed, place a small test piece of soutache in the mixture. The longer it stays in the dye, the darker the color will be. Add a little more dye to the mixture and test again. When you have a color you like, place the whole piece of soutache in the mixture and leave it for the amount of time determined from your test.

Dispose of the dye mixture as directed on the package. Place the soutache on some old towels or several layers of paper towels to dry. If you do not have soutache, the stems can also be embroidered with a stem stitch. (See page 20.)

Point Turner

Several of the patterns require you to sew fabric pieces together and then turn them inside out. After the piece is turned, use a point turner to smooth the edges.

Table Roll

An inexpensive paper, the kind used on examination tables in doctors' offices, is ideal for tracing block designs and border patterns. When designing borders, you can cut the paper the full length of the border and not have to tape paper pieces together. You might be able to purchase a roll from your doctor, medical supply store, or office supply store.

Tulle

This type of fabric can be found in the bridal section of many fabric stores. Purchase the smallest amount they will sell you. It is not expensive, but you need only a little for the dragonfly and bumblebee wings. I use off-white. Be careful when ironing tulle because it melts easily. For best results, press with light heat and a pressing cloth.

Ultra-Suede®

Ultra-Suede® is a very interesting fabric because the edges do not fray. I used it to make the ladybugs on the Lazy Daisy block. Ultra-Suede® is rather expensive, but I have found small bags of scraps in vendors' booths at quilt shows. It was a less expensive way to get a lot of different colors without having to purchase the full width of the fabric.

Bias Press Bars

There are several brands of bias press bars on the market. I like the heat-resistant plastic type. If you cannot find them in your area, refer to the Resource section on p.143 to order.

The metal press bars are okay, but they stay hot a lot longer. Be careful not to burn yourself when removing them from the fabric.

Feathers

This might seem like an unusual item to use on a quilt block, but they work great for the antenna on the moth and the wooly booger! When I was designing the moth, I was trying to come up with a way to make the antenna look like feathers when I thought, "Why not use feathers?" My husband is a fly fisherman and uses feathers to make his flies, so I borrowed a few. I hope he does not miss them.

These feathers are the only items on the quilt that might not hold up well when washing. The feathers can be removed and stitched back in place after washing. Or, the antenna could be embroidered.

If you decide to use feathers, look for Grizzy #2 grade. Since our area is world-renowned for trout fishing, it is easy to find these feathers in stores. Or, if you know anyone who ties flies, ask them for a couple of feathers. It is like asking a quilter for a little fabric, they are happy to share. ❀

SECTION
2

Appliqué
Methods

Spray Starch & Template Method

This method requires a lot of ironing. Before you begin, put on your favorite music, lower your ironing board, and have a seat. You might as well get comfortable. This step will take a while but is well worth the time spent.

This is my favorite appliqué method, the one I use whenever possible. Pat Andreatta introduced me to this method years ago. One of the biggest advantages of this technique is that the seam allowance is nicely turned under before you start to sew. It makes the appliqué process very easy.

You need a few supplies to get started.

Iron: Work with a dry, hot iron. You do not want steam shooting from the iron because your fingers will be so close to it. I do not recommend an automatic shut-off iron because they frequently turn off before you need them.

Templar: A heat-resistant plastic that does not melt when ironed. Used for cutting templates, its accuracy is based on how well the shape is cut.

Spray starch: Magic Sizing brand works great for this method. This will add some stiffness to the seam to hold it down when pressed but not so much stiffness that it is hard to sew through.

Emery board: Use this to smooth the edges of the templates.

Press cloth: Scraps of muslin or other cotton fabric placed over an ironing surface will serve this purpose nicely. Starch can build up on your ironing surface, and it is much easier to toss the scraps of muslin in the washer than to replace your ironing board cover.

Stencil brush: Apply the spray starch with a stencil brush or cotton swab. A stencil brush can be used repeatedly; cotton swabs need to be replaced regularly.

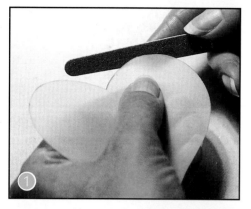

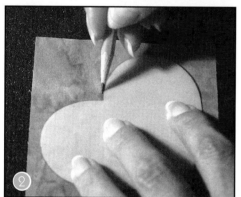

Applique Basics – Procedure Guide

Now that all your supplies are together, you are ready to get started. Let's walk through the procedure using a heart shape.

Place a sheet of plastic over the heart pattern. Using a pencil, trace the heart onto the Templar. With paper scissors, cut along the line you just drew. Do not add a seam allowance. If there are rough spots along the edge of the template, smooth them with an emery board ❶.

Place the template on the back side of your fabric and trace around the heart ❷. Cut the shape from fabric, adding a little less than ¼" seam allowance ❸.

Place the fabric heart face down on your ironing surface. Center the plastic template over the fabric. Cut into the seam allowance at the inner point of the heart until you are about two threads from the template. If you cut right

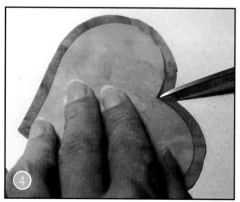

up to the template, your edges may fray. It is always a good idea to clip seam allowances as you go, being careful not to shift the plastic template ❹.

Coat the seam allowance at the inner point with starch using the stencil brush or a cotton swab ❺.

With a dry, hot iron on a medium heat setting, push the seam up and over the edge of the template, straight into the point. Keeping the iron close to the folded edge helps keep the edge smooth, free of bumps and unwanted points ❻.

The iron has to be hot enough to dry the starch, but not so hot that it warps the plastic. I call this the "happy setting" on the iron. If your iron is too hot, the template will warp and you will have to make another one. It takes a little experimenting to find this "happy setting." Start at a wool setting and make adjustments from there.

Allow the starch to dry! The hardest part of this technique is leaving the iron on the fabric long enough to dry the starch. Do not slide or press down hard on the iron. Your arm will get tired and the starch will not dry any faster.

Move from the inner point along the curve on one side of the heart pressing small sections of fabric as you go ❼. If the seam does not lie flat, you probably did not leave the iron on the fabric long enough, or your iron was not hot enough.

If any part of the pressed seam allowance does not turn out the way you want, moisten that area with a little more starch and iron it again. Be sure the seam allowance is tight against the template on the side you just ironed, then repeat the process around and down the other side ❽.

For a sharp bottom point, place your fingernail, point turner, or anything that has a sharp point and will not melt, on the seam allowance of the point. Paint the allowance with spray starch. Pleat in the fullness at the point and hold it with your fingernail. Then slide the iron over the point. Hold it in place long enough to dry the starch. The point takes a little longer to dry because of the thickness. Do not trim away any of the seam allowance. After all the edges are turned under and ironed, remove the template. The heart is ready to appliqué.

If you have a piece with smooth inner curves, the seam allowance might not require clipping. Center the template over the fabric shape. Start with the inner curves or points and moisten with starch. Push the iron into the point. The moisture opens the seam allowance, and the seam may not require any clipping. When the inner curves are all pressed, work on the outer curves. ✿

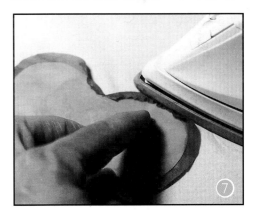

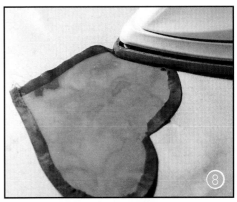

Needle-Turn Method

I like to use a basic needle-turn method when the spray starch and heat-resistant plastic method will not work well. In each block section I will tell which method I used; however, do whatever works best for you. Following are two different ways to approach needle-turn.

Freezer paper: Make a freezer paper template by placing the paper, waxy side down, over the pattern piece. Trace the shape with a pencil and cut on the pencil lines. Do not add a seam allowance. Iron the waxy side of the paper template to the right side of your fabric ❶. Cut outside the shape, adding a little less than ¼" all around the edge for a seam allowance ❷.

With this method, there is no need to mark the right side of your fabric. The edge of the freezer paper is the guideline for your seam allowance. The folded fabric edge, when appliquéd, should be just beyond the edge of the freezer paper. This means the size of the shape will be slightly *larger* than the original pattern size.

Plastic template: If freezer paper feels too stiff and the edges are hard to handle, try the plastic template method. Trace the pattern you have chosen onto a piece of template plastic. Cut the shape and place the template on the right side of your fabric. Trace around the shape using a washout marker. Remove the template, and cut a little less than a ¼" outside the lines for your seam allowance. When you use a plastic template and trace around the edges, make sure the line you draw is tucked under the fabric's folded edge. The finished shape will be slightly *smaller* than the template.

With the needle-turn method you will use your needle to tuck under small sections of the seam allowance. Only tuck in as much of the seam allowance as you can hold with your thumb. If you are right-handed, the needle will be in your right hand, and you will hold the seam with your left thumb. If you are left-handed, the needle will be in your left hand, and you will use your right thumb to hold the seam allowance.

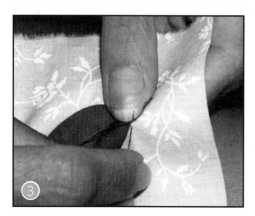

Try holding the appliqué shape so you are pulling the seam allowance toward your body. I find it much easier to control when I pull it toward my body rather than pushing it away.

After the section you are holding with your thumb is stitched, tuck in the seam allowance on the next small section. Keep stitching until the piece is secured to the background. ❀

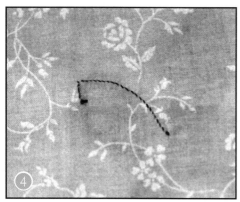

Appliqué Stitch

This stitch should be virtually invisible. Start with knotted thread, bring the needle up from behind the appliqué, through the background fabric and the folded edge of the appliqué. Stay very close to the edge of your appliqué .

Take the needle into the background fabric beside the folded edge, making a straight stitch from the folded edge of the appliqué to the background fabric. Bring the needle up into the folded edge of the appliqué. Now pull the needle through ❸.

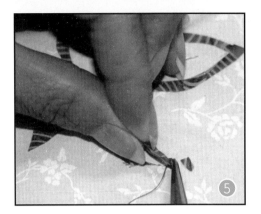

When you look at the back of your block, the stitches will be slightly slanted ❹. On top, they should be perfectly straight. The stitches on top will not be noticeable if the stitch is done correctly. When you finish stitching around the shape, insert the needle and thread through the background fabric and knot the thread. You should have 10 to 12 stitches per inch.

If your thread should break in the middle of a shape, pull the tail to the back of the block. Rethread your needle, and start stitching about 1" back from where you stopped. The overlap will secure the loose thread. The thread is so fine that even double stitching is not noticeable.

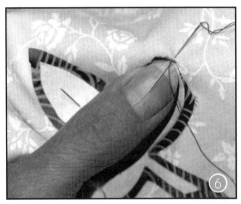

How to Handle Inner & Outer Points

Outer points: When using the needle-turn method, the point is a bit more tricky than the template and starch method, but not difficult. Stitch up along the side of the point. Just before the point, take one stitch off to the side to secure the seam. Reposition the fabric so you can lift the fabric from the opposite side. Trim away the seam allowance from the side where you have already stitched. This will reduce the bulk, making it much easier to tuck the seam in on the remaining side ❺.

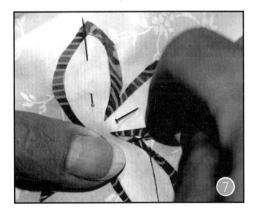

With your needle, pull the seam allowance across the point horizontally. It should be straight across the top. Tuck the seam allowance in on the remaining side. Take one straight stitch out on the point, then continue stitching down the side ❻.

Inner points: This is a weak spot for hand appliqué because of the potential for the raw edge to fray. For the needle-turn method, stop when you are about 1" away from the inner point, clip straight into the seam allowance at the point, cutting so that equal amounts of seam allowance remain on both sides ❼. Sweep your needle under the other side of the point area, and bring it down into the point. With your needle, sweep the seam allowance down under the fabric. Sweep as many times as needed. When it is tucked under the way you want, take three tack stitches in the inner point to secure it in place. The freezer paper ❽ can be removed as you go. ✤

Perfect Circles

One of the compliments I frequently get from judges is "perfect circles." If the judges knew how easy they are, I would never get those compliments.

Once when I was teaching a quilting class and explaining how I make larger circles from Templar and smaller ones using coins as patterns, a student asked if metal washers would work for making small circles. I thought it was a great idea, so I stopped at the hardware store on the way home and purchased two washers of every size they had.

Several years later, I asked my husband Joe if he would stop at the hardware store and get 25 of a specific size washer for a workshop I was teaching. He came home with plastic washers. I thought they would melt under the iron but decided to try one anyway. Guess what? It did not melt. They are made from Mylar®, a heat-resistant plastic, and work better than metal washers or coins because they are thinner and do not stay hot as long. I have been thanking Joe ever since!

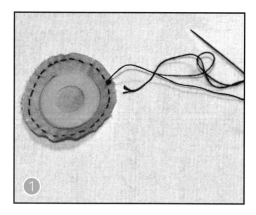

To make a perfect circle, trace around a washer on the back side of the fabric. Cut the circle, leaving a full ¼" seam allowance all the way around. The only exception is with really small circles, which need narrower seam allowances.

With knotted thread, sew a running stitch around the circle midway through the seam allowance. Place the fabric circle on your pressing cloth right side down. Place the washer in the center of the fabric circle ❶. Pull on the thread and the seam allowance will gather around the washer ❷. To keep the seam snug, hold tightly, and pull the thread across the washer.

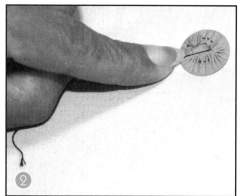

While holding the thread, moisten the seam allowance with starch. Slide a dry, hot iron onto the back of the circle, being careful not to burn your fingers. The iron will need to remain on the fabric long enough for the starch to dry. This takes a little time because the starch soaks into the gathers. As this circle is drying under the iron, I start a running stitch in the seam allowance of the next circle. It is a little assembly line process.

After the starch dries on the first circle, loosen the seam where you finished your running stitch and remove the washer ❸. The end of the running stitch is easy to find if you left a tail of thread. After removing the washer, pull on the tail again to close the circle. All the patterns in this book are based on standard size Mylar® washers ❹.

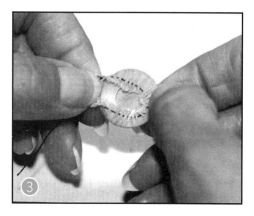

When I first started recommending washers, several students informed me they were hard to find in some areas. I have since started packaging and selling them. See the Resource section on page 143 if you cannot find the washers in your area. ❁

Appliqué Basics: Flower Wreaths, Karen Kay Buckley

Bias Strips for Stems

Many of the stems in this book are made using bias press bars. If you have a stem that curves, the fabric must be cut on the bias. The bias has a lot more give and allows the stem to lie flat. If the fabric is cut on grain, it will buckle.

To cut bias strips, place your ruler on top of the fabric with the 45-degree angle on the edge of the fabric. The side of the ruler will be on the bias of the fabric. Cut along the ruler with your rotary cutter or trace a line to be cut with scissors.

Even though some stems are smaller than others, *all the stems in this book will be cut in strips 1¼" wide*. To determine the length, measure the stem on each block pattern. Press the strip in half, wrong sides together. Place the press bar tight against the fold and slide it under your sewing machine's presser foot. You can use a zipper, top, or edge stitching foot. If you use a zipper foot, try riding the foot on top of the press bar while sewing down the right side. Guide the fabric and bar into the machine with your fingers. On a few occasions when stitching stems with a zipper foot, I stitched into the plastic bias press bar, leaving small nicks. The nicks can be smoothed with an emery board. This is a benefit of plastic. With metal bars, your needle would break immediately.

A top or edge stitching foot has a plastic or metal insert which rests along the edge of the press bar so you cannot accidentally sew into the bar.

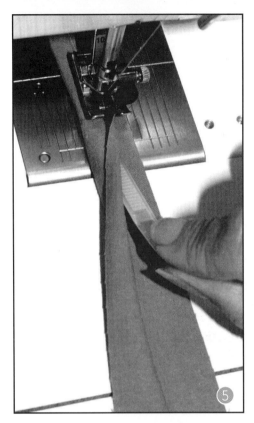

If the strip of fabric is longer than the press bar, stop sewing with the needle down and lift the foot. Pull the press bar toward you, drop the foot, and continue sewing ❺.

Keep the press bar inside the strip. With scissors, trim the seam allowance as close to the sewing line as possible without cutting into the seam ❻.

Push the seam toward what will become the back of the stem. Moisten the seam with starch. Slide your iron onto the seam and leave it until the starch is dry. If your fabric strip is longer than the press bar, press the section around the bar, making sure the starch is dry, then slide the press bar down to the next area. Moisten with starch and iron dry as before ❼. When the strip is completed, remove the press bar.

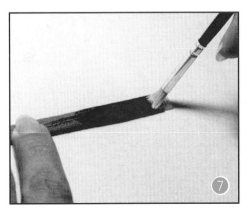

When stitching a bias strip onto background fabric, pin the stem in place and sew the *inside* curve first, followed by the *outside* curve. The stem will lie flatter if the inner curve is sewn first. After the inner curve is completed, travel the needle and thread to the other side of the stem and appliqué the outer curve. Then stitch the next inner curve area. ✿

Embroidery Stitches

The main embroidery stitch used on these blocks is the stem stitch. You may also choose to use French knots instead of beads on some of the blocks. There are a few other embroidery stitches used on one block; these will be explained later.

Unless otherwise noted, the embroidery stitches are worked with two strands of embroidery floss. Cut about 18" from the skein and separate two strands from the others. An embroidery needle is recommended, but quilting needles also work well.

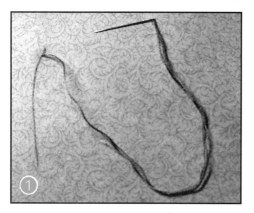

Stem Stitch

I always say the Embroiders Guild would kick me out because I knot my embroidery floss. Most embroiderers prefer to leave a tail of thread that will be caught or woven into the stitching. Do whatever you prefer. Knots are absorbed into the quilt batting and will not be noticed.

Bring the thread up from behind the background fabric. Start about ¼" down from the actual starting point of the line.

Insert your needle at the start of the line, and bring it out down past the stitch. The first stitch you took should be in the middle of this stitch ❶.

Continue until you have reached the other end of the line. Keep stitches close together so the line you drew is covered ❷.

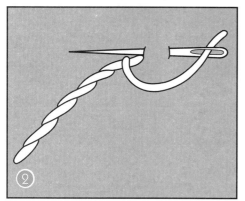

French Knots

Tie a knot in the end of your thread. Insert the needle from behind the background fabric so the knot is on the back.

On the front side, wrap the thread around the needle three times ❸. Insert the needle into the same spot it just came through and pull the needle down through the fabric ❹.

Knot on the back to secure the stitch. In most areas where beads or French knots are required, they are clustered to fill an area. ❀

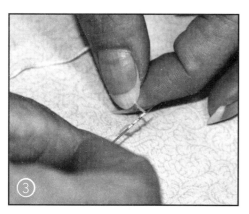

Pressing

After all the shapes have been appliquéd to your background and embroidery added, the block needs to be pressed. Place a terry cloth towel on your ironing surface. Put the completed block *face down* on the towel. With a dry, hot iron press the back of the block. When the pressing is complete, you will be ready to trim the block. ❀

Preparing the Block

Cut: Cut squares from your background fabric 16" x 16". After doing a lot of dimensional appliqué, the background fabric sometimes pulls and becomes uneven. The distorted edges can be trimmed to 14½" x 14½" when the block is complete (see below).

Trace: For tracing the pattern onto paper, cut a square of table or freezer paper 15" x 15". Fold it in half in both directions and crease. Place the folds over the dotted lines shown on the pattern page. Trace each section. Transferring the pattern to one large sheet of paper will make it much easier to transfer to the fabric.

Transfer: Begin by finding the center of your background fabric. If you are placing your blocks on the *horizontal/vertical* layout, fold your fabric in half across the horizontal and finger crease or gently iron the fold. Open the square and fold it in half in the vertical direction. You should have a large plus sign creased in your fabric, dividing it into four equal quadrants. If you are planning a *diagonal* layout, fold your background fabric in half on the diagonal and crease the fold. Do the same on the other diagonal. You should have an "X" creased in the fabric to use as a placement guideline.

How to Transfer & Trim the Patterns

Light box or window method: Tape the pattern to a light box, glass door, or window ❶. Center the background fabric, right side up. Align the dotted lines on the pattern with the fabric's creases. Tape or pin in place.

With a washout marker that you have tested, trace the pattern onto your background fabric. There are some instructions on the patterns indicating which lines do and do not need to be traced.

Saral® paper method: Tape your fabric, right side up, to a hard, flat surface. Center and pin the pattern over the fabric. Slide a sheet of Saral® paper between the pattern and fabric with the dark side of the paper against the right side of the fabric ❷. Remember to test the Saral® paper on a scrap of fabric first for washability.

Using a blunt-tipped object, firmly trace over the pattern. Items that work well for tracing are a stiletto (embossing tool), a pen that has run out of ink, and the tip of a seam ripper. Do not use a pen with a spring or a felt tipped marker because you cannot push hard enough. After you have traced a small section, peek underneath to be sure the pattern is transferring.

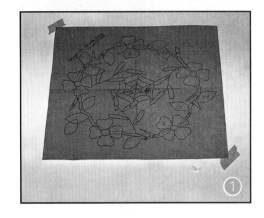

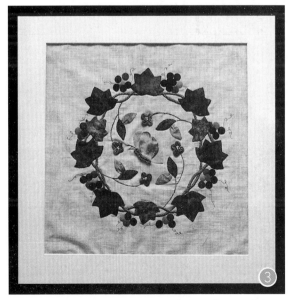

Lytle Markham, Carlisle, PA

Trim: When the block has been appliquéd and pressed, it needs to be trimmed. Use a window template (refer to page 10) and fabric marker for this step. Visually center the design ❸, then measure to be sure. Trace a line around the inside edge of the square. This line is your cutting line (seam allowance is already included). Cut with scissors or rotary cutter. The block is now ready to be sewn into the setting of your choice. ❀

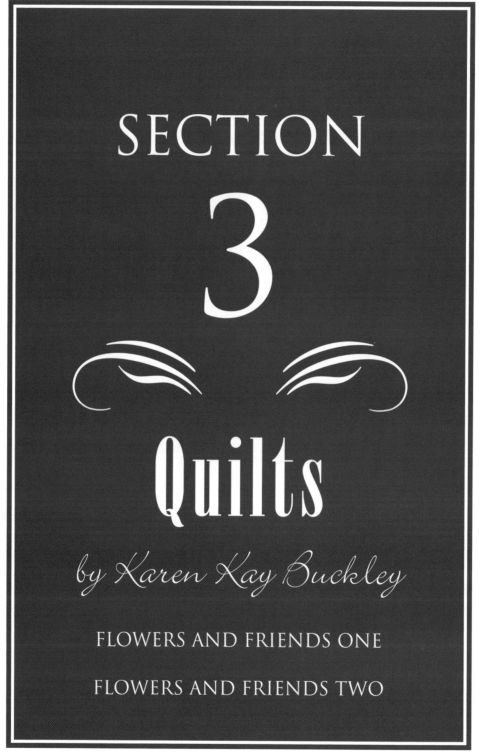

SECTION

3

Quilts

by Karen Kay Buckley

FLOWERS AND FRIENDS ONE

FLOWERS AND FRIENDS TWO

Flowers And Friends One

FLOWERS AND FRIENDS ONE, 88" x 88"
Made by the author, 1997

*H*ere is an original setting design that showcases nine blocks presented in this book. It features a twice-outlined octagon center block with an appliquéd hand-drawn sun. The solid royal blue fabric coordinates with the swirl print used in the borders and in the interlocking star points. Notice how the darker wood grain fabric (when used for the interlocking pieces and inner-border strips) sets apart the earth-tone background of each block. These are set off with a sky-blue fabric used to frame the blocks, four of which have been set on point.

Pansies & Other Posies block
Directions are on pages 118 – 120.
Patterns are on pages 122 – 125.

Lazy Daisies block
Directions are on pages 97 – 100.
Patterns are on pages 102 – 105.

Heard It Through the Grapevine block
Directions are on pages 36 – 39.
Patterns are on pages 40 – 43.

Appliqué Basics: Flower Wreaths, Karen Kay Buckley

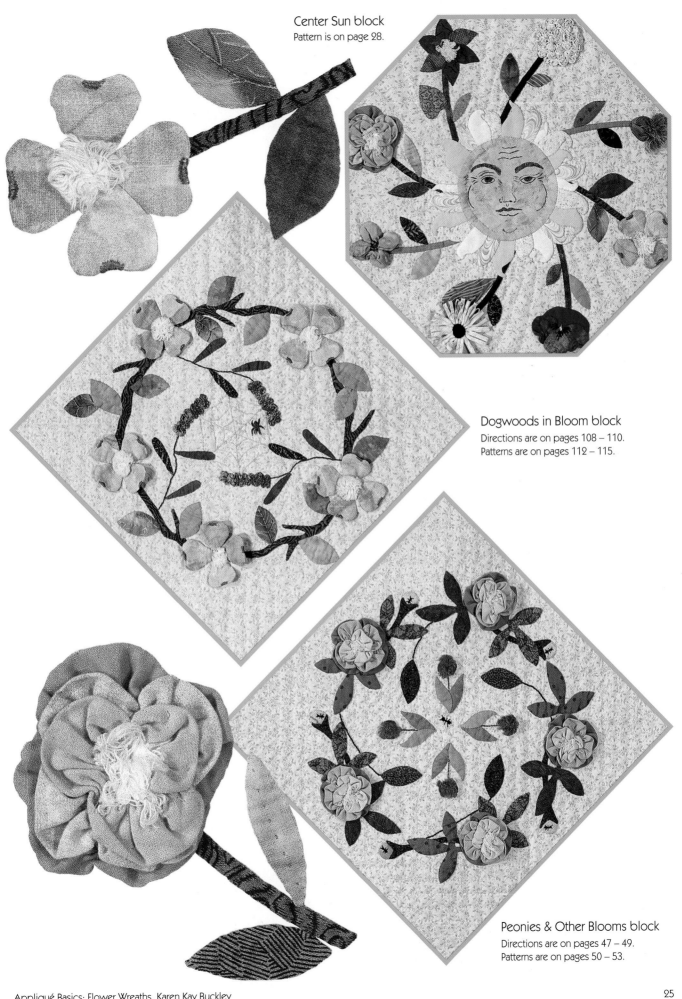

Center Sun block
Pattern is on page 28.

Dogwoods in Bloom block
Directions are on pages 108 – 110.
Patterns are on pages 112 – 115.

Peonies & Other Blooms block
Directions are on pages 47 – 49.
Patterns are on pages 50 – 53.

Orchids & Bluebells block
Directions are on pages 77 – 79. Patterns are on pages 80 – 83.

Marigolds on My Mind block
Directions are on pages 57 – 59.
Patterns are on pages 60 – 63.

Clematis, Bee Plants & Bee block
Directions are on pages 67 – 69. Patterns are on pages 70 – 73.

Appliqué Basics: Flower Wreaths, Karen Kay Buckley

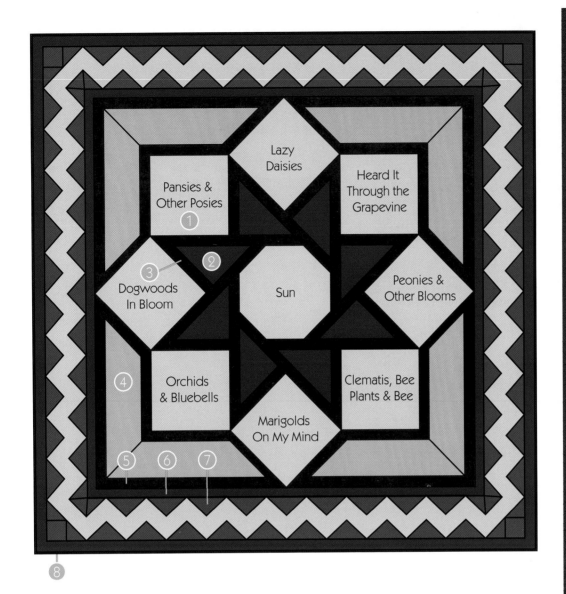

Flowers And Friends One Placement Chart

Finished measurements after quilting blocks are 13¾" **❶**, star-point triangles 13" x 9½" **❷**, framing strips 2" **❸**, cloud-blue mitered corners 5¾" **❹**, first inside border 2" **❺**, and second outside solid border 1⅝" **❻**. The triangles are 3½" right angles **❼**. The quilt has matching ⅜" straight-edge binding **❽**.

For added appeal, a zigzag garden maze encircles the entire quilt. The appliquéd three-dimensional flowers, gathered leaves, straight stems, and nature's own insects meander across the 1¼" lattice-pieced background fabric enhanced with narrow ¼" bands.

Detail of Sun block, FLOWERS FROM FRIENDS ONE, by the author

All the individual flowers sewn radiating out from the sun are discussed in the following chapters. The change in directions is that the Bluebell flower (p.79) is made from a 3" square, and the Daisy flower (p.97) is cut from yellow fabric 2" x 3½". Changing the flower's proportion was necessary to make them all the same size in the center block as shown on page 25.

Alternate sun-rays as shown in illustration.
Add seam allowances.

This sun pattern can be appliquéd or used alone as a quilting design (refer to Gallery, page 138).

Flowers And Friends Two

FLOWERS AND FRIENDS TWO (shown on the cover), 53" x 53"
Made by the author, quilted by Sandra Chambers, 1998

*A*fter making FLOWER AND FRIENDS ONE, I wanted to try some of the same blocks but on a darker background. With solid navy blue fabric as the background, it was necessary to select more vibrant colors for the appliqué. These five blocks are set side-by-side and on-point. I used templates from each wreath to draw my border design. After the quilt top was completed, I spoke with Sandra Chambers about my ideas for quilting the large open area in the center. I have an antique Baltimore Album style quilt and its background was quilted in a random fashion with leaves, flowers, and stems from the appliqué patterns themselves. Sandy had never done anything free-form before but agreed to try it, and she did a wonderful job!

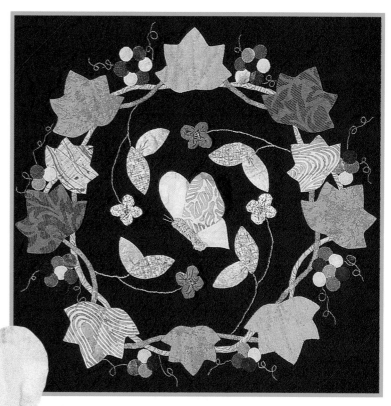

Heard It Through the Grapevine block
Directions are on pages 36 – 39.
Patterns are on pages 40 – 43.

Lazy Daisies block
Directions are on pages 97 – 100.
Patterns are on pages 102 – 105.

Appliqué Basics: Flower Wreaths, Karen Kay Buckley

Pansies & Other Posies block
Directions are on pages 118 – 120.
Patterns are on pages 122 – 125.

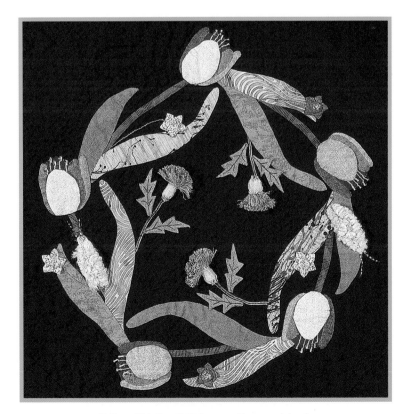

Tulips, Thistles & Tobacco Flowers block
Directions are on pages 87 – 89.
Patterns are on pages 90 – 93.

Dogwoods In Bloom block

Directions are on pages 108 – 110.
Patterns are on pages 112 – 115.

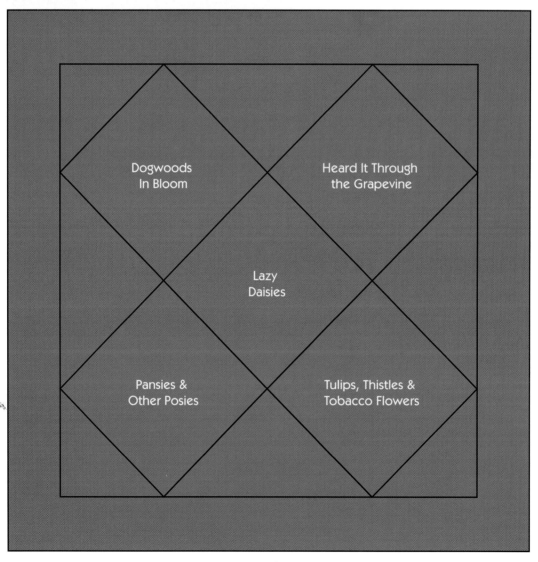

Dogwoods
In Bloom

Heard It Through
the Grapevine

Lazy
Daisies

Pansies &
Other Posies

Tulips, Thistles &
Tobacco Flowers

SECTION
4

Blocks

Heard It Through the GRAPEVINE

Block by Barbara J. Schenck
Camp Hill, PA

HEARD IT THROUGH THE GRAPEVINE

SUPPLIES

■ **Basic sewing supplies**
needles, template material, thread, pins, fabric markers, and scissors

■ **Embroidery thread on a skein**
for stems, grape squiggles, and butterfly antenna

■ **Pigma™ marker, brown**

■ **Rotary cutter, ruler, and board (optional)**

■ **Small piece of batting**

■ **Tapestry needle, size 18**

■ **Water soluble glue stick**

■ **Safety pin**

■ **Seed beads or embroidery thread**
for centers of violets

FABRIC

■ **16" x 16" background fabric**

■ **Scraps for leaves**
use a variety of green fabrics

■ **Scraps for grapes**
when making your selection, remember grapes are red, purple, and white. Your color decision might also be based on the background fabric you are using.

■ **Yardage for stems**
use ¼ yard of one or more brown fabrics

■ **Scraps for violet flowers**
use one or two blue fabrics

■ **Scraps for butterfly**
use two different yellow fabrics. Check the back side of the fabric, sometimes it will offer you just the right shade to complement the front side so you can get everything you need from the same piece. Or look for a fabric with butterflies and take advantage of the printed design.

The Grapevine

Stems and Leaves

These stems could be made with bias press bars, but I decided to stitch them with the needle-turn technique so they are slightly uneven and look more realistic.

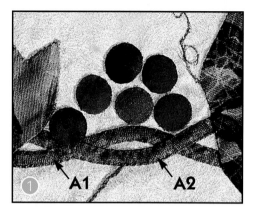

Stems: Follow the placement guide as shown on page 40. There are some stems labeled "**A1**" and some labeled "**A2**."

Sew **A1** stems first. Cut strips on the bias ⅜" wide. These can be cut with a rotary cutter or mark your fabric and cut with scissors. Pin the stem to the background fabric and needle-turn a scant seam allowance on the inner curve first and then the outer curve. The finished stem will be about ⅛" wide ❶.

Leave ¼" to ½" raw at the beginning and end of each stem. These raw edges will be covered later by the leaves.

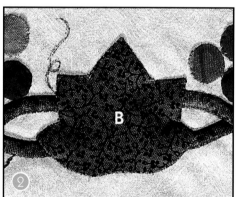

Stuffing the Stems (optional technique): After the **A1** stems are stitched in place, they are ready to be stuffed. Thread a tapestry needle with yarn. Any color will do since it will not be seen. Bring the needle up through the background fabric. Leave a tail of thread about 1" long on the back; it will be trimmed later. Push the threaded tapestry needle through the stem channel and out the opposite side. You may have to scrunch the stem a little to get the needle and yarn through.

Smooth the stem if necessary. Insert the needle through the background fabric. Trim the yarn so there is about ¼" extra left at the beginning and end.

After all the bottom stems are stitched and stuffed, follow the same procedure with the top stems.

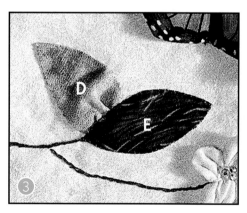

Leaves: I used the spray starch and template method to turn under the edges of the grape leaves ❷. Use the method that works best for you.

The templates for this project are on pages 40 – 43. Cut 3 **B** medium leaves and 7 **C** large leaves. There are 4 **D** small leaves in the center of the block. Turn under seam allowances on two sides of the **D** shape, but leave the straight edge unturned. The straight raw edge will be covered ❸ by the **E** leaf. *The slash marks on a pattern piece indicate an edge that remains raw.*

Before stitching the **D** leaves in place, gather the raw edge to add fullness. With regular sewing thread or quilting thread that matches your leaf fabric, knot the end of the thread and sew a running stitch about ⅛" from the raw edge. When you get to the end, pull the thread tight and knot the thread to hold the gather. This leaf is ready to appliqué in place. Appliqué all the **D** leaves before proceeding to the **E** leaves. ✿

Stuffed Grapes

Grape Circles

Use an assortment of colors and fabrics to make each bunch of grapes. Please refer to page 18 for advice for making perfect circles. The size of the washer used for the grapes in this project is ½".

Stuffing the Grapes: The grape circles can simply be stitched in place, or you can stuff the grapes. I like to stuff some of them to add dimension to the block. I tried stitching part of the way around a shape and then pushing some stuffing in from the side, but my finished shapes were too irregular. After some experimentation, I found a way that gives nice smooth grapes.

Cut a circle from cotton batting slightly smaller than the finished size of the circle. Place the batting circle on the background block. Center the grape circle over the batting and stitch around the grape circle. The batting will be enclosed. When sewing circles this small, it is helpful to glue rather than pin them in place. Just dab the back of the circle with a very small amount of water-soluble glue. You can also use glue to hold the batting in place.

Grape Squiggles

Try adding a curly tendril to the vines for a touch of realism. They can be drawn freehand on the finished block with a Pigma marker ❹. For darker background fabrics, you will need to use an embroidered stem stitch. Refer to page 20 for instructions. ❀

Close-up detail,
BUGS & BLOOMS,
by Peggy S. Meyers, Newville, PA

Gathered Violet Flowers

To make the gathered violet flowers , first cut a template of a 1" circle (refer to template on top of page 41.) Trace the circle onto the back of your fabric. Place two pieces of fabric right sides together. Cut ¼" outside the line through both pieces of fabric. Sew a running stitch on the line you drew. Start and stop with a knot. Do not gather the thread.

To turn the shape inside out, slit the back circle. Be careful not to cut through the front circle. Pinch the back circle and pull it toward you. Grab onto the fabric and put a little snip in the back circle with your scissors. Now that you have a small slit in which to place your scissors cut an "X" through the fabric 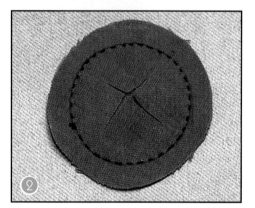.

Turn inside out and place four small marks on the outer edge of the circle. Imagine your circle as a clock, and place marks at 12, 3, 6, and 9 o'clock .

Using regular sewing thread in a color that matches your fabric, knot the end of your thread and bring your needle up through the center of the circle.

Wrap the thread up and over the mark at 12. Take the thread over the circle edge and back up through the center. Be sure the thread loops over the folded edge right on the 12 o'clock marking. Knot but do not cut the thread .

Do the same thing at 3, 6, and 9 o'clock. Be sure to pull the thread tight each time. You will have created a four-petal flower which closely resembles a violet. To finish the flower, stitch some seed beads in the center or embroider some French knots (see color photograph.)

When attaching the violets to the block, you can allow the beads or French knots to hold the flower in place. If you think your quilt will get a lot of use, appliqué around the outside edge of the flower to hold it in place.

Stems: The stems for the violets in the center of the block are embroidered with a stem stitch (page 20). Use two strands of green embroidery thread. Try threading your needle with two different shades of green, light and dark, to give the stem some subtle shading. ❀

Butterflies

Everyone appreciates a butterfly! Their color combinations and patterns are always unique. Consider using a special fabric for the wings. Search through your stash of fabric for something that looks like veins on a butterfly wing ❶.

Wings: I used the starch and heat-resistant template method to turn under the edges on the **J** and **K** shapes. Patterns for the wings are on the following pages. Make one each of the **J** and **K** shapes. The pattern pieces can be combined into one template, as shown here in the student's block, or used individually ❷ to create movement of color and form.

Reduced Butterfly Wings

Dimensional Wing: Use the **L** template and trace it on the back of your fabric. Place two pieces of fabric right sides together, cut outside the line ¼".

Before you begin to sew, pin a safety pin between these two pieces of fabric, through one side of the wing fabric only. This will make it easier to turn the pieces right side out.

Sew a running stitch on the line you drew. Remember *do not stitch* on the side with the slash marks. Pull the safety pin through the opening and turn the wing inside out ❸. Use a point turner to smooth the edges.

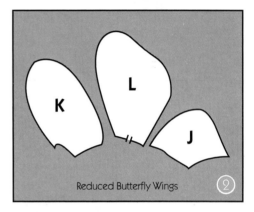

Place the wing in position over the background fabric. Start your appliqué stitch halfway down one side. When you reach the bottom raw edge, tuck ¼" up and under the wing. Continue stitching halfway up the other side. The top of the wing will remain loose.

Body of the Butterfly: Cut 3 strips of fabric 4" long and slightly less than ¼" wide, *on the bias*. Stack these three pieces on top of each other. With matching thread, sew a running stitch down the center of the layers of strips. Because this is going to be gathered, it is a good idea to use regular sewing thread or quilting thread. Pull the thread to gather the strips ❹.

Sew the gathered piece **M** down the center to the background fabric. A stab stitch (taking one stitch at a time) should be easier than a regular running stitch because this is so thick. After the strip is stitched in place, rub it gently with your fingers to open the edges and fill in the body area with the frayed threads.

Antennae on Butterfly: The antennae could be sewn with a stem stitch or drawn with a Pigma™ marker. The decision might be based on the color of your background fabric. If you are working on a dark background fabric, you will need to use a stem stitch. Try using one strand of thread instead of two for a softer look. If you are working on a light background fabric, the antennae could be drawn or embroidered. The choice is yours. ✿

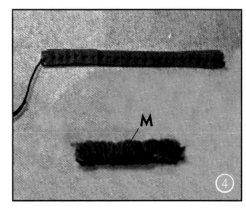

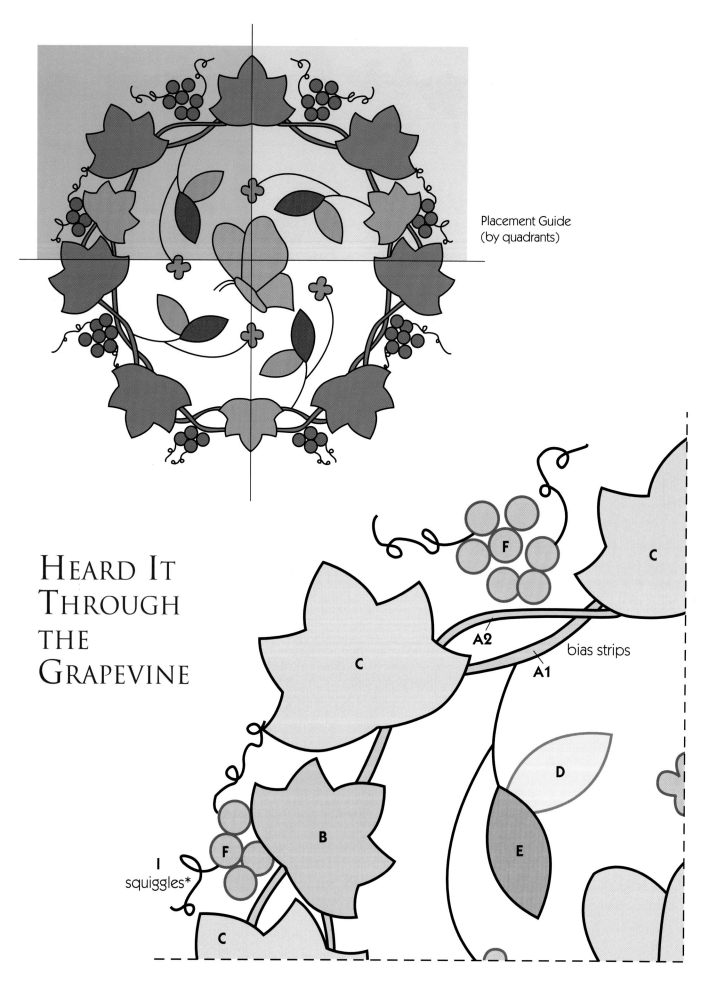

Placement Guide
(by quadrants)

Heard It Through the Grapevine

F

C

A2

bias strips

A1

D

C

E

B

I
squiggles*

F

F

C

Appliqué Basics: Flower Wreaths, Karen Kay Buckley

Pattern shapes are identified with letters and indicate the order in which to appliqué. The written directions refer to the corresponding letters. Some edges will be left raw and covered by another shape; these edges are marked with small slash marks or drawn open ended.

A1 & A2 (9 each)	H (4)
B (3)	I* squiggles
C (7)	J (1)
D (4)	K (1)
E (4)	L (2)
F (44)	M (1)
G* stems	N* antennae

*embroidered or drawn

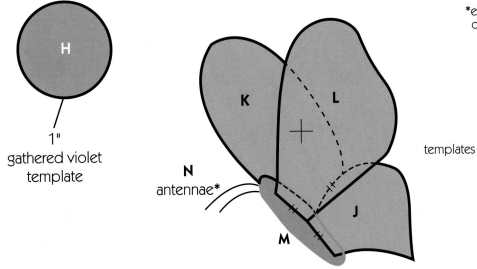

H

1"
gathered violet
template

N
antennae*

templates

Assembly Diagram

HEARD IT THROUGH THE GRAPEVINE

Add seam allowances.

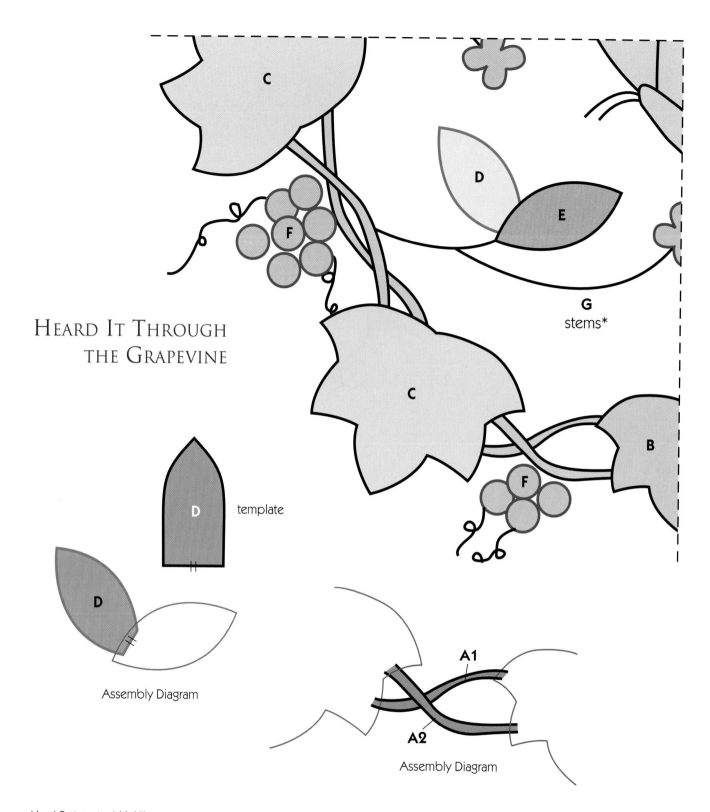

Heard It Through the Grapevine

template

Assembly Diagram

Assembly Diagram

Al & A2 (9 each)	H (4)
B (3)	I* squiggles
C (7)	J (1)
D (4)	K (1)
E (4)	L (2)
F (44)	M (1)
G* stems	N* antennae
*embroidered or drawn	

Pattern shapes are identified with letters and indicate the order in which to appliqué. The written directions refer to the corresponding letters. Some edges will be left raw and covered by another shape; these edges are marked with small slash marks or drawn open ended.

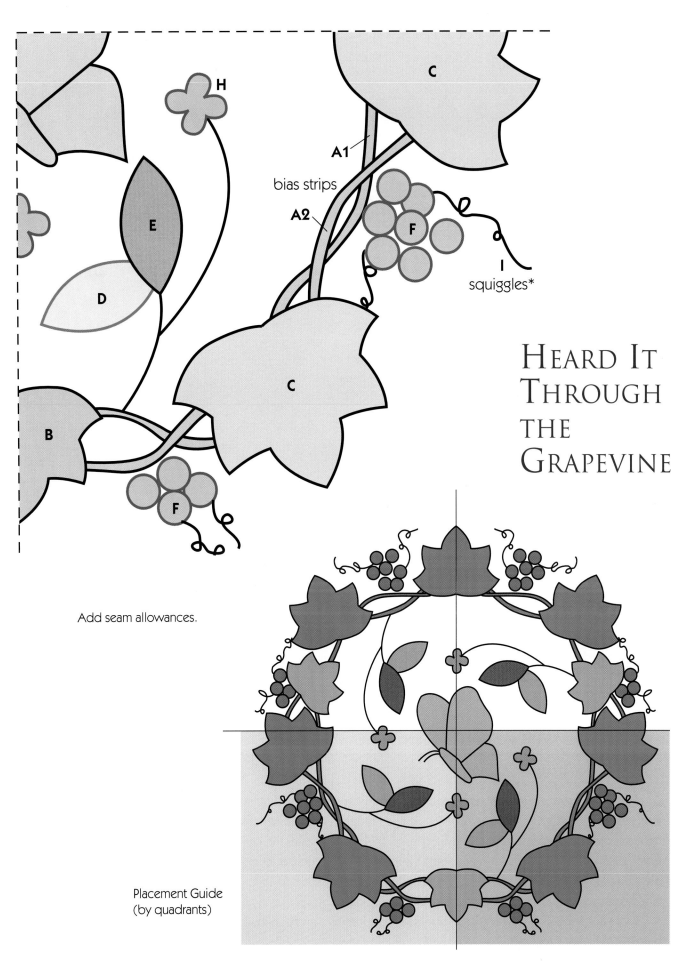

H

A1

bias strips

A2

C

F

I

squiggles*

E

D

B

C

F

F

HEARD IT THROUGH THE GRAPEVINE

Add seam allowances.

Placement Guide
(by quadrants)

Planning Chart One

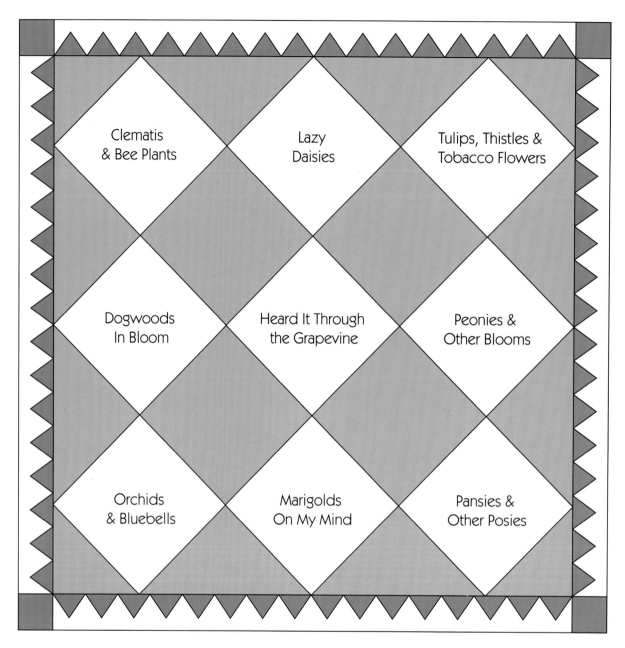

Clematis & Bee Plants

Lazy Daisies

Tulips, Thistles & Tobacco Flowers

Dogwoods In Bloom

Heard It Through the Grapevine

Peonies & Other Blooms

Orchids & Bluebells

Marigolds On My Mind

Pansies & Other Posies

FLOWERS AND FRIENDS
70" x 70", Barbara J. Schenck, Camp Hill, PA

*A*ll nine flower wreaths are nicely arranged within this large square quilt top. This chapter's featured pattern, HEARD IT THROUGH THE GRAPEVINE, is placed in the center and set on-point with alternate squares cut from a coordinated green and purple swirling print. This square creates the perfect area in which to display any large quilting motif, gridlines, or meandering swirls. A sawtooth border in purple fools the eye by appearing pieced together, when in reality it was appliquéd on top of the tone-on-tone white print 3" border. This white fabric is also used as the background of the appliquéd blocks.

Barbara Schenck and I have much in common – our love for hand appliqué and our agreeing that green and purple look fantastic together!

PEONIES
& Other Blooms

Block by Natalie H. Shaffer
Hanover, PA

Peonies & Other Blooms

SUPPLIES

- **Basic sewing supplies**
  needles, template material, thread, pins, fabric markers, and scissors

- **Rotary cutter, ruler, and board (optional)**

- **Tape**

- **Batting, 3" square**

- **Embroidery thread on the skein**
  for ants (black), for stems (two shades of green)

- **Freezer paper, 1" x 4"**

FABRIC

- **16" x 16" background fabric**

- **Scraps for leaves**
  use seven different green fabrics

- **Scraps of yellow**
  for center of peony

- **Scraps of pink**
  use for peony buds

- **Three shades of pink**
  for peony flowers. Use one light, one medium, and one dark fabric.

- **Small pieces of blue**
  for clover flowers in center of block

The Peony

Peony Flower: There are five of these dimensional flowers ❶ in the block. From your lightest pink, cut 5 strips 6½" x 1½". From your medium fabric, cut 5 strips 8½" x 1½". From the darkest of your pink fabrics cut 5 strips 8½" x 1½". Sew three strips together (on the short side) with a ¼" seam allowance from the lightest to the darkest color. The medium shade will be in the center. Press the strip in half wrong sides together. Place a small slash mark every two inches down along the raw edge of the strip. You do not need to place a slash mark at the seams but still use them as guidelines.

With regular weight sewing thread or quilting thread, sew a running stitch as shown in the illustration. The thread will show a little when the flower is completed, so change the thread color to match the fabric as you sew.

At each slash mark, gather and knot the thread ❷. If your thread breaks, you only need to go back and sew one petal, not the entire row. When you reach the folded edge of the fabric, take the thread up and over the fold. If your last stitch before the fold finished in the front, take the thread back in the fabric from behind so the thread is looped over the fold to make a nicer petal.

There should be eleven petals in all. The petals on the outside will be larger than those on the inside. Gather the center six petals tightly. The outer five petals should be gathered gently. After all of the strips are gathered, coil each strip around itself, keeping the small petals in the center. Continue until the flower looks similar to the one in the sample block. Firmly tack the back of the flowers to hold it together. Secure the peony to the background fabric by stitching around the outer petals.

Frayed Peony center: Cut a square on grain 1½" x 1½". Pull threads from all four sides until the edges are frayed equally. Fray about ⅜" from each edge. Next, fold the square in half on the diagonal. Then fold it again on the diagonal ❸. Repeat five times.

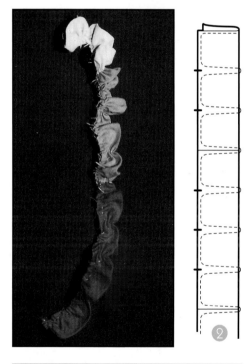

With matching thread, stick your needle and thread down through the center of the folded square. Stitch the square into the center of the peony flower. Tack the frayed edges where necessary to hide the raw edges of the center peony flower. ❀

The idea for this flower came from a demonstration given by Cindy Zlotnick Oravecz. I recommend her book (listed in the Bibliography Section on page 143) if you are looking for more dimensional flower ideas.

Peony Flowers & Leaves

Stuffed Peony Buds: These are made as perfect circles. Follow the directions on page 18. Use a ¾" washer and cut 5 circles of fabric **A**.

You may stuff the buds ❶ or sew them as they are. I used a little stuffing cut from a piece of batting, slightly smaller than the circle. Position the batting circle on the background fabric. Place your fabric circle on top of the batting and appliqué around the circle. The batting will be enclosed in the fabric circle. Refer to page 37 on stuffed grapes.

Stems and Leaves: Make a freezer paper template by placing freezer paper over the pattern shown on pages 50 – 53 and trace the stem onto the paper side of the freezer paper. Cut on the lines you drew. Iron the freezer paper, waxy side down, to the right side of your fabric. Trace around the shape. Cut a rectangular area around the shape. With a shape this narrow, work with a bigger piece of fabric, trimming the seam allowance as you sew ❷. With this method, your fabric edges will not fray.

Pin the rectangular piece in place. Trim a small section of seam allowance off the leaf or stems (refer to example). Appliqué the section you just trimmed. Cut the next seam allowance area. Sew that section. Keep moving around the shape until it is completed. By working with a larger piece of fabric and cutting the seam allowance as you sew, it controls the shape and prevents the seams from fraying. Repeat the steps, moving all the way around.

Leaves: For the peony leaves, I used the needle-turn method of appliqué. Refer to the general directions on page 16. You could also make a template from Templar or freezer paper if that is the method you prefer.

Cut 10 large **C** leaves, cut 4 medium **E** leaves, and cut 8 in total of the small **F** leaves (reverse half of the pieces) ❸. To appliqué, I chose the starch and template method. Use the method you like the best.

Stems: With two strands of embroidery thread, sew the stems ❹ from the base of the **E** leaves. ❀

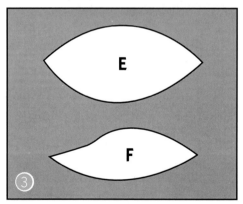

Clovers & Ants

Clover Flowers: The blue clover flowers in the center of the block are fun and easy to make ❶. Cut a strip of fabric on grain, ¾" x 4". Refer to the illustration and fray both sides of the strip. You want to fray about ¼" from each side, leaving ¼" in the center ❷.

Starting with a knot, sew a running stitch down the center of the strip. When you reach the opposite side pull on the thread to gather the strip. Knot the end. Grab each end and twist the strip around itself a few times ❸. Secure the clover flowers to the background by stab stitching down the center of each piece. Repeat four times.

Stems: With two strands of embroidery thread, sew the straight stem from the base of the clover flower to the point on the leaves.

Ants: Use two strands of embroidery thread on the body and head. Use one strand for the legs. Refer to the illustration on page 51. You might want to sew a practice ant first.

The stitch used for the body and head of the ant is called a satin stitch. The stitches ❹ should be side by side but not overlapping. ❀

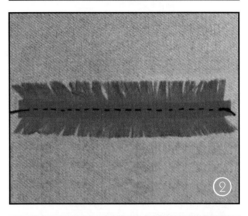

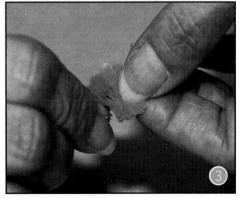

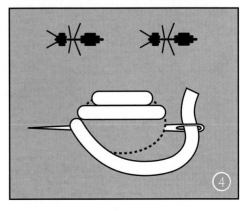

Placement Guide
(by quadrants)

PEONIES
& OTHER
BLOOMS

Appliqué Basics: Flower Wreaths, Karen Kay Buckley

Pattern shapes are identified with letters and indicate the order in which to appliqué. The written directions refer to the corresponding letters. Some edges will be left raw and covered by another shape; these edges are marked with small slash marks or drawn open ended.

A (5)	F & Fr (4 each)
B (5)	G (4)
C (10)	H* stems
D (5)	I* ants
E (4)	

*embroidered
 or drawn

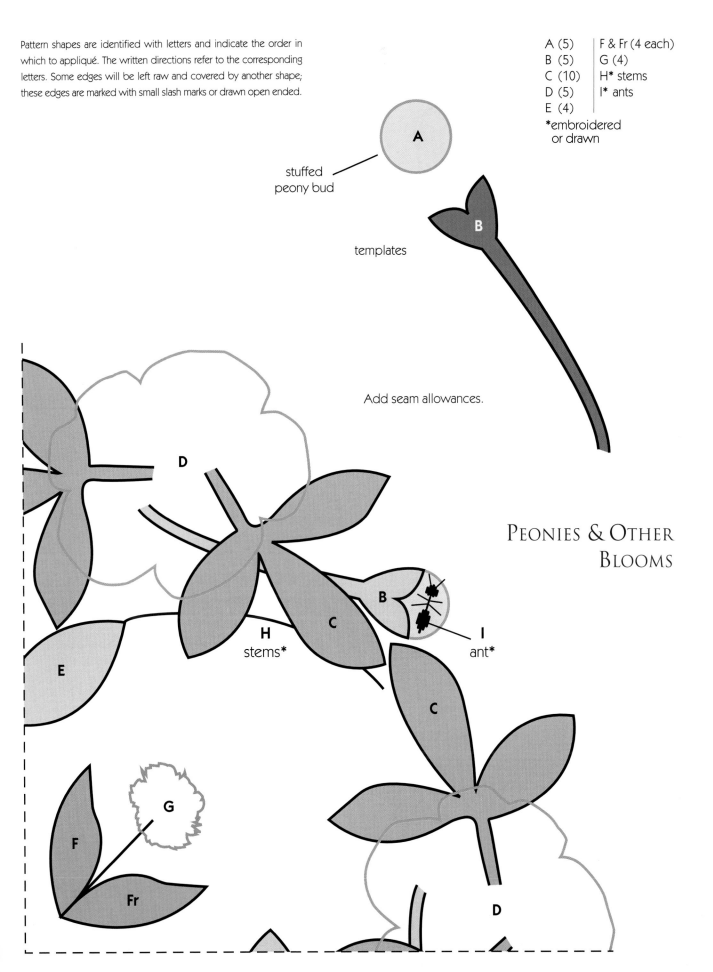

stuffed
peony bud

templates

Add seam allowances.

PEONIES & OTHER
BLOOMS

stems*

ant*

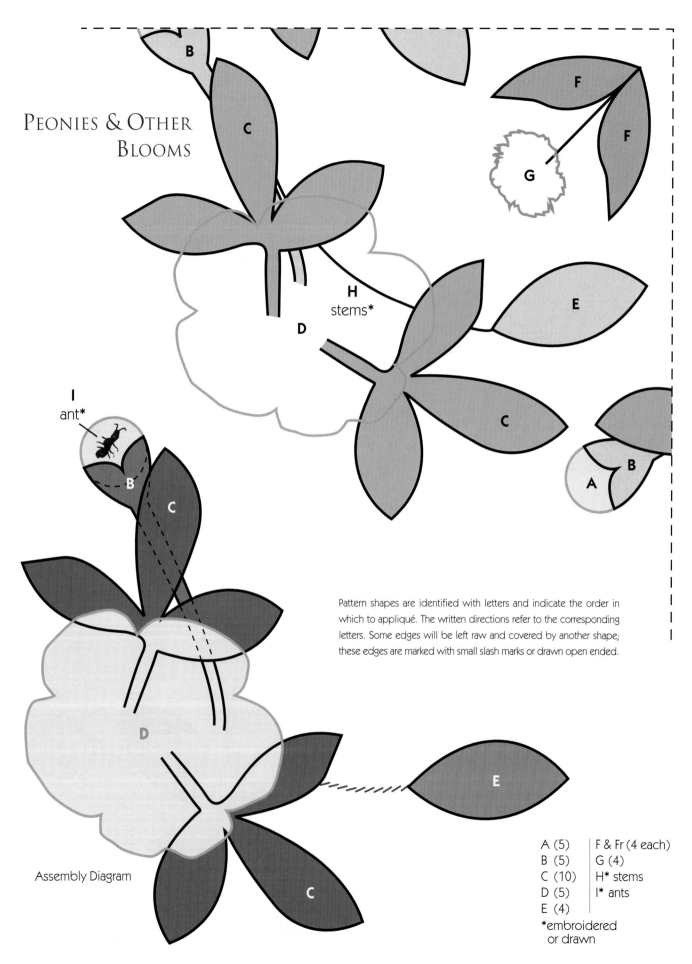

PEONIES & OTHER BLOOMS

B

C

F **F**

G

E

H stems*

D

C

E

A **B**

I ant*

B

C

Pattern shapes are identified with letters and indicate the order in which to appliqué. The written directions refer to the corresponding letters. Some edges will be left raw and covered by another shape; these edges are marked with small slash marks or drawn open ended.

C

D

E

Assembly Diagram

C

A (5) | F & Fr (4 each)
B (5) | G (4)
C (10) | H* stems
D (5) | I* ants
E (4) |

*embroidered
  or drawn

Appliqué Basics: Flower Wreaths, Karen Kay Buckley

F

Fr

E

G

H
stems*

C

B

A

C

PEONIES
& OTHER
BLOOMS

C

D

Add seam allowances.

Placement Guide
(by quadrants)

PLANNING CHART TWO

BACKYARD BEAUTIES AND BEYOND
83" x 83", Natalie Hixson Shaffer, Hanover, PA

The pieced sawtooth strips around the nine blocks create a square frame for the designs. The light gray background fabric and the subtle mini print allow the colorful appliquéd blocks to become the main focus of the quilt. By using the background fabric for the large border triangles, it appears as though the center area extends into the pieced border. Even though this border is composed of straight lines, visually it looks like a smooth curved line. When Natalie Shaffer came to the class reunion with this top, which she had designed on her own, we were all impressed!

Natalie felt she let many of her domestic responsibilities slide and wanted to thank her family for allowing her the time to work on this project. She said they were glad when she was finished – but I think she's just starting!

Appliqué Basics: Flower Wreaths, Karen Kay Buckley

MARIGOLDS
On My Mind

Block by Lytle Markham
Carlisle, PA

MARIGOLDS ON MY MIND

SUPPLIES

- **Basic sewing supplies**
  needles, template material, thread, pins, fabric markers, and scissors

- **Seed beads**
  use for honeysuckle flowers

- **Pigma™ markers in black and brown**

- **Small piece of batting**

- **Embroidery thread**
  varigated shades for stems

- **Freezer paper, 1" x 4"**

FABRIC

- **16" x 16" background fabric**

- **Scraps for leaves**
  use a variety of green fabrics

- **Scraps for berries**

- **¼ yard orange-gold fabric**
  for marigolds

- **Scraps for honeysuckle flowers**

- **Scraps of muslin**
  use for potato beetle

Marigold Flowers & Leaves

Leaves: Make a template of the small leaf shape on page 60. I used about ten different fabrics to make these leaves. Because of the size, I prefer the needle-turn method.

Before you start on these shapes, here are a few ideas from former students for making the leaves quicker. Their ideas do not require turning under the edges! These are the smallest shapes on any of the blocks in this book. Because they are so small, they can be challenging to get the seam allowance turned under properly.

One student stitched all of the leaves with silk ribbon. They looked fantastic! Another student embroidered all of the leaves with wool yarn using a satin stitch. They looked great. Another used the Wonder-Under™ method shown here ❶. Do what is comfortable for you and looks good.

Stems: The stems connecting the marigold leaves are sewn using a stem stitch (refer to page 20). Again, consider two shades of embroidery thread instead of one.

Marigolds: The four marigold flowers are made by ruching your fabric. Cut 4 strips of fabric on the grain 22" long and 1¼" wide. Use regular sewing thread or quilting thread since they will be gathered.

Press each strip flat so the raw edges meet down the center back of the strip. Start with a knot. Using a running stitch, sew a zigzag down the strip. When you reach the fold, take the thread up and over the folded edge ❷. If the last stitch finishes on the back of the strip, take the thread up and over the fold, and bring the needle in on the right side of the fabric. When the thread loops over the fold, it makes a nicer petal.

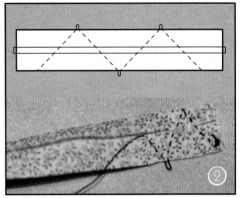

After you have 2" – 3" of stitching complete, pull the thread to gather the fabric ❸. Knot but do not cut the thread. Sew several more inches, pull, gather, and knot. Continue until you have reached the opposite end. To complete the marigold you need to coil the gathered strip around itself. Start in the middle, and tuck the raw edge under. Stitch the strip to itself. Continue until you reach the end of the gathered strip. Form this into a nicely shaped circle ❹ as you coil it around the center. Attach the flower to your background fabric by tacking the outer petals. ❀

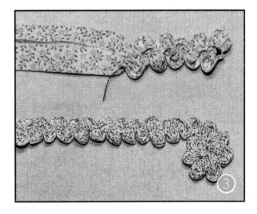

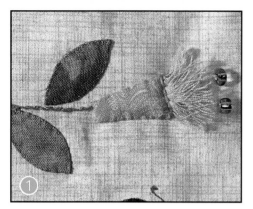

Honeysuckle Flowers

Honeysuckle Flowers: These dainty flowers ❶ are made using the template shape **H** provided on page 62. Cut 4 and finger crease the seam along the bottom edge. Appliqué only the two sides and top of the shape. The bottom will remain open temporarily until stuffed with batting to give added dimension to the flower. A portion of the fringe will also be placed in this opening.

To make the honeysuckle fringe, cut a piece of fabric on grain 2" x ¾". Fray ⅜" from one side of the strip as shown ❷. Stitch across the unfrayed edge with a running stitch. Pull and gather the thread. Push this up inside the flower and stitch it in place ❸.

Stamen: To make the stamen of the honeysuckle flower stitch with regular sewing thread and sew two straight stitches out from the frayed edge. Sew a seed bead to the end of each straight stitch.

Leaves: There are many leaves in the MARIGOLDS ON MY MIND block, I used the spray starch and template method to appliqué on both the **D** and **E** shapes. You need to cut 8 **D** large leaves, 4 **E** medium leaves and 16 **G** small leaves. (Refer to page 57 for **G** instructions.)

Berries: To make the small berries **F** use a ½" washer. Make 16 berries. Instructions for making perfect circles are on page 18.

Stems for berries: To give them a little more dimension, these stems were sewn with a stem stitch ❹ using wool yarn. If you cannot find wool yarn, the stems also look great sewn with two strands of embroidery thread. ✿

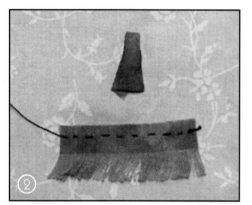

Potato Beetles

Peg Myers is a professional photographer as well as a quilter. The potato beetle photograph ❶ that she brought to class inspired everyone. It is the perfect insect to appear within the honeysuckle and marigold flowers.

Potato Beetles: To complete the block MARIGOLDS ON MY MIND, you need to make the potato beetles. These are my favorite insects in the whole project, and they are fun and easy to make. You might want to make a practice one before working on your finished block. The drawings take a little practice.

To make the beetle's body, make a template of the shape **C** provided on page 61. Trace the shape onto the right side of a piece of muslin. Cut outside these lines adding slightly less than a ¼" seam allowance.

Position the muslin/potato beetle body on the background fabric ❷. Using the needle-turn method, appliqué the body in place. Stitch about three-quarters of the way around the body. Push a small piece of batting inside the body ❸, and appliqué the rest of the way around the shape.

Draw the lines on the body with black and brown permanent Pigma markers, as shown in the illustration below ❹. Complete the potato beetle by drawing the legs and antennae with a black Pigma marker.

The legs and antennae could be stitched with embroidery thread if you prefer. It may depend on your choice of background fabric. ✿

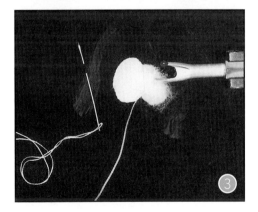

Placement Guide
(by quadrants)

MARIGOLDS
ON MY
MIND

B

A

A

A

A

E

F

G

G

G

G

A

F

D

C
potato
beetle*

D

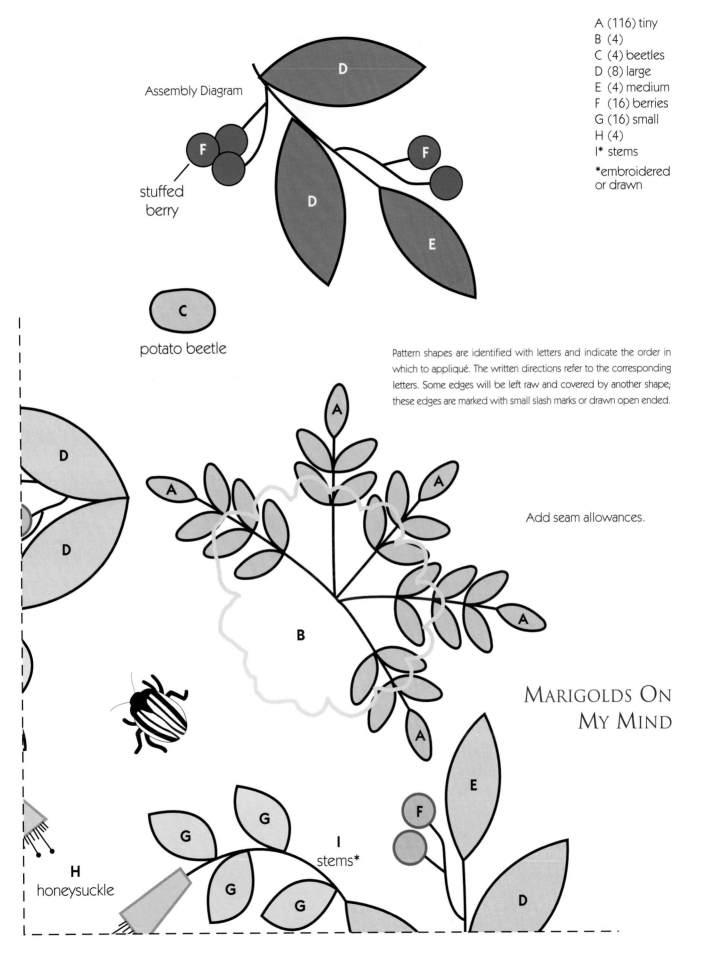

A (116) tiny
B (4)
C (4) beetles
D (8) large
E (4) medium
F (16) berries
G (16) small
H (4)
I* stems

*embroidered
or drawn

Assembly Diagram

stuffed
berry

potato beetle

Pattern shapes are identified with letters and indicate the order in
which to appliqué. The written directions refer to the corresponding
letters. Some edges will be left raw and covered by another shape;
these edges are marked with small slash marks or drawn open ended.

Add seam allowances.

MARIGOLDS ON
MY MIND

stems*

honeysuckle

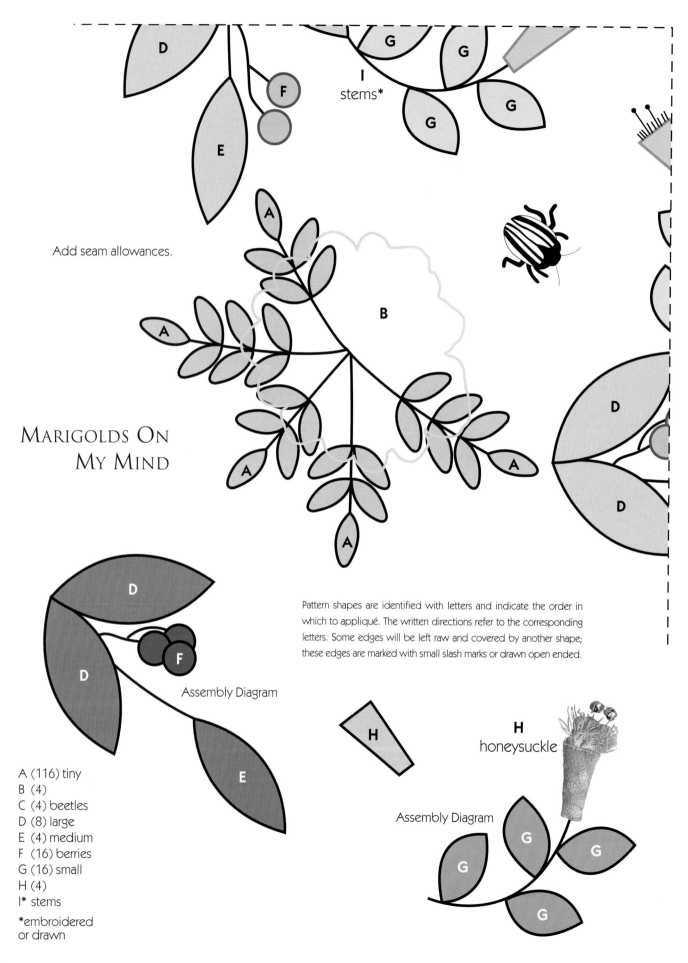

Add seam allowances.

I
stems*

B

MARIGOLDS ON
MY MIND

Pattern shapes are identified with letters and indicate the order in which to appliqué. The written directions refer to the corresponding letters. Some edges will be left raw and covered by another shape; these edges are marked with small slash marks or drawn open ended.

Assembly Diagram

H
honeysuckle

Assembly Diagram

A (116) tiny
B (4)
C (4) beetles
D (8) large
E (4) medium
F (16) berries
G (16) small
H (4)
I* stems

*embroidered
or drawn

Appliqué Basics: Flower Wreaths, Karen Kay Buckley

C
potato
beetle*

MARIGOLDS ON MY MIND

Placement Guide
(by quadrants)

PLANNING CHART THREE

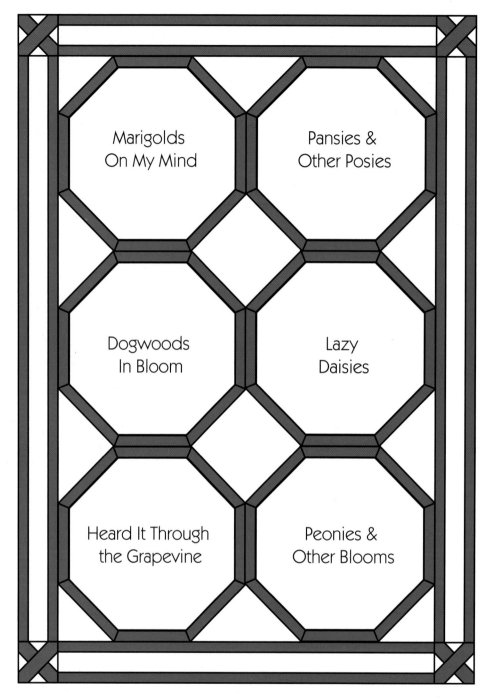

Marigolds
On My Mind

Pansies &
Other Posies

Dogwoods
In Bloom

Lazy
Daisies

Heard It Through
the Grapevine

Peonies &
Other Blooms

DREAM GARDEN
41" x 57", Lytle Markham, Carlisle, PA

Because her time is limited, Lytle Markham wanted to keep the layout and border simple, but do something that would complement the blocks. She chose a small floral print that had the same colors as the appliquéd blocks. This fabric really worked to her advantage. Since the fabric had flowers and leaves, she felt that no additional appliqué was needed on the border. The dark fabric around each of the six octagons and in the border gives this wall quilt nice clean lines and helps to tie everything together.

I have always thought that Lytle was an excellent quilter. She has a great eye and likes to try different things. Her only problem is she works too much which cuts into her sewing time!

Appliqué Basics: Flower Wreaths, Karen Kay Buckley

CLEMATIS,
Bee Plants & Bee

Block by Sandra Moore
Harrisburg, PA

CLEMATIS, BEE PLANTS & BEE

SUPPLIES

- **Basic sewing supplies**
  needles, template material, thread, pins, fabric markers, and scissors

- **Sewing machine**

- **Small piece of freezer paper**

- **Seed beads**

- **Embroidery thread**
  for stems (green), antennae (black), and center of clematis (yellow)

- **Perle cotton (size 8) or embroidery thread**
  for stamen of bee plants

- **Yarn, wool yarn, or embroidery thread**
  for body of bee

- **Metallic thread**
  for wings of bee

FABRIC

- **16" x 16" background fabric**

- **Scraps of purple fabrics**
  for the clematis flowers

- **Scraps of yellow fabrics**
  for the center of clematis

- **Scraps of green fabrics**
  for leaves

- **Scraps of blue (optional)**
  or use color of your choice for bee plants in center of block

- **Scraps of yellow**
  for body of bee

- **Tulle fabric**
  for wings on bumblebee

Clematis Flowers

Leaves: There are 10 of the clematis leaves. Each leaf has two pieces. Half of these leaves are in reverse so remember when marking and cutting your fabric to do half in the opposite direction. I used four different green fabrics for these leaves.

The templates for this pattern are on page 72. The leaf **B1** will be appliquéd in place first. The slash marks on the side indicate those edges remain raw because they will be covered later. Using the method of your choice, turn under the curved edge on each leaf. When you appliqué **B2** in place, make sure it covers the raw edge of the under side of the leaf ❶.

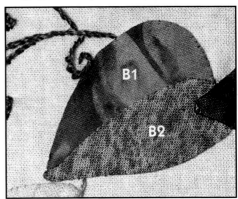

Petals: There are 30 of the clematis petals (template **C**). It sounds like a lot, but they are not difficult to make. I used three different purple fabrics in my petals. Remember there are many different colors of clematis flowers. Your choice might depend on your background fabric.

Before sewing the clematis petals on the background, place a ¾" square of yellow fabric in the center of the clematis flower ❷. This can be basted in place or pinned. The center of the flower is made using thread and sometimes does not cover the entire opening. It looks better if the yellow fabric shows through, rather than your background fabric. Choose a yellow fabric that will closely match your yellow embroidery thread.

When sewing the clematis petals, work in a circular direction. I planned my flowers using three different purple fabrics placing matching fabrics across from each other. It is the "balanced" side of me! After the first petal is sewn in place, the second petal will go over the first in the center area. The third petal will overlap the second petal, and so on. With this in mind, keep a section on the first petal open so the last petal can be tucked under it.

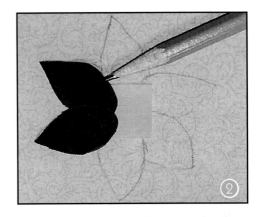

Clematis Centers: Cut a 4" length of yellow embroidery thread. Set it aside. Pull another length approximately 18 – 20" from the skein. Do not cut the thread. Wrap the thread in its full thickness of six strands around a 1" ruler or the handle of a seam ripper. (Anything about that size that will work.) Wrap the thread around eight times. Pull it from the ruler and cut the thread even with the looped end. Take the 4" length and tie it around the center of the looped thread. Cut the loops open and trim the 4" section of thread even with the other ends ❸.

Turn it sideways, so one of the cut edges is open and flat against the center opening of the clematis petals. Secure the threaded center to the clematis flower by tacking it ❹ in several places. ✿

Bee Plant Flowers & Stems

Leaves: The templates for this project are on pages 70 – 73. There are three **A** leaves used on each plant, and five bee plant flowers arranged around the center of the block. I used three different green fabrics for these leaves, all cut from template **A**. I used the starch and template method to make 15 leaves from a variety of green fabrics. Use the method of your choice to appliqué this shape in place.

Embroidery: With a stem stitch embroider the stem of the bee plants ❶. Use two strands of embroidery thread and follow the directions on page 20 to do this stitch. The curlicue vines of the clematis plant can also be added at this time ❷. Refer to the placement diagram for this block.

Flowers: I used the needle-turn method for the flowers. Cut 5 **D** flowers. After the flower is sewn in place, sew four to five straight lines out from the pointed area of the flower. I used a perle cotton thread for these lines, but two strands of embroidery thread would work nicely. To complete these flowers, sew one seed bead ❸ at the end of each of your straight stitches.🐝

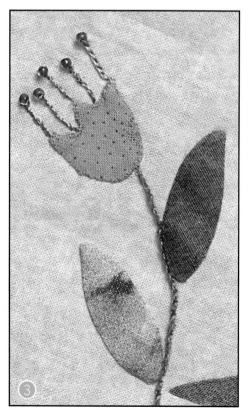

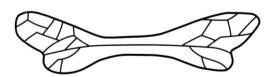

Bumblebee Wing Pattern

The Bumblebee

What garden would be complete without a buzzing bumblebee **❶**?

Wings: To make the wings, refer to the pattern on page 68. Trace the outline of the wings and the veins in the wings on the paper side of a piece of freezer paper. This paper will act as a stabilizer and will be torn away when the stitching is complete.

Cut, layer, and place 4 pieces of tulle the same size as the freezer paper. Place the tulle against the waxy side of the freezer paper. Baste around the outside edge to hold the layers together.

These wings, like the wings on the dragonfly (page 120), are made using the sewing machine. Thread your machine with metallic or iridescent thread in the top*. Place cotton machine embroidery thread, from a spool, in the bobbin. Use an open embroidery foot on your machine for this stitch so you can easily follow your drawn lines.

Practice stitching along the outer edges of the tulle and freezer paper before sewing on the wings. Set your machine for a very small satin/zigzag stitch. The stitches should be very close together but not overlapping **❷**. The width on this should be small as you can get it.

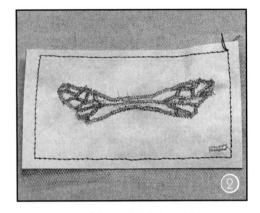

Sew the veins first. Start with the short veins, and watch your lines of stitching. The longer vein lines will cover the raw edges on the inside. Extend the veins out past the edges of the wings. They will be trimmed later and secured with more satin stitching. After all of the veins are sewn, increase the width of your stitch slightly and sew around the outside of the wing. Remove the freezer paper from the inside vein area **❸**. Cut around the outside edges being careful not to cut through your stitching. Pin the wings in place.

Body: Make template **E** for the body of the bumblebee and position the body over the wings **❹**. Appliqué the body leaving a small opening in which to stuff some batting then close the remaining seam.

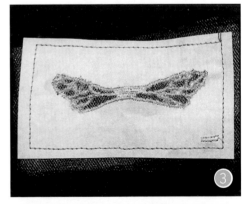

Using yellow yarn or three strands of yellow embroidery thread from the skein, sew over the back section of the body with a satin stitch. Referring to the photograph above add black lines to the body and legs on the bumblebee. These can also be sewn with yarn or three strands of embroidery thread.

Antennae: Stitch the antennae on the front of the bumblebee body with two strands of black embroidery thread. ❀

*You might want to try this with a regular sewing machine needle in an 80/12 size. If the thread breaks, switch to a metallic or metafil needle or try a product called *Sewers Aid*. It is a liquid that is squeezed down the side of the spool of thread (directions on bottle).

Placement Guide
(by quadrants)

CLEMATIS, BEE PLANTS & BEE

B1

B2

F

A

A

B1

B2

A

D

F

C
petals

E

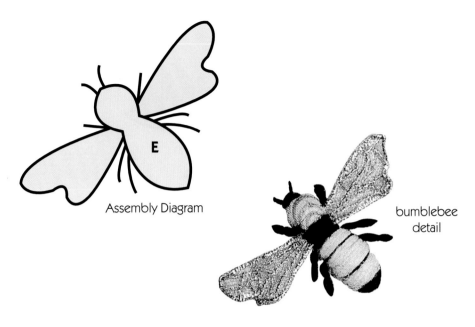

Assembly Diagram

A (15)
B1 & B2 (10 each)
C (30)
D (5)
E (1)
F (5) yellow squares
G (5) frayed centers
H* stems

*embroidered
or drawn

bumblebee
detail

Pattern shapes are identified with letters and indicate the order in which to appliqué. The written directions refer to the corresponding letters. Some edges will be left raw and covered by another shape; these edges are marked with small slash marks or drawn open ended.

CLEMATIS,
BEE PLANTS & BEE

Add seam allowances.

Clematis, Bee Plants & Bee

G frayed center

B1

B2

Assembly Diagram

A (15)
B1 & B2 (10 each)
C (30)
D (5)
E (1)
F (5) yellow squares
G (5) frayed centers
H* stems

*embroidered
or drawn

Pattern shapes are identified with letters and indicate the order in which to appliqué. The written directions refer to the corresponding letters. Some edges will be left raw and covered by another shape; these edges are marked with small slash marks or drawn open ended.

E

A

A

A

B1

B2

B2

B1

D

C
petals

B2

B1

F

A

B2

A

B1

CLEMATIS,
BEE PLANTS
& BEE

Add seam allowances.

Placement Guide
(by quadrants)

PLANNING CHART FOUR

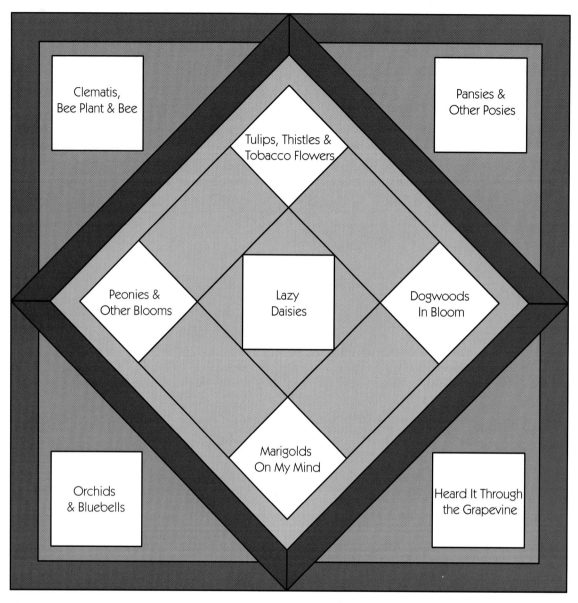

CIRCLES OF SPLENDOR
80" x 80", Sandra Moore, Harrisburg, PA

This layout allows you to expand the quilt top to fit any bed size and is really easier than it looks. The darker fabric around the center five blocks makes a wonderful frame and taking the inner border into the outer border creates a very interesting visual effect. The larger open areas would be a great place to use some wonderful quilting designs.

If you decide to try this layout, keep in mind that some blocks are set on the diagonal which will determine how you position them on your background fabric when you transfer the patterns.

Sandy Moore is a newer quilter and deserves a lot of credit for her initiative and innovative work. She has developed a real love for appliqué which comes across in her work.

Appliqué Basics: Flower Wreaths, Karen Kay Buckley

ORCHIDS & BLUEBELLS

Block by Eleanor L. Karper
Carlisle, PA

Orchids & Bluebells

SUPPLIES

- **Basic sewing supplies**
  needles, template material, thread, pins, fabric markers, and scissors

- **Ruler, rotary cutter, and board (optional)**

- **Bias press bars**

- **Embroidery thread**
  for stems of bluebells

- **Small piece of batting**

- **Fly fishing feathers (optional)**

FABRIC

- **16" x 16" background fabric**

- **Scraps of green fabrics**
  use four or five different greens for stems

- **¼ yard green for stems**

- **Scraps of purple fabrics**
  use two different fabrics for orchid flowers

- **Scrap of yellow**
  for center of orchid

- **Scraps of blue**
  for bluebells

- **Scrap of brown**
  for moth. Use two different fabrics for the wings and one for the body.

The Orchids

Stems: To make the stems for the orchid flowers, use the ³⁄₁₆" bias press bar. Be sure the raw edge of the stem extends ¼" under the flower and the petal.

Leaves: When making the orchids you need a template of each leaf shape. Refer to the pattern on page 81. Half of the 10 **B** leaves need to be cut in reverse. Cut 5 **C** leaves. I used the starch and template method to turn under the edges of these leaves ❶.

Orchid Buds: Make a template of the flower bud shape **D**. Cut the shape from fabric adding a little less than a ¼" seam allowance. Since this shape will be stuffed, you also need to cut a piece of batting. Place the template over a piece of batting which has been cut slightly smaller than the template.

Pin the **D** fabric shape to your background fabric. Stitch from the raw edge along one side up to the point of the bud. Slide the batting under the bud and stitch down the other side. The batting will be enclosed in the bud. Repeat five times.

Calyx: You need to cut 5 **E** pieces. To make the shape of the calyx, or bud's covering, for the orchids, I used the needle-turn method of appliqué ❷.

Petals: Make the smaller petal pieces first. There are three of these in each flower therefore cut 15 **F** pieces. I used the starch and template method on this shape.

To make the shape of the larger orchid petals **G** I again used the starch and template method because the moisture from the starch makes the nice gentle curves look great ❸.

Centers: There are several steps to making the dimensional centers of the orchids and it may seem a little strange at times, but go with it. It looks good in the end! Complete instructions are provided on the following page. ✿

Dimensional Orchids

How to make the dimensional center of the orchid ❶

- There are five dimensional centers **H**, so you need to cut 5 pieces of purple fabric 4" x 2½" and 5 pieces of yellow fabric 4" x 1½". Sew one purple strip to one yellow strip with a ¼" seam allowance. Press the seam to one side.

- Fold and press these units in half, wrong sides together. Place a mark 1" in from the raw edge on the yellow fabric. Do this on each side.

- Line your ruler up from the outer point on the folded edge to the 1" mark. Cut off that corner. Do the same on the other side ❷.

- Open the above unit, and fold it in half right sides together. Sew with a ¼" seam allowance along the purple fabric and halfway down the yellow fabric. Turn the unit inside out, using a point turner to smooth the edges ❸.

- Push the yellow fabric inside the tube.

- Using quilting or regular sewing thread and a running stitch, start along the seam and sew in a zigzag manner around the upper edge of this shape. You will only sew through two thicknesses of fabric at one time. The uppermost point of the zigzag should be ¼" from the folded edge.

- When you are back at the seam, pull the thread gently to gather the edge.

- Pull the orchid fabric back to expose a small portion of the yellow fabric ❹. Tack the purple fabric in place.

- Position the shape in place over the stems, leaves, and petals. Stitch along one side of the gathered flower. When you reach the raw edge section, use your needle to tuck the seam under. Round the edge and stitch up along the other side (refer to photo at top.) Repeat five times. ❀

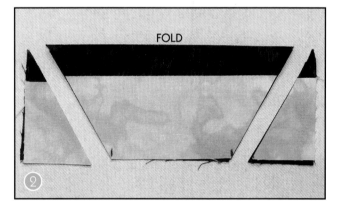

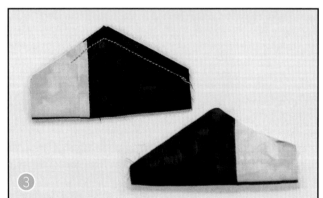

The Bluebell

Stems: Use two strands of embroidery thread to sew the stems.

Bluebells: After making the orchids these flowers will be a breeze! There are four short steps to making the bluebells ❶.

• Cut 10 squares of fabric, 1" x 1" on the grain. Fray a small section from each side of the square.

• With a running stitch, using matching thread, sew just inside the frayed edge. Start in one corner with a knot and stitch until you are back to the same corner **a**.

• Fold the square in half on the diagonal, wrong sides together.

• Pull the thread to gather the square **b**, **c**. Knot the thread and appliqué the bluebells in place. ❀

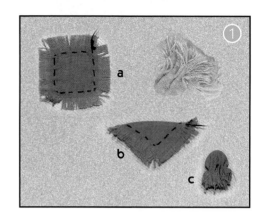

The Moth

Back Wings: To make the back wings of the moth **L** and **Lr**, I used the starch and template method. Do not worry about the point on this shape because it will be covered by the body of the moth. Using the template on page 82, cut 1 **L** and 1 **Lr** shape.

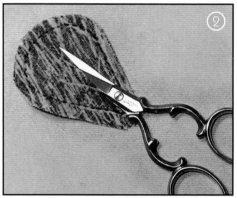

Dimensional Front Wings: Make a template of the shape **M**. These wings are meant to be dimensional. Place two pieces of fabric right sides together and trace a wing on the back of the fabric. Trace the second wing in reverse.

Cut slightly less than a ¼" beyond the lines you drew. Sew on the lines. Do not sew across the small straight edge with the slash marks. Cut half way up the back of the wing so it can be turned inside out ❷. Be careful not to cut through the front of the wing.

Use a point turner to smooth the edges. Stitch the slit closed. Appliqué the wings in place. Only stitch half way down each side so the wings look more dimensional.

Body: To make the body of the moth cut a strip of fabric, on grain, ¾" x 6". Fray ¼" from each edge. Using matching thread, start with a knot and sew down the center of the strip ❸. Pull the thread to gather the strip. Knot the thread. Twist the strip around itself ❹. Stab stitch in place through the center of the body.

Antennae: I used fly-fishing feathers for the antennae. See the Supplies section on Feathers, page 12. The antennae can also be stitched with embroidery thread. ❀

Placement Guide
(by quadrants)

ORCHIDS
& BLUEBELLS

Add seam allowances.

C

J
stems*

A

B

Br

D

E

H

F

F

G

K
bluebell

F

G

Mr

G

F

N

templates

A (5)
B & Br (5 each)
C (5)
D (5)
E (5)
F (15)
G (10)
H (5) dimensional orchid centers
I* antennaes
J* stems
K (10)
L & Lr (1 each)
M & Mr (1 each)
N (1)

*embroidered or drawn

Pattern shapes are identified with letters and indicate the order in which to appliqué. The written directions refer to the corresponding letters. Some edges will be left raw and covered by another shape; these edges are marked with small slash marks or drawn open ended.

ORCHIDS & BLUEBELLS

antennaes*

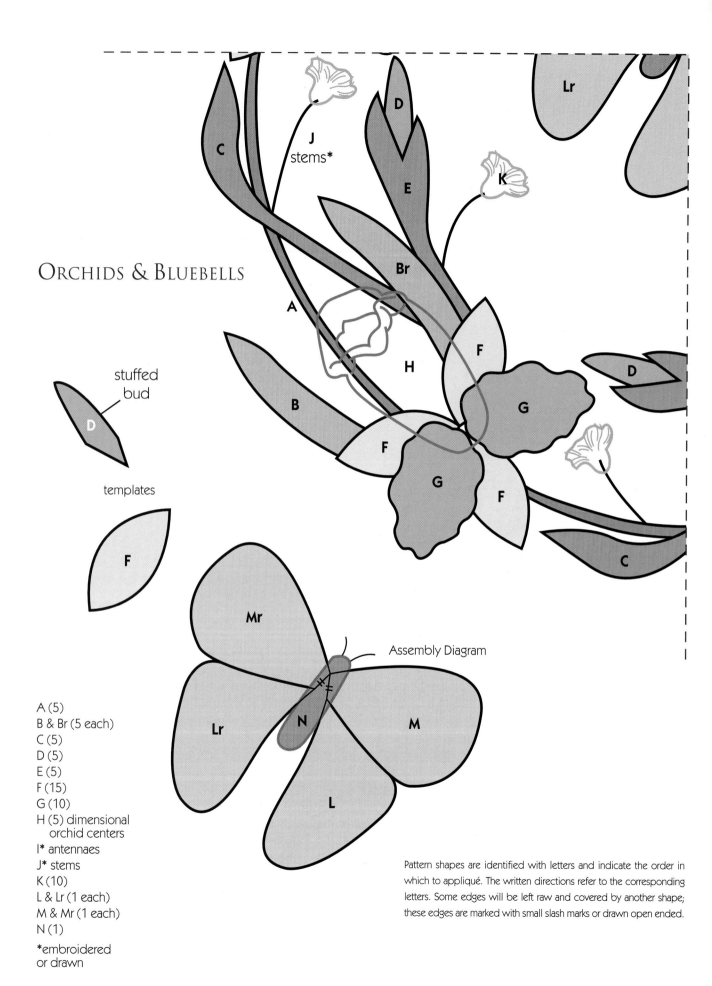

ORCHIDS & BLUEBELLS

stuffed
bud

D

templates

F

J
stems*

C

D

E

Br

A

H

F

B

F

G

D

F

G

C

Lr

K

Lr

Assembly Diagram

Mr

N

M

L

A (5)
B & Br (5 each)
C (5)
D (5)
E (5)
F (15)
G (10)
H (5) dimensional
    orchid centers
I* antennaes
J* stems
K (10)
L & Lr (1 each)
M & Mr (1 each)
N (1)

*embroidered
or drawn

Pattern shapes are identified with letters and indicate the order in
which to appliqué. The written directions refer to the corresponding
letters. Some edges will be left raw and covered by another shape;
these edges are marked with small slash marks or drawn open ended.

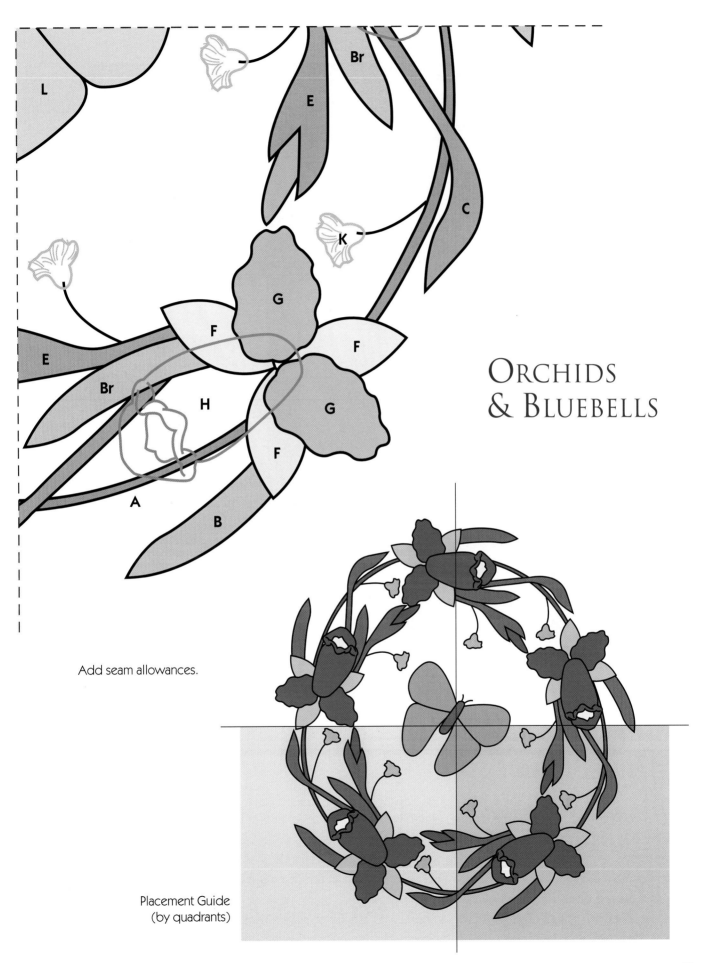

Orchids & Bluebells

Add seam allowances.

Placement Guide
(by quadrants)

PLANNING CHART FIVE

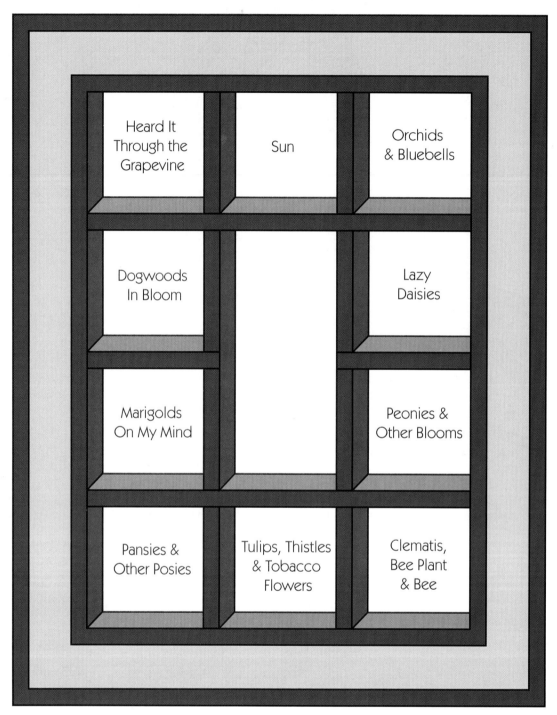

THROUGH THE WINDOW
67" x 81", Eleanor L. Karper, Carlisle, PA

*A*n enlarged Attic Windows patchwork pattern was used to set together the floral wreaths. When you stand back and view this quilt you see all the beautiful flowers through the window sashings. The classic window frame uses dark and medium value fabrics which give a nice perspective of depth to the quilt. Eleanor Karper created a superb center medallion by taking flowers from each wreath to create a new floral arrangement. Her use of the Sun block (page 28) at the top center seems to bring those rays of sun down through the entire quilt.

Eleanor's quilt THROUGH THE WINDOW, can be viewed in color on page 137 of the Gallery section. Eleanor comes from a family of stitchers, and she has been sewing for many years. Her quilts reflect her considerable talent.

Appliqué Basics: Flower Wreaths, Karen Kay Buckley

TULIPS, THISTLES & TOBACCO FLOWERS

Block by Annie P. Johnson
Littlestown, PA

TULIPS, THISTLES & TOBACCO FLOWERS

SUPPLIES

■ **Basic sewing supplies**
needles, template material, thread, pins,
fabric markers, and scissors

■ **Yellow embroidery thread**
for stems of tobacco flowers

■ **Seed beads**
for center of the tobacco flowers

■ **Larger beads**
for ends of tulip stamen

■ **Small piece of batting**

■ **Fly fishing feathers (optional)**

■ **Yarn**
for wooly boogers

■ **Wonder-Under™**

■ **Soutache**
for thistle stems (optional)

■ **⅓ yard of ⅝" wide ribbon**
(wire or regular)
for pod of thistle

FABRIC

■ **16" x 16" background fabric**

■ **Scraps of green fabrics**
use different greens for stems and leaves

■ **One color in several shades**
for tulips

■ **Scraps of blue fabric**
for tobacco flowers

The Thistles

Thistle: To make a thistle shown in the TULIPS, THISTLES & TOBACCO FLOWERS block, you need to make the pod area first, and then the flower ❶.

Pod Area: Use ⅝" wide ribbon for the pod area. Cut 3 pieces of ribbon 1½". Remove the wire, if necessary. Fold the ribbon in half and sew with a ¼" seam allowance. Start and stop with a knot. Turn the ribbon inside out so the seam is on the inside. Sew around what will be the top of the pod with a small running stitch. Sew through one thickness only. With a knot in your thread start sewing at the seam. When you are back at the seam, pull the thread to gather the ribbon. Secure with a knot ❷. For added dimension, stuff a small piece of batting inside the ribbon.

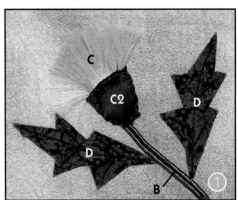

Thistle Flower: You need ⅞" wide grosgrain ribbon to make the thistle*. Cut 3 sections 4", one for each of the flowers. Remove the selvage from one side of the ribbon. Pull the threads, and fray until about ¼" of the ribbon remains. Roll the ribbon around itself ❸. Stitch the ends to hold the roll in place. Push the grosgrain ribbon into the pod, then stitch the pod and the flower together around the end of the pod/ribbon.

Thistle Leaves: Make a template of the leaf pattern **D** on page 92. Fuse two pieces of fabric together. Cut 2 squares 4" from green fabric. Iron a piece of Wonder-Under™ slightly less than 4" x 4" to the back of one piece of the green fabric. Remember to use a press cloth over and under your fabric to avoid damaging your iron and ironing surface. Allow the fusible web to cool for a few seconds before peeling the paper away.

Center the other 4" square of green fabric over the fusible web and iron. The back sides of the fabric will now stay together. Trace the leaf shape onto the fused square. Cut just inside the lines you drew ❹.

Secure the leaf to your background fabric with a stab stitch down the center vein. After the leaf is secure, trace the center and side veins with a Pigma marker. I used a brown marker, but choose one that contrasts with the color of your leaf fabric.

Thistle Stems: You could use your ⅛" bias press bar to make these stems. I added another dimension to this block using soutache braid. Since it often comes in just three basic colors, I purchased white and dyed my own. It was very easy to do. This was one of the last blocks I designed in this series. If I had thought of it sooner, I would have used soutache in several other blocks. If you are going to dye a package of soutache, consider using it for some of the other stems as well (refer to pages 11 – 12.) ❀

* Several years ago, I saw Camela Nitschke demonstrating how to make these flowers. She has numerous dimensional flower pattern ideas.

Tulips & Leaves

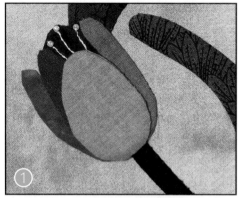

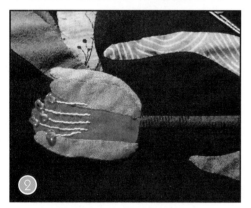

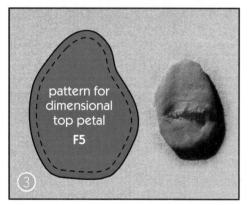

pattern for
dimensional
top petal
F5

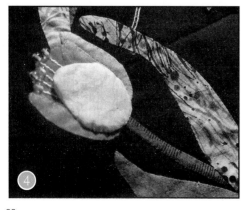

Tulip Leaves: Make a template of the leaves **E1** and **E2**, on page 92. Cut 5 each of these tulip leaves. Remember the slash marks indicate raw edges, which do not need to be turned under. I used the starch and template method to appliqué these shapes.

Tulip Stems: Use your ¼" bias press bar to make the **A** stems. Be sure to extend the stem at least ¼" into the flower area and ¼" into the leaf.

Flowers: Each tulip flower ❶ consists of four flat pieces, **F1**, **F2**, **F3**, and **F4** and one dimensional piece **F5**. To start the flowers, make a template of each of the flat shapes. These shapes appear on page 91.

Appliqué in place in the order they are numbered, using the method of your choice. I used the starch and template method. After these four shapes are appliquéd in place, the next step is to stitch the stamen. Referring to the photo ❷, sew the stamen with a stem stitch and two strands of embroidery thread. Sew a bead to the end of each stamen.

Make a template of the shape **F5**. Trace the shape onto the back of your fabric. Place the fabric right sides together with another piece of fabric in the same color, and cut ¼" beyond the lines you drew. Sew on the drawn lines, starting and stopping with a knot. Clip a slit in the back of the petal. Turn the fabric inside out ❸, using a point turner to smooth the edges.

If the open slit is on the lower half of the petal, it does not need to be stitched closed. Appliqué the dimensional petal to the top of the previous tulip shapes. Stitch to attach only half of the way up each side so the top of the petal ❹ has more dimension. ✿

Appliqué Basics: Flower Wreaths, Karen Kay Buckley

Tobacco Flowers

Tobacco Stems: With wool yarn, or two strands of embroidery thread, sew a stem stitch to create the stems **G** for the tobacco flowers ❶.

Flowers: There are a few simple steps to follow to make the petals for this flower. First, make a template of the shape **H1**, page 91. There are five of these flowers, each with five petals. Trace 25 circles on the back of your fabric using the template. *Do not add seam allowance.* Cut on the line you drew. Fold the circle in half, wrong sides together. Then fold it in half again. Sew with a running stitch across the bottom raw edge. Be sure to start with a knot. Pull and gather the thread. Stitch the remaining circles in the same manner connecting them all to one piece of thread. Connect the first and last petal with a couple of extra stitches ❷.

Stuffed Center: To add dimension to the center of the tobacco flowers use the **H2** circle. Trace the circle on the back of your fabric, and cut on the line you just drew. Using a running stitch, sew slightly inside that line. Roll a small piece of batting into a ball, and place it on the back of the circle ❸. Gather the thread so the batting is enclosed inside the circle. Stitch the stuffed circle to the center of the five petals.

Appliqué the flower in place, and stitch several seed beads in the center or embroider French knots. Refer to the first illustration. ❀

The Wooly Booger

Some of you are thinking, "What is a wooly booger?" In my area that is what we call caterpillars. It is also the name used by fly fishermen for a type of fly designed by Barry Beck. It is amazing what we learn from each other!

Wooly booger: Use yarn to make the wooly booger. Wrap it around your index finger 20 times. Pull the yarn from your finger, and place the yarn on a piece of fabric the same color as the leaf (in case some of it shows). On the sewing machine, stitch down the center of the looped yarn. Backstitch at beginning and end of stitches ❹. Cut the loops open on each side. Now give the wooly booger a haircut! Make the head a little smaller than the body to give it some definition even though the head and tail look the same on the real ones! Cut the base fabric away so very little remains, being careful not to cut through your stitching. Stitch the wooly booger in place with a stab stitch down the center.

Antennae: For the wooly booger, I used fly fishing feathers, which I explain on page 79, for the antennae. If you do not want to use feathers, you can embroider the antennae or draw it on with a Pigma marker. ❀

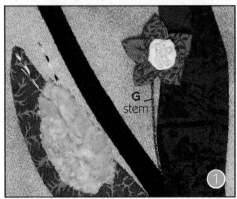

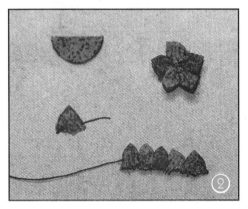

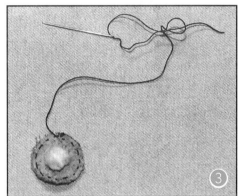

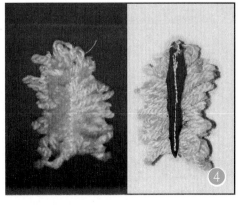

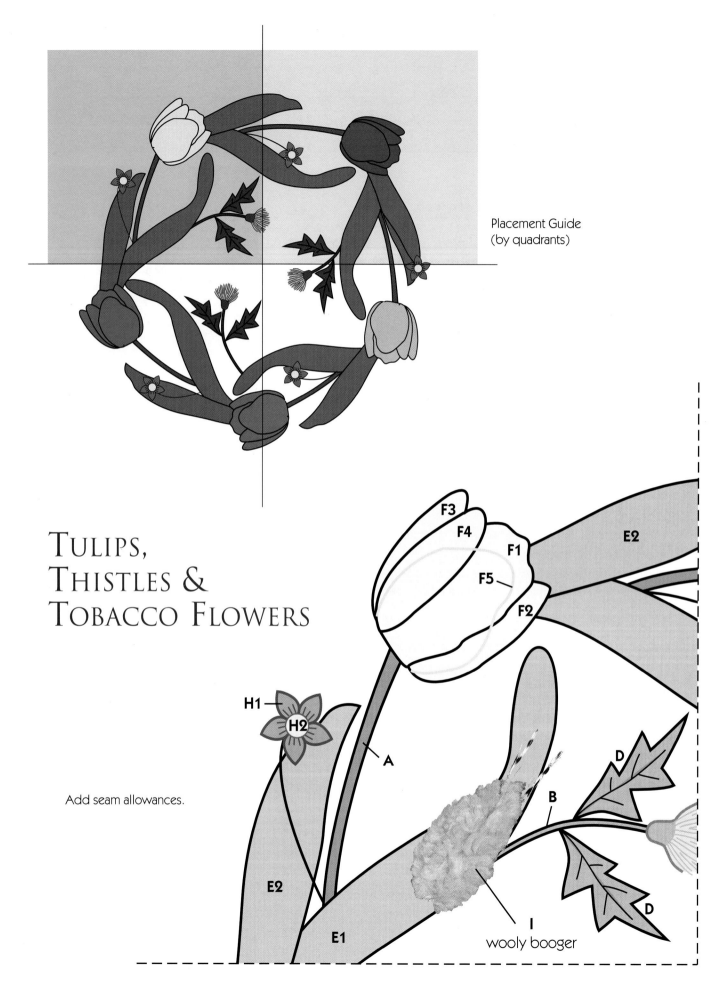

Placement Guide
(by quadrants)

TULIPS,
THISTLES &
TOBACCO FLOWERS

Add seam allowances.

F3
F4
F1
F5
F2
E2

E2

H1
H2
A

E2

E1

D

B

D

I
wooly booger

Appliqué Basics: Flower Wreaths, Karen Kay Buckley

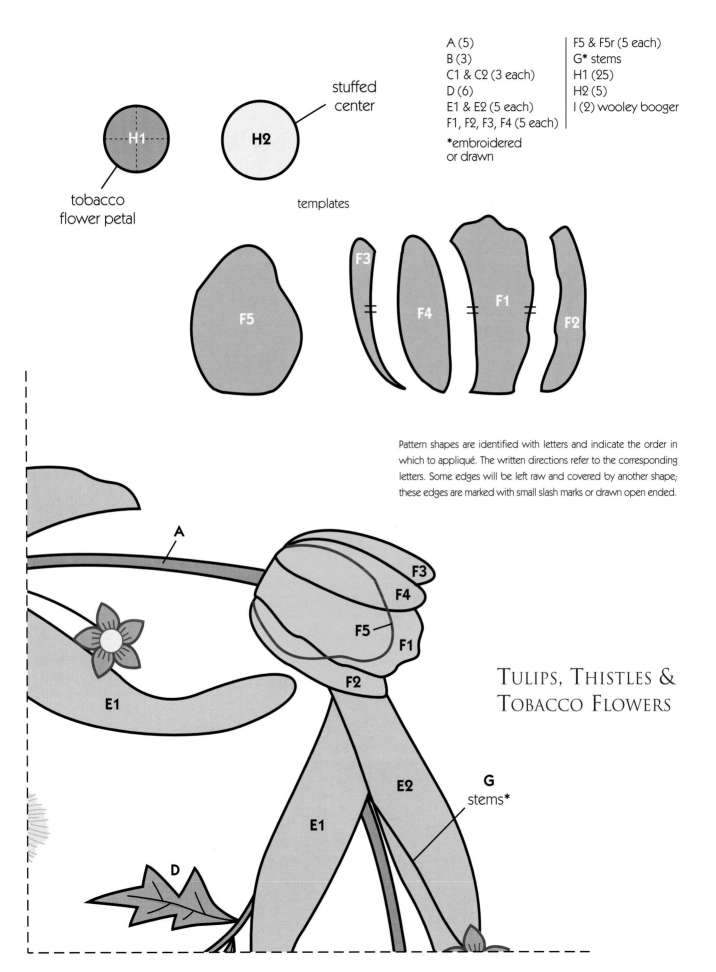

A (5)
B (3)
C1 & C2 (3 each)
D (6)
E1 & E2 (5 each)
F1, F2, F3, F4 (5 each)

F5 & F5r (5 each)
G* stems
H1 (25)
H2 (5)
I (2) wooley booger

*embroidered
or drawn

stuffed
center

H1

H2

tobacco
flower petal

templates

F3

F4

F1

F2

F5

Pattern shapes are identified with letters and indicate the order in
which to appliqué. The written directions refer to the corresponding
letters. Some edges will be left raw and covered by another shape;
these edges are marked with small slash marks or drawn open ended.

A

F3
F4
F5
F1

F2

E1

TULIPS, THISTLES &
TOBACCO FLOWERS

E2

G
stems*

E1

D

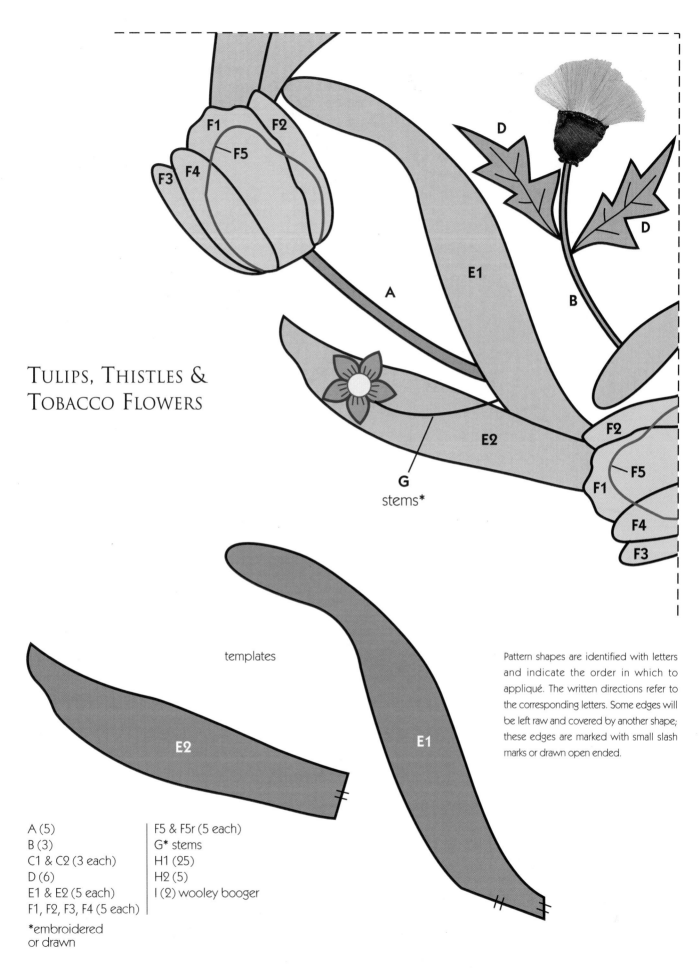

TULIPS, THISTLES & TOBACCO FLOWERS

F1 F2 F5 F3 F4

D D

E1 B

A

G
stems*

E2

F2 F5 F1 F4 F3

templates

E2

E1

Pattern shapes are identified with letters and indicate the order in which to appliqué. The written directions refer to the corresponding letters. Some edges will be left raw and covered by another shape; these edges are marked with small slash marks or drawn open ended.

A (5)
B (3)
C1 & C2 (3 each)
D (6)
E1 & E2 (5 each)
F1, F2, F3, F4 (5 each)

F5 & F5r (5 each)
G* stems
H1 (25)
H2 (5)
I (2) wooley booger

*embroidered
or drawn

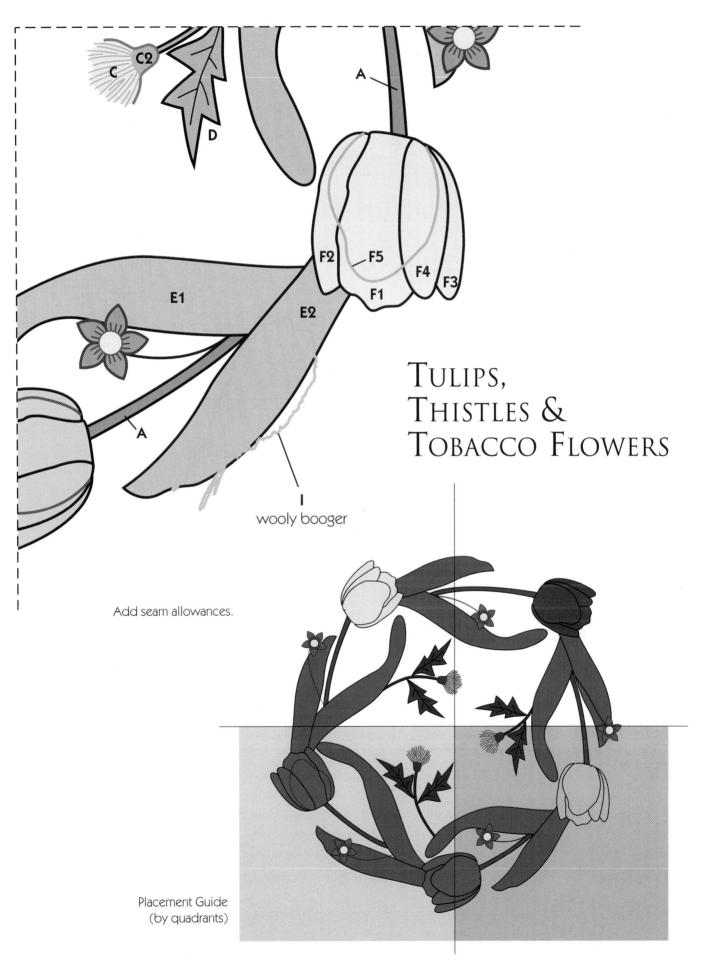

C2
C
D

A

F2 F5
E1
E2 F4 F3
F1

A

wooly booger

TULIPS, THISTLES & TOBACCO FLOWERS

Add seam allowances.

Placement Guide
(by quadrants)

PLANNING CHART SIX

Marigolds On My Mind	Orchids & Bluebells	Peonies & Other Blooms
Heard It Through the Grapevine	Tulips, Thistles & Tobacco Flowers	Pansies & Other Posies
Dogwoods In Bloom	Clematis, Bee Plants & Bees	Lazy Daisies

VISITORS IN MY GARDEN
62" x 62", Annie P. Johnson, Littlestown, PA

This simple but elegant idea of setting the blocks side-by-side with no sashing works beautifully in this project. I absolutely love Annie's use of light blue-green fabric! It creates a whole different mood for the blocks and gives the illusion that these flowers are growing in a lush field. A portion of each wreath was used to create the border. By doing the appliqué work first on border strips and attaching them to the center, it is only necessary to appliqué small sections at each miter to finish the quilt top.

When you view the close-up of her TULIP, THISTLE & TOBACCO FLOWER block on page 85, and border detail on page 5, you can truly appreciate Annie's talent as an expert appliquér.

Appliqué Basics: Flower Wreaths, Karen Kay Buckley

$\mathcal{L}$AZY $\mathcal{D}$AISIES

Block by Susan Sterner Platt
Hanover, PA

LAZY DAISY

SUPPLIES

■ **Basic sewing supplies**
needles, template material, thread, pins,
fabric markers, and scissors

■ **Thread to match daisy fabric**

■ **Thread to match daisy center fabric**

■ **Black embroidery thread**
for ladybug legs

■ **Pigma™ marker**

■ **Green embroidery thread**
for rose leaves and bluebell stems

■ **¼ yard of 1⅜" wide wire or regular ribbon**
for bluebells

■ **Small piece of batting**

■ **Bias press bars**

FABRIC

■ **16" x 16" background fabric**

■ **¼ yard**
for daisy stems

■ **⅛ yard rose**
use for stems

■ **Scraps**
for rose buds

■ **⅛ yard yellow**
for daisies

■ **Small piece of fabric**
for daisy center

■ **Scraps of green fabrics**
several different green fabrics for leaves

■ **Ultra-suede®**
for ladybugs

Roses & Leaves

Rose Stems: Use your ⅛" bias press bar and follow the directions on page 19.

Rose Leaves: I used the starch and template method to turn under these edges. Use template **E** and cut 8 leaves. After the leaves were stitched in place I added some embroidery stitches to the edges of each leaf ❶. I used a single strand of embroidery thread. Refer to the pattern on page 104 to complete the stitching.

Daisy Leaves: Make templates and cut 12 **B1** and 4 **B2** leaves (shown on the following page). I used the starch and template method for appliquéing these leaves. After the edges are pressed under on the **B1** leaf, the bottom raw edge will be pleated. Pinch the raw edge to make a pleat. Tack the pleat in place.

Note: There will be excess fabric at the bottom of some leaves. Wait until you are ready to stitch the daisy stems in place to trim the excess.

Daisy Stems: Make the daisy stems using the ¼" bias press bar. (Refer to page 19 for instructions.) These stems will cover the bottom raw edges of the **B1** and **B2** daisy leaves ❶. As you are stitching the stems in place, trim any excess from the bottom of the leaves.

Dimensional Buds: Make a template of circle **F** on page 104. Trace the circle onto the back of your fabric, and cut on the line. *Do not add a seam allowance.* Cut 4. Fold the circle in half. Fold the left side in toward the center. Refer to the illustration. Fold the right side in toward the center. It should over-lap the left fold and the bottom raw edges should remain relatively even. The top fold should be about ¼" across. Sew across the bottom raw edge starting with a knot. When you reach the opposite side, pull on the thread and gather gently ❷.

Position the bud in place on your background fabric, and stitch around the outside folded edges.

Rosebud Base: Make a template of the shape **G**, cut 4. I used the starch and template method to turn under these edges.

Position the base over the raw edge of the rose bud. Be sure the raw edge of the stem and the raw edge of the rose bud ❸ are covered. ✿

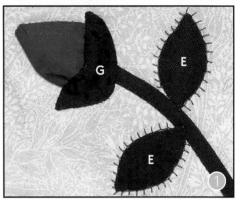

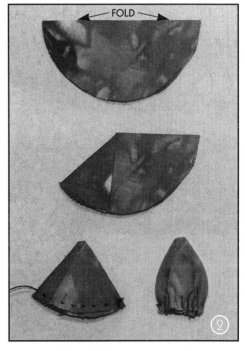

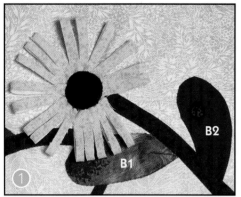

The Daisies

Daisy Flowers: Cut 8 pieces of yellow fabric 2½" x 3¼" and cut 4 pieces of fusible web 2" x 3" (I prefer to cut fusible web slightly smaller than the piece of fabric). The bottom edge of the fabric is ¼" larger than the fusible web because you need to sew through this area and by cutting the web smaller, it keeps it out of the area to be stitched.

Remember to use a press cloth over and under your fabric when working with fusible web. Center and iron one piece of fusible web to the back of one piece of yellow fabric ❷. Give it a couple of seconds to cool and remove the paper. Center another piece of yellow fabric back sides together and iron in place. It will now be fused to the other piece of yellow fabric. Trim ⅛" from the two sides. Do not trim the top and bottom edges.

Fold your fabric in half, and stitch about ⅛" from the raw edge. You will be stitching through four thicknesses of fabric. Leave the needle and thread hanging. This fabric will be gathered later. Cut ⅛" parallel lines into the folded edge. Be very careful not to cut through your line of stitching. You can cut these lines with scissors or your rotary cutter ❸.

After the ⅛" sections are cut, pull on the thread and gather the fabric. Pull tightly and knot your thread. Connect the beginning and ending by placing the strip right sides together and sewing along the ¼" seam at the bottom. You will now have a beautiful daisy flower*.

To stitch the daisy flower to the background fabric, sew a single stitch through the lower part of each petal. This seems like a lot of work, but if flowers are not tacked in this manner they can become crinkled when folded.

Stuffed Centers: Make a template of the circle on page 104. Trace this circle onto the back of your fabric. Cut ¼" beyond the line you drew. Sew a running stitch ⅛" from the cut edge. Cut a small piece of batting about 1¼" x 1¼", and roll it into a ball. Place the batting inside the circle, and pull on the thread. Gather the seam up and around the batting. Knot the thread. Sew the stuffed center to the center of your daisy flower. ✿

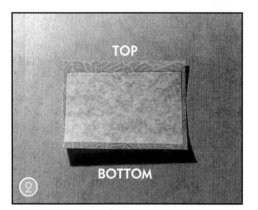

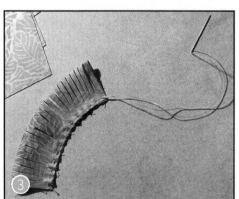

*During the quilting process the edges frayed terribly. I thought the fusible web alone would prevent that from happening. I had to remove all of the daisy flowers and replace them. Now I apply Fray Stop (or Fray Check) to the raw edges by placing the daisy over the waxy side of freezer paper. Allow it to seep into all parts of the fabric. Let dry completely. (Directions on product.). Refer to page 143 for supplier.

The Ladybugs

Ladybugs: These bugs were so much fun, and they were extremely easy. I used Ultra-Suede to make dainty little ladybugs **H ❶**. Trace a circle on the right side of your Ultra-Suede with a black Pigma marker. Sometimes the marks are absorbed into the Ultra-Suede, and it might be necessary to go over the lines a second time to darken them.

You can make a template of the ¼" circle, or use a circle template sheet pictured here ❷. If you use the circle template as shown, a 9/32"-size circle works great. If you decide not to use Ultra-Suede, an alternative method is explained below.

Ultra-Suede® Body: Trace 4, or as many ladybugs you want, but *before* you cut the circles from the Ultra-Suede, draw the head, dots, and center line on the body ❸. It is much easier to trace while on a larger piece of fabric.

With your embroidery scissors cut around the circle to include the black line around the body and head. Place the ladybug on a leaf and with one strand of black embroidery thread, stitch the legs. These straight stitches should catch a small piece of Ultra-Suede along the outside edge of the circle. Also, stitch down the black center line to help hold the ladybug in place.

Alternative Method: If you do not have Ultra-Suede, use the circle size on page 103, and make a perfect circle using regular fabric as explained earlier. (I recommend using a washer as close to a 9/32"-size circle as possible.)

Appliqué the fabric circle to the background fabric ❹. With your Pigma marker, add the head, dots, and center line. You might also want to draw the legs with your Pigma marker or use embroidery thread as mentioned above for the legs. ❀

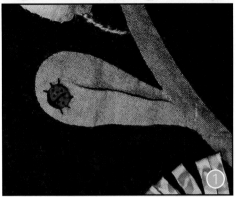

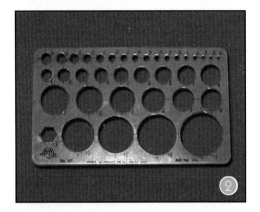

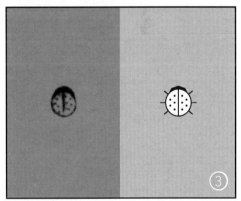

The Bluebells

Bluebells: These pretty little flowers are easy to create ❶. Use a 1⅜" wide wire-edge ribbon to make the bluebells. (If not available, regular ribbon is fine.)

Cut 6 pieces of ribbon 1½", one for each bluebell. Fold the ribbon in half wrong sides together. Sew along the cut, raw edge. Referring to the illustration, start at the bottom and stitch to the "X." Do not cut your thread, but make a knot ❷.

Now stitch across the top to the fold. Pull and gather the thread. Only the top portion of the ribbon should be gathered. Cut a piece of batting 1" x 3" for each bluebell. Roll the batting and push it into the ribbon. Use a closed pen or a pencil to push the batting inside ❸. The seam of the ribbon will be on the back of the bluebell.

Fringed Bottom: Cut 6 pieces of fabric, 1" x 1" on the grain, one for each bluebell. Fringe the edges on all four sides. Fold the square in half on the diagonal, wrong sides together. Then fold the square in half again. It will now be a triangular shape. Place the fringed square inside the open end of the ribbon. Stitch across the bottom edge of the ribbon just up from the wire and gather gently ❹.

Stems: I used wool yarn to make the stems, but two strands of embroidery thread would work great. Refer to page 20 for the stem stitch. ✿

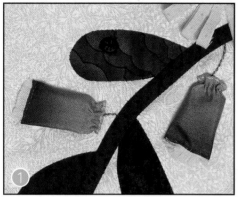

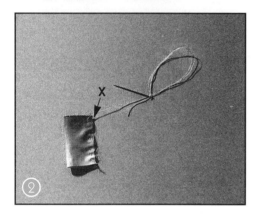

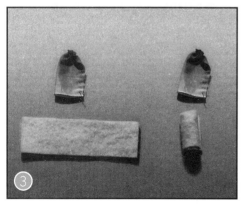

PLANNING CHART SEVEN

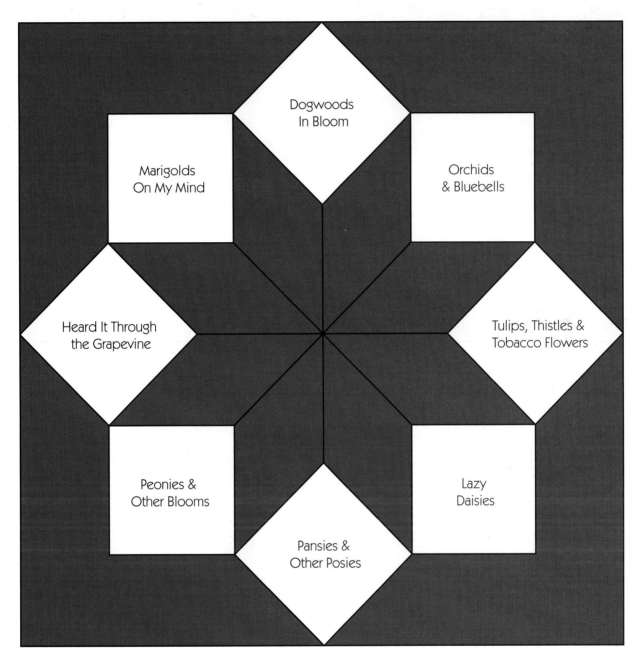

Dogwoods
In Bloom

Marigolds
On My Mind

Orchids
& Bluebells

Heard It Through
the Grapevine

Tulips, Thistles &
Tobacco Flowers

Peonies &
Other Blooms

Lazy
Daisies

Pansies &
Other Posies

FLOWERS AND FRIENDS
77" x 77", Susan Sterner Platt, Hanover, PA

Combining the floral wreaths with Hawaiian style appliqué (not shown) makes this a stunning quilt! Susan said she was working on her blocks and thinking about layout possibilities when she saw a quilting show on television about Hawaiian designs. Even though she had never done anything like this before, she was so intrigued with the idea she designed her own pattern and went to work.

The center star is a great showcase for the eight blocks. The contrast of the light backgrounds against the dark blue fabric forms a breathtaking arena for her expert appliqué skills. If Susan Sterner Platt cannot find this quilt, it might be at my house!

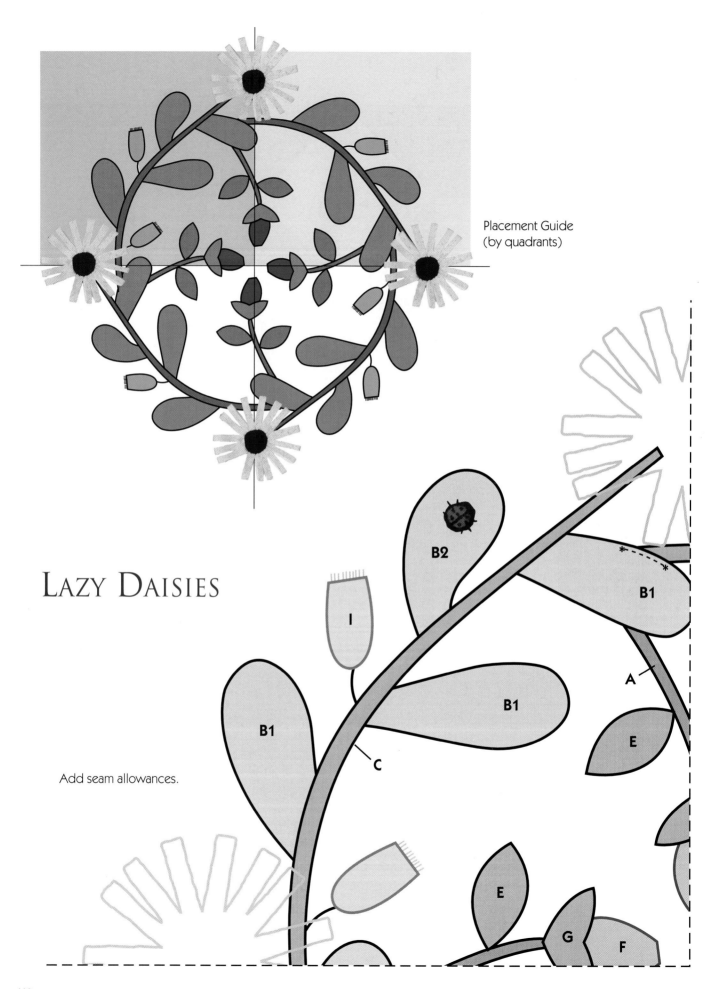

Placement Guide
(by quadrants)

Lazy Daisies

Add seam allowances.

B2

I

B1

C

B1

A

E

E

G

F

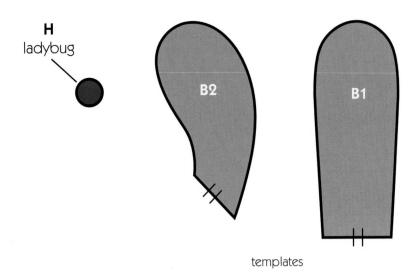

H
ladybug

B2

B1

A (4)	F (4)
B1 (12)	G (4)
B2 (4)	H (6)
C (4)	I (6)
D (4)	J* stems
E (8)	

*embroidered or drawn

templates

Pattern shapes are identified with letters and indicate the order in which to appliqué. The written directions refer to the corresponding letters. Some edges will be left raw and covered by another shape; these edges are marked with small slash marks or drawn open ended.

Lazy Daisies

Note: Please notice the asterisk on four of the B1 leaves. This portion of the seam must remain unstitched until the daisy stem is stitched in place. It will be closed after the stems are stitched.

D

B1

C

B1

B2

E

G

F

E

B1

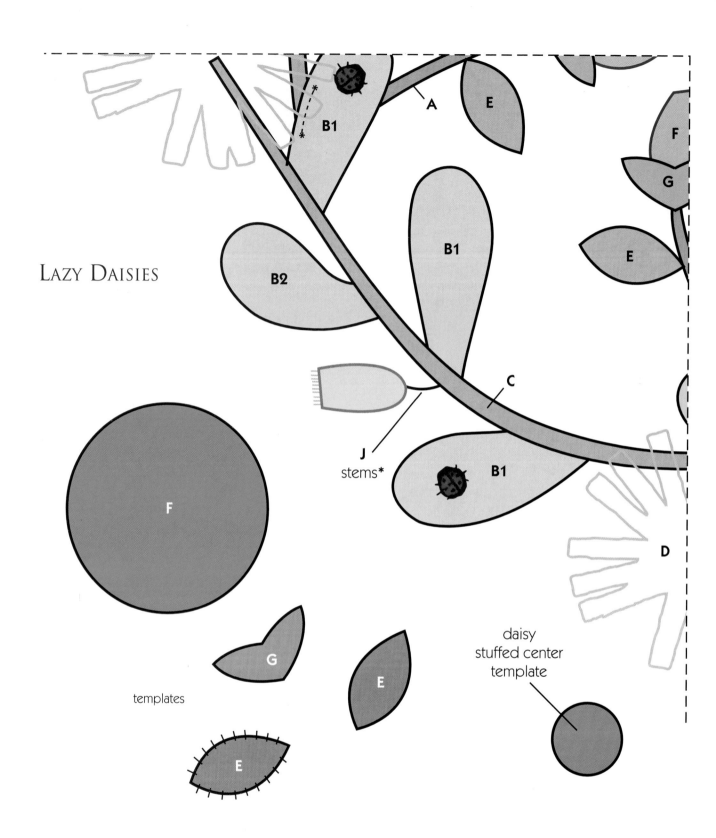

Lazy Daisies

B1

B2

E

F

G

A

C

J
stems*

B1

D

E

F

G

E

templates

G

E

E

daisy
stuffed center
template

A (4) | F (4)
B1 (12) | G (4)
B2 (4) | H (6)
C (4) | I (6)
D (4) | J* stems
E (8)

*embroidered
or drawn

Pattern shapes are identified with letters and indicate the order in
which to appliqué. The written directions refer to the corresponding
letters. Some edges will be left raw and covered by another shape;
these edges are marked with small slash marks or drawn open ended.

Appliqué Basics: Flower Wreaths, Karen Kay Buckley

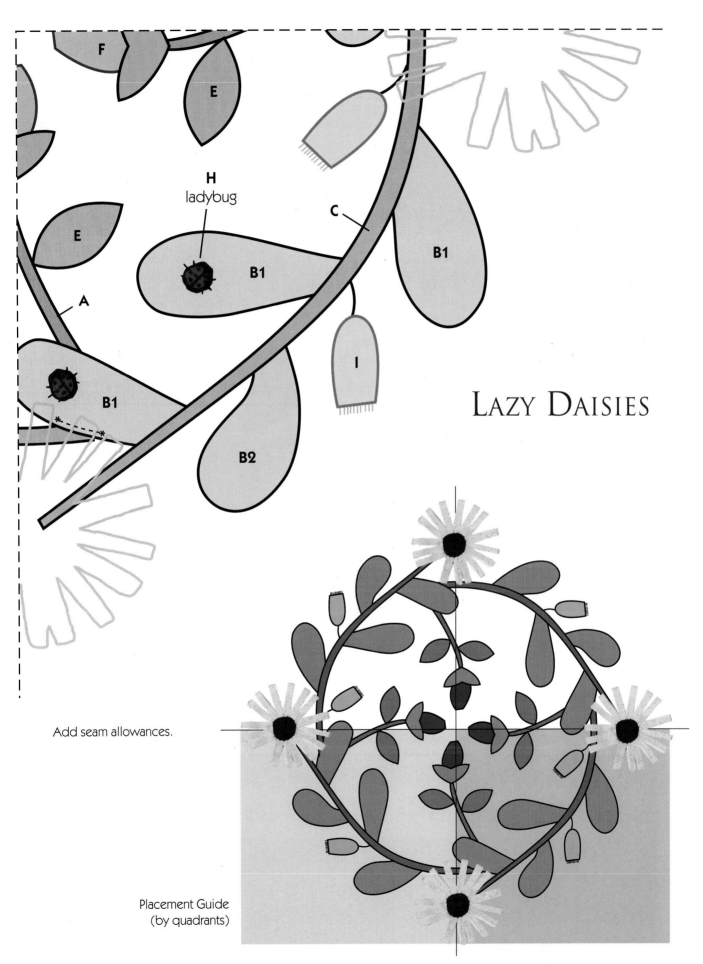

F

E

H
ladybug

E

C

A

B1

B1

B1

I

B2

LAZY DAISIES

Add seam allowances.

Placement Guide
(by quadrants)

DOGWOODS In Bloom

Block by Marilyn R. Eckert
New Bloomfield, PA

DOGWOODS IN BLOOM

SUPPLIES

■ **Basic sewing supplies**
needles, template material, thread, pins, fabric markers, and scissors

■ **Brown embroidery thread**
for outer edge of dogwood petals

■ **Green embroidery thread**
for stems

■ **Brown and black embroidery thread**
for spider (optional)

■ **Pigma™ markers**
for spider (optional)

■ **Freezer paper**

■ **Embroidery thread**
for spider web

■ **Seed beads**
for spider web (optional)

FABRIC

■ **16" x 16" background fabric**

■ **Scraps of brown**
for branches

■ **Scraps of blue**
for squill flowers in center

■ **Scraps of pink**
for dogwood petals

■ **Scraps of yellow**
for center of dogwood flowers

■ **Scraps of green**
for leaves

Branches & Leaves

Branches: There are two different branches in this wreath. They are all labeled. For the DOGWOODS IN BLOOM block, cut 3 **A1** and cut 2 **A2** branches. I used the needle-turn method on all of the branches ❶. Refer to page 16 for detailed instructions.

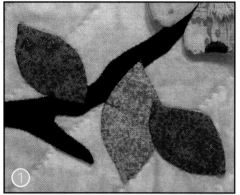

I liked making these shapes with a freezer paper template rather than template plastic. Place a piece of freezer paper waxy side down over the branch shapes shown on pages 112 – 115. Trace the shapes onto the paper side of the freezer paper with a pencil. Cut on the lines you drew. Iron the freezer paper to the right side of your fabric. Trace around the freezer paper with a washout marker. Cut around the shape. (See illustration #2 on page 48, Peonies.)

Position the branch on your background fabric. If you work with the larger piece of fabric, it is still very easy to position. Take a pin through two to three areas of the branch and line it up with your traced pattern. I like to pin at the point areas. Trim the seam as you stitch. Cut about 1" to 1½" of seam at a time. Turn under that part of the seam. Trim the next 1" to 1½", and turn under as necessary, continuing around the branch. Leave those edges raw that will be covered later by another piece.

I like working with a larger piece of fabric on shapes like this, because the branches are so skinny, I do not want my fabric to fray before it is turned under. If you do not like working with a piece of fabric this large try cutting a generous ¼" seam allowance, and trim as you sew ❷. Follow whichever method seems easier to you.

Leaves: I used the starch and template method to turn under the edges of the dogwood leaves. I found a large piece of fabric that had some leaves on it and used the veins from those leaves for my block. You need to cut 7 **C1** leaves and cut 4 **C2** leaves from your fabric. These leaves will overlap ❸ so refer to the placement quadrants as you work. ✿

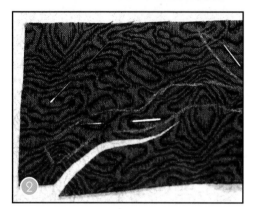

C1

C2

The Dogwoods

Dogwood Petals: Make a template of the shape **B** on page 113. You need four petals for each flower ❶. There are five flowers on the wreath so you need to cut 20 petals. Fold your fabric right sides together and trace the petal shape on the back of the fabric. Cut outside the lines adding a little less than a ¼" seam allowance. The lines you drew will be your sewing lines. Remember do not stitch the side marked with the slash marks.

After you have reached the opposite side, knot your thread and cut a slit in the back about halfway up the petal. Be careful to cut through only one thickness of fabric ❷. Clip into the seam allowance all the way around the shape. Turn the petal inside out. Smooth the edges with a point turner.

Using two strands of embroidery thread stitch across the top of the petal. Start with a knot in your thread. Bring the needle up through the middle of the petal and pull it out where you want to start stitching. The knot will be inside the seam allowance. Place stitches side-by-side as shown in the illustration. Instead of knotting the thread on the back of the petal, take the needle through the back side of the stitches. Push the needle in the side where you finished stitching and across to the opposite end. Cut the thread. Stitch the back slit closed ❸.

Turn the bottom raw edge under the petal, and pin it to your background fabric. Stitch ½" down each side and across the bottom. Do the same with the remaining three petals for each blossom.

Frayed Dogwood Centers: To make this frayed center ❹, cut 5 pieces of fabric on the grain 3" x ½", one for each of the dogwood flowers. Fray one edge about half way down the strip. Sew across the bottom edge of the strip. Pull on the thread and gather the strip. Connect the beginning and ending of the strip. Push the unfrayed section of the strip down into the middle of the petals. Tack some of the frays to hold the center in place. Refer to the frayed portion of the honeysuckle flower, illustration #2 on page 58 for a visual reference of this method. ❀

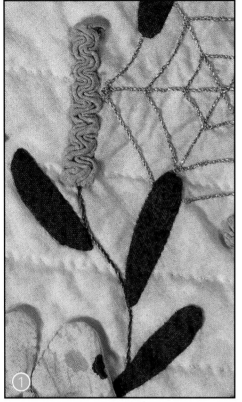

Squill Flowers

Stem: Before you can add the flowers you need to embroider the stems ❶. Using the stem stitch, sew with two strands of embroidery thread. Refer to the placement diagrams on pages 112 – 115.

Leaves: Make a template of the shape **F**. Cut 9 leaves. I used the needle-turn method of appliqué on the squill leaves.

Squill Flowers: There are three of these squill flowers in the block, and they are made with a ruching technique. Cut 3 strips of fabric 1" x 4". Press the raw edges of the strip toward the back so they meet in the center of the strip. With a running stitch sew in a zigzag manner down the strip. Start with a knot. Remember to use a double strand of sewing thread, or use quilting thread, since this will be gathered. Also, be sure to take the thread up and over the folded edge of the strip. Refer to MARIGOLDS ON MY MIND for ruching information, illustrations #2 and #3, page 57. When you have reached the other side, pull on the thread and gather the fabric tightly. Knot the end.

Position the ruched flowers on the stems and stitch each squill flower in place. Use your needle to turn under the raw edges at the top and bottom of the flower.❀

Spider & Web

Spider Web: To make the spider web ❷, sew with a stem stitch. Use two strands of thread for the spider web. On my light background block, I used a light gray thread so the web is hardly visible. On my dark background block, I used a silver metallic thread. On each of the webs I stitched in some seed beads to create the illusion of dew on the web.

Spider: You might want to draw or sew a practice spider on some scraps of fabric before you work on your block. I did some practice sewing and drawing to build some confidence.

On my quilt FLOWERS AND FRIENDS ONE, with the light background fabric, I drew the spider in the web with black and brown Pigma markers. Refer to the DOGWOODS IN BLOOM block on page 25.

When I was working on FLOWERS AND FRIENDS TWO, which has a navy blue background (page 32), I knew the spider would never show if I drew it with Pigma markers. So I chose to embroider the spider on one of the leaves ❸. The contrast of stitching on the green fabric worked nicely.❀

PLANNING CHART EIGHT

Heard It Through the Grapevine	Dogwoods In Bloom	Pansies & Other Posies
Marigolds On My Mind	Tulips, Thistles & Tobacco Flowers	Lazy Daisies
Clematis, Bee Plants & Bee	Peonies & Other Blooms	Orchids & Bluebells

POLLINATION
60" x 60", Marilyn R. Eckert, Bloomfield, PA

*T*his is an easy combination to make with the nine blocks surrounded by a pieced border. Marilyn was looking for a simple border that would frame her appliquéd blocks without detracting from them. She selected a 3" isosceles triangle border using the light background fabric in half the triangles, and the dark colors from her appliquéd flowers in the other triangles. A darker print was also used as a bias binding edge.

Marilyn Eckert used a subtle background fabric that had good light and dark shades which made it a great choice on which to display her appliqué abilities. Marilyn's years working as a nurse have given her patience with such small pieces. Her daughter, Jayne Eckert, was the graphic artist for this quilt project.

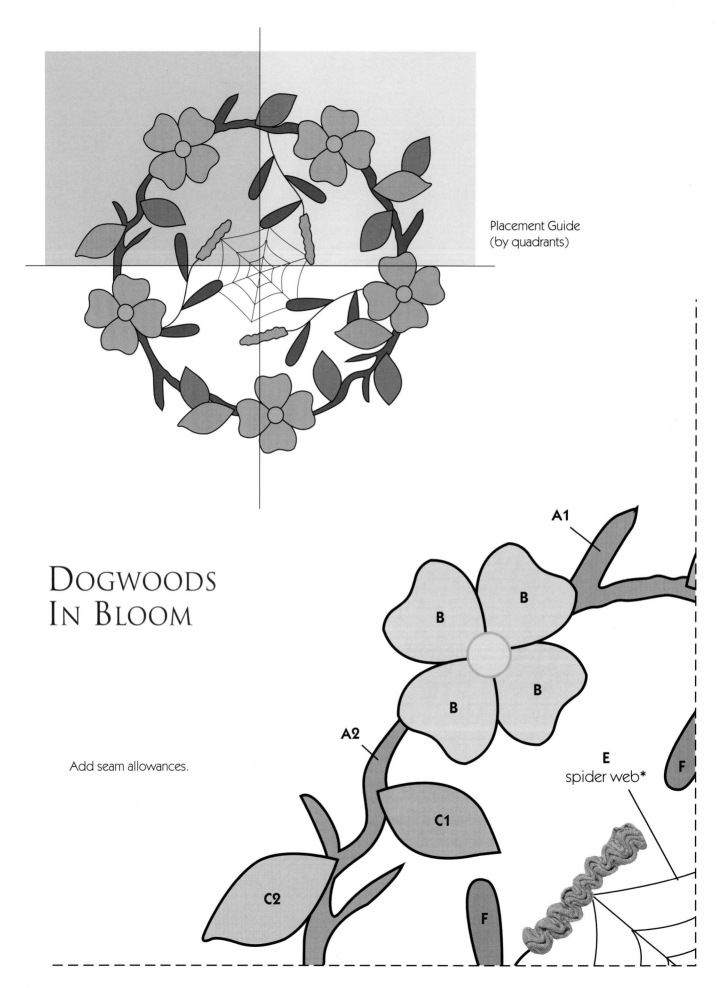

Placement Guide
(by quadrants)

Dogwoods
In Bloom

Add seam allowances.

A1

B

B

B

B

A2

C1

C2

E
spider web*

F

F

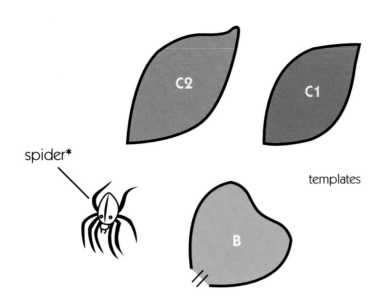

A1 (3)	D* stems
A2 (2)	E* (1) web
B (20)	F (9)
C1 (7)	G (3)
C2 (4)	

*embroidered
or drawn

spider*

templates

Pattern shapes are identified with letters and indicate the order in which to appliqué. The written directions refer to the corresponding letters. Some edges will be left raw and covered by another shape; these edges are marked with small slash marks or drawn open ended.

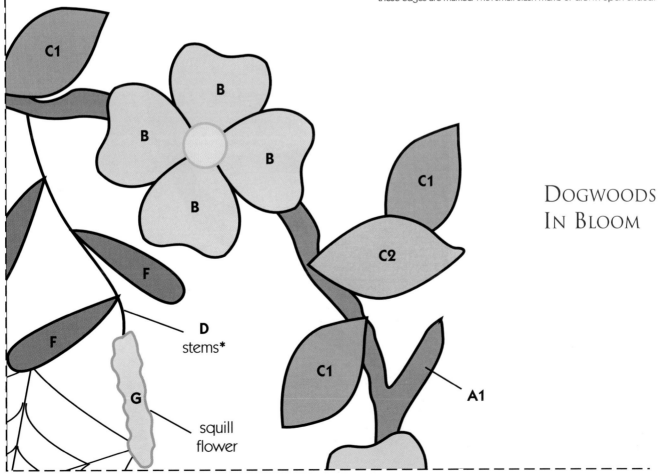

D
stems*

squill
flower

DOGWOODS
IN BLOOM

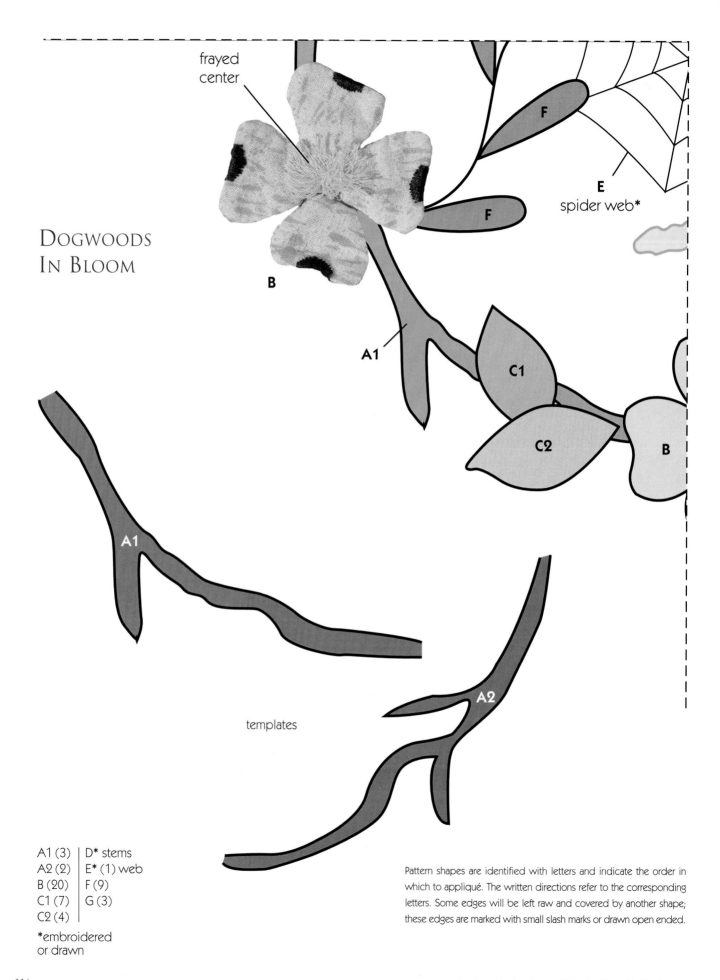

frayed center

F

F

spider web*

E

Dogwoods
In Bloom

B

A1

C1

C2

B

A1

templates

A2

A1 (3)   D* stems
A2 (2)   E* (1) web
B (20)   F (9)
C1 (7)   G (3)
C2 (4)

*embroidered
or drawn

Pattern shapes are identified with letters and indicate the order in which to appliqué. The written directions refer to the corresponding letters. Some edges will be left raw and covered by another shape; these edges are marked with small slash marks or drawn open ended.

DOGWOODS
IN BLOOM

Add seam allowances.

Placement Guide
(by quadrants)

PANSIES

& Other Posies

Block by Peggy S. Myers
Newville, PA

Pansies & Other Posies

SUPPLIES

■ **Basic sewing supplies**
*needles, template material, thread, pins,
fabric markers, and scissors*

■ **Embroidery thread on a skein**
*one or two shades of green, yellow for pansy flower,
black for pansy flower*

■ **Perle cotton thread size 8**
for the little forget-me-not embroidery flowers

■ **Metallic or iridescent thread**
for wings of dragonfly

■ **Wool yard**
for body of dragonfly

■ **1 yard of ⅜" wide ribbon**

■ **Seed beads**

■ **Freezer paper**

■ **Pigma™ markers**
for eyes and legs of dragonfly

■ **⅝ yard of 1½" wide ribbon
(wire edged or regular)**

FABRIC

■ **16" x 16" background fabric**

■ **Scraps of green fabrics**
use three different greens for leaves

■ **Small scrap**
for body of dragonfly

■ **Scraps**
for pansy flowers

■ **Tulle**
for wings of dragonfly

Forget-Me-Nots

Stems: All of the stems for the PANSIES & OTHER POSIES block were embroidered with a stem stitch using two strands of embroidery thread. It provided a nice vine and stem effect ❶ and the stems were also used with the ribbon flowers shown on page 120.

Leaves: The placement guide by quadrants and full-size patterns can be found on pages 122 – 125. Make a template of the shape **A** and cut 19 leaves. Position as shown. I used the starch and template method to turn under the edges on these leaves.

Forget-Me-Not: These 45 little flowers are fun to make using a daisy stitch. You could use two strands of embroidery thread or perle cotton, size 8. I like the perle cotton because it gives me another texture ❷. Variegated thread is recommended for shading the flowers. It is best to do some practice stitching on some scraps before sewing on the actual block. It allows the opportunity to even out the stitches so the petals on one flower will all be the same size. Try creating the three spokes of a "Y" first, and then go back and fill-in the last two daisy stitches ❸.

After the forget-me-not flowers are embroidered, add a seed bead ❹, small button, or French knot to the center of each flower for an additional dimension. ✿

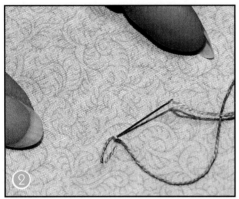

Pansies & Leaves

No garden is ever complete without some perky little pansies ❶.

Ribbon Leaves: There are 11 of these leaves. Cut 11 pieces of 1½" wide wire or regular ribbon into 2" sections. To make a leaf, fold a 2" section in half and sew across one end, starting and stopping with a knot. Turn the seam you just sewed inside out. Use a point turner to push the point open. Sew across the bottom raw edge of the ribbon. Gather your stitching and knot the thread ❷. This gathered edge will be under the pansy flowers. The ribbon leaves are now ready to sew to your background block.

Pansy Flowers: There are five of these flowers on the block. Each flower has four pieces, some flat and some dimensional. I used three shades of purple with the base being darkest and the front being the lightest shade. Make a template of the shape **E1** on page 123. This is the base of each pansy flower so you need to cut 5 of these. I used the starch and template method to turn under these edges. Appliqué these shapes in place making sure to overlap and cover the raw edges of the ribbon leave.

Make a template of the circle **E2**, 2½". Trace this circle on your fabric, and cut on the line you drew. *Do not add seam allowance.* You can layer your fabric so you can cut several of these at one time. You need two for each flower for a total of 10 circles. Using a running stitch, sew about ⅛" in from the raw edge of the circle. Gather tightly and knot the thread. (It should resemble the flat side of a yo-yo circle.) Take one stitch from the center, where you finished stitching, and loop the thread over the edge of the fold. Bring the thread back through the center and pull tightly ❸. Knot the thread.

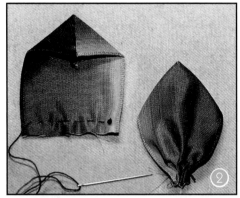

Position two of the small circles/petals over the larger one. Appliqué half of the way around this shape. Leave the front part of the petal unstitched for more dimension.

Make a template of the **E3** circle, 1⅞". This is for the smaller petals in the front of the pansy. You need to make five of these. *Do not add seam allowance.* Follow the same procedure for the large petal to make the small petal ❹. Appliqué this shape in the same manner as the larger circles.

Embroidery: To complete the pansy flowers, add embroidery stitching to the petals as shown in the color photograph. Use two strands of black and two strands of yellow to do this stitching (refer to stitch pattern on page 123). ❀

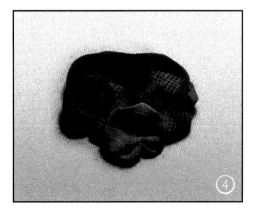

Posies

Ribbon Flowers: To make the ribbon flowers **F ❶**, use the ⅜" wide ribbon and matching thread. Do not trim this ribbon down to any size. Work with your one-yard piece. Start with a knot and sew in a "U" pattern across the ribbon. Take the thread up and over the ribbon at the top of the "U." When you have stitched five of the "U" shapes, gather the ribbon and knot your thread.

Join the beginning to the end of the ribbon. Leave a ½" tail of ribbon at the end to tuck under the center of the flower ❷. Stitch the ribbon flower in place and add some seed beads, buttons, or French knots to the center. ✿

The Dragonfly

Dragonfly: Follow the same instructions for these wings as shown for the bumblebee on page 69, illustrations #2 and #3. After the wings are stitched and the freezer paper is removed, glue the wings in place with water-soluble glue. Use just a dab of glue.

To make the body of the dragonfly, make a template of the shape on page 124. You can appliqué this shape with a regular appliqué stitch or satin stitch it by hand or machine. Or you might want to use yarn as shown in ❸.

After the body and wings are appliquéd in place, you need to add the eyes and the legs ❹. This could be completed with embroidery stitching or drawn with a Pigma marker. ✿

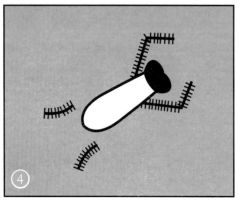

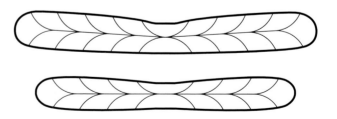

Dragonfly Wings Pattern

Planning Chart Nine

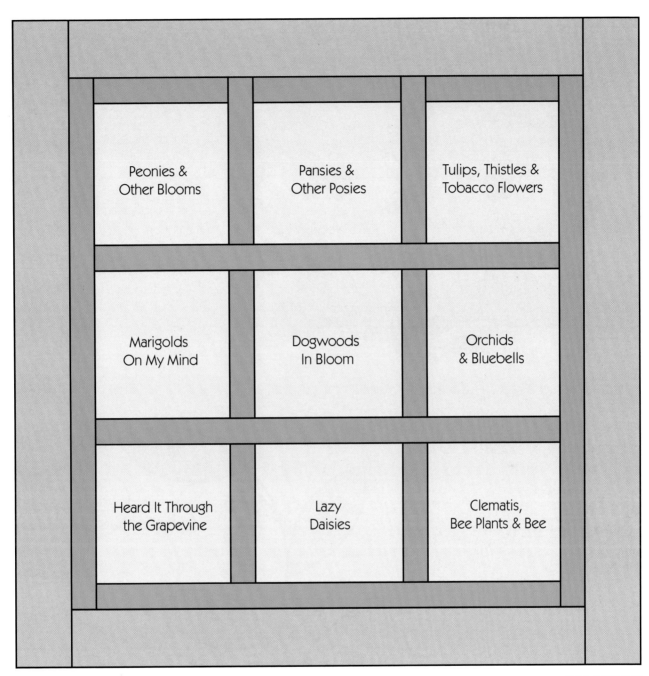

Peonies & Other Blooms	Pansies & Other Posies	Tulips, Thistles & Tobacco Flowers
Marigolds On My Mind	Dogwoods In Bloom	Orchids & Bluebells
Heard It Through the Grapevine	Lazy Daisies	Clematis, Bee Plants & Bee

BUGS & BLOOMS
70" x 70", Peggy S. Myers, Newville, PA

This was a great project for Peg Myers to combine her greatest passions, quilting and the great outdoors. Being a professional outdoor photographer, she used sky fabric for the PANSY and other wreath backgrounds, and a grass-green fabric in her quilt BUGS & BLOOM. The nine wreaths are set with 2" sashing strips and inner border. Peg then added wide 8" outer borders. The top and bottom have a grapevine motif (see page 37). The two sides are appliquéd in her original, large-sized flowers and bugs designs *(not drawn in sketch, details are shown throughout the book)*.

When I was designing my blocks to make them more interesting, I thought of Peg, whom we affectionately call the "bug lady." She's interested in insects and brought to class a dazzling photograph of a potato beetle (page 59) which inspired everyone. I thank her again for sharing her many talents and showcasing her bugs!

Placement Guide
(by quadrants)

PANSIES & OTHER POSIES

Add seam allowances.

A

A

A

B

A

B

E3
E2
E1

E2

E3
E2
E1

D
forget-me-nots*

Appliqué Basics: Flower Wreaths, Karen Kay Buckley

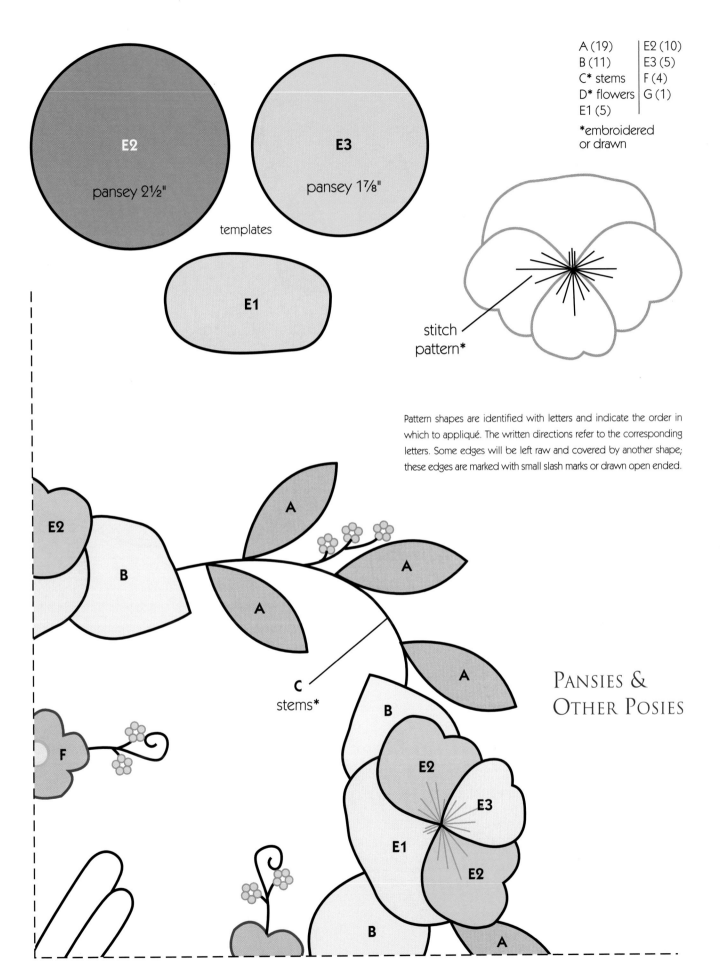

E2

pansey 2½"

E3

pansey 1⅞"

templates

E1

A (19)   E2 (10)
B (11)   E3 (5)
C* stems F (4)
D* flowers G (1)
E1 (5)

*embroidered
or drawn

stitch
pattern*

Pattern shapes are identified with letters and indicate the order in which to appliqué. The written directions refer to the corresponding letters. Some edges will be left raw and covered by another shape; these edges are marked with small slash marks or drawn open ended.

E2

B

A

A

A

A

C
stems*

B

E2

E3

E1

E2

F

B

A

PANSIES & OTHER POSIES

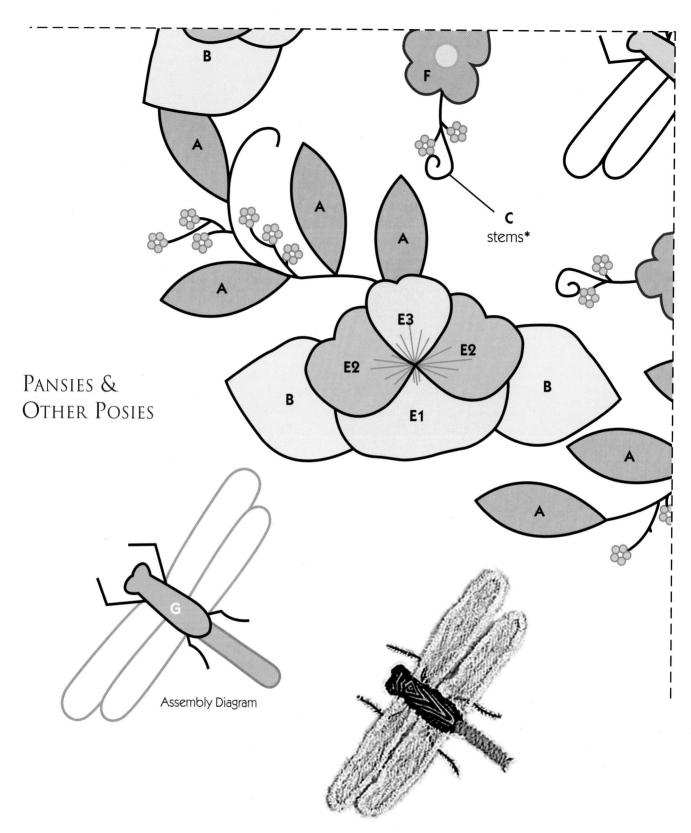

PANSIES & OTHER POSIES

Assembly Diagram

A (19) | E2 (10)
B (11) | E3 (5)
C* stems | F (4)
D* flowers | G (1)
E1 (5) |

*embroidered
or drawn

Pattern shapes are identified with letters and indicate the order in which to appliqué. The written directions refer to the corresponding letters. Some edges will be left raw and covered by another shape; these edges are marked with small slash marks or drawn open ended.

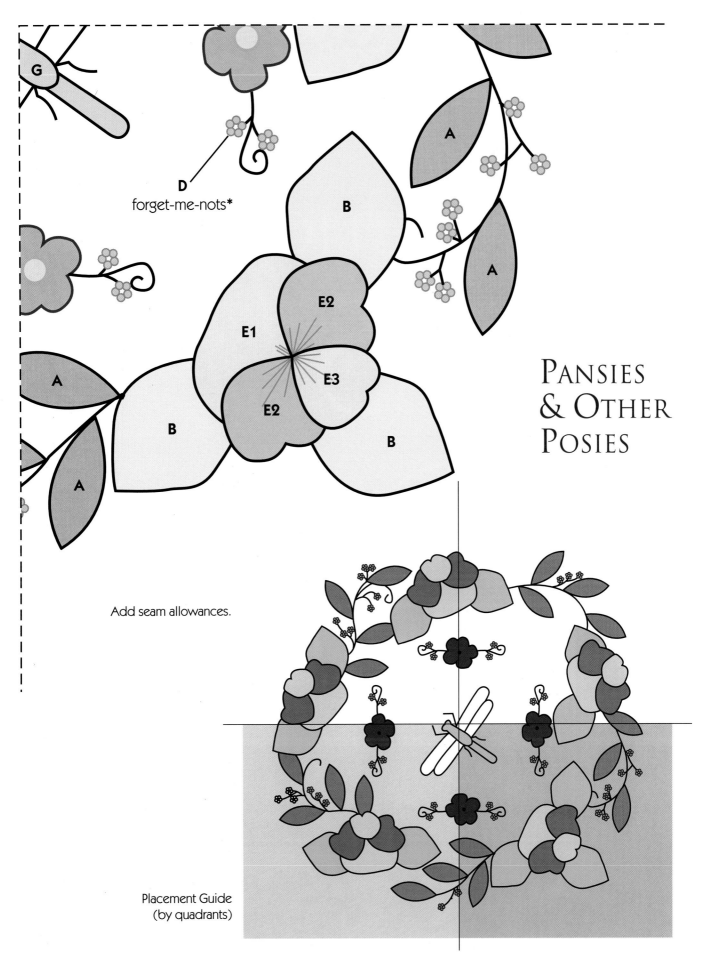

D

forget-me-nots*

B

A

A

A

E2

E1

E3

E2

B

A

B

A

PANSIES
& OTHER
POSIES

Add seam allowances.

Placement Guide
(by quadrants)

SECTION

5

Borders

Borders from Flowers & Friends Two

There are endless possibilites to enhance the center of your quilt. Please refer to the Gallery (pages 136 – 142) for examples of my students' work. Some chose to add a single band of fabric around the outside edges, another used a fabric that fits the theme of the blocks and carries the colors into the border. Either choice is a great way to finish the outside edge of the quilt. For a theme quilting design, a lattice border will create the illusion that you are standing in a garden, and the elements of a special flower (such as the orchid) can be redrawn and repeated as a border motif. (See FLOWERS FOR MOTHER, page 141.)

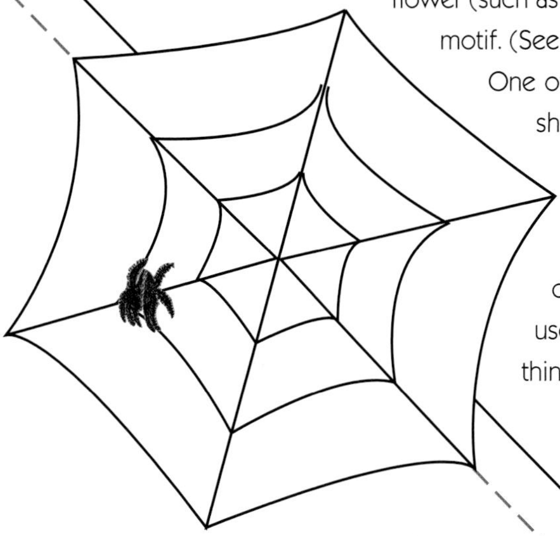

One of my favorite methods of designing a border is to use shapes from the center of the quilt in the border. The pattern that starts on this page and continues to page 132 is the border I designed for my FLOWERS AND FRIENDS TWO quilt. What better way to pull the quilt together than to use the same shapes as were used in the wreaths! Keep an open mind and try something new. You might be pleasantly surprised.

from DOGWOODS IN BLOOM

pages 112–115

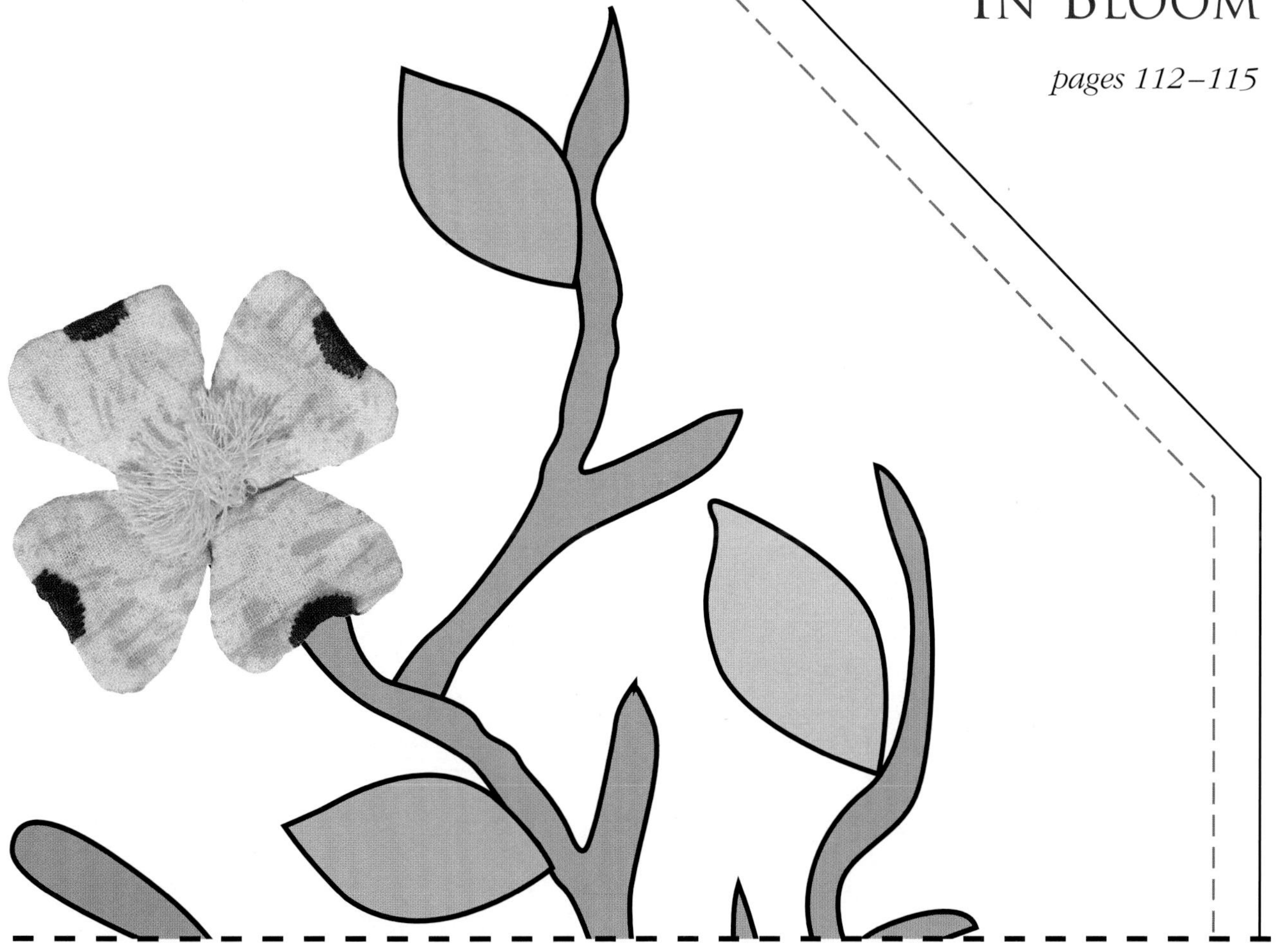

from PANSIES
& OTHER
POSIES

pages 122–125

Appliqué Basics: Flower Wreaths, Karen Kay Buckley

from LAZY
DAISIES

pages 102–105

from TULIPS,
THISTLES &
TOBACCO FLOWERS

pages 90–93

from HEARD IT
THROUGH THE
GRAPEVINE

pages 40–43

Moth from
ORCHIDS & BLUEBELLS

page 82

*Combining Patterns
in a Border*

What works extremely well for me when planning the border is to cut a piece of table paper to the finished size to see exactly how things will look and fit on the border. When thinking about a border with curved stems and vines, I recommend using French curves. They give a vast amount of options. Work in pencil and plan to remove and replace some curves as you design. The French curves will give you a good start. Some of you can just draw a good curve for a stem without using a tool. Go for it.

Place all the templates used in the blocks on the table. Pick them up, one at a time, and start to draw. I often work with clusters of templates that came from the same block, but do whatever feels right to you. Many of my students are amazed at their capabilities when they do this. Most of them think they cannot design their own borders. They soon start to feel more relaxed and realize it is pretty easy. I highly recommend you give it a try. ❀

SECTION

6

Lesson Plans

Flower Wreath Lesson Plans

I have been teaching these classes for a couple of years and the results have been wonderful. This is the monthly lesson plan I use and it has worked very well. The class meets for ten sessions and each session is two hours. After teaching Baltimore Album classes I realized how important it was to give the students enough time to complete each block. Most of them feel better about continuing if they can get the block from the last session completed before starting a new block. In some cases you can have them sew directly on their wreaths, and sometimes it is good to provide the class with scraps of fabric for them to make a sample. Always start each class with the students showing the blocks they have completed during the previous month. This is very motivational for everyone, even the teacher!

LESSON ONE – FLOWER WREATHS
1. Discuss how different background fabrics affect the look of the quilt and show samples of this idea.
2. Show different theme fabrics and discuss how to work with them.
3. Discuss layout and show ideas for settings.
4. Review supplies needed for class.
5. Talk about how to cut the background fabric.
6. Explain supplies needed for the first block.

LESSON TWO – DOGWOODS IN BLOOM
1. Transfer pattern to background fabric.
2. Make one branch and sew part of it in place.
3. Make one dogwood petal.
4. Make one dogwood center.
5. Demonstrate the starch and template method of appliqué.
6. Demonstrate and have students sew a little of the stem stitch.
7. Make one squill flower.
8. Discuss supplies needed for next class.

LESSON THREE – LAZY DAISIES
1. Discuss daisy leaves.
2. Demonstrate and have students make stems.
3. Discuss working with fusible web and make one daisy flower.
4. Make one daisy center.
5. Discuss rose leaves.
6. Make one dimensional rose bud.
7. Discuss ladybug.
8. Make one bluebell flower.
9. Discuss supplies needed for next class.

LESSON FOUR – HEARD IT THROUGH THE GRAPEVINE
1. Discuss different ways to make stems.
2. Demonstrate and have students make and stuff a stem.
3. Discuss leaves.
4. Make a perfect circle with washers.
5. Make one gathered flower.
6. Discuss the butterfly.
7. Make the body of the butterfly.
8. Discuss supplies needed for next class.

LESSON FIVE – MARIGOLDS ON MY MIND
1. Discuss options for making the small "A" leaves.
2. Ruch one marigold flower.
3. Discuss appliqué methods for other leaves.

4. Make one honeysuckle flower.
5. Make one potato beetle.
6. Discuss supplies needed for next class.

LESSON SIX – PANSIES & OTHER POSIES
1. Make one ribbon leaf.
2. Demonstrate and have students sew a sample of the daisy stitch.
3. Make some pansy petals.
4. Make one ribbon flower.
5. Demonstrate and discuss how to make the wings on the dragonfly.
6. Discuss how to finish the dragonfly.
7. Discuss supplies needed for next class.

LESSON SEVEN – PEONIES & OTHER BLOOMS
1. Discuss making circles and stems.
2. Make one peony flower.
3. Make one peony center.
4. Make one clover flower.
5. Sew an ant.
6. Discuss supplies needed for next class.

LESSON EIGHT – ORCHIDS & BLUEBELLS
1. Discuss leaves.
2. Make one orchid flower.
3. Make one bluebell flower.
4. Discuss how to make the moth.
5. Review supplies needed for next class.

LESSON NINE – TULIPS, THISTLE & TOBACCO FLOWERS
1. Discuss using soutache.
2. Make one thistle flower.
3. Discuss making leaves with fusible web.
4. Review how to make tulip flowers.
5. Make one tobacco flower.
6. Demonstrate process of making the wooly booger. Make sample.
7. Review supplies needed for next class.

LESSON TEN – CLEMATIS, BEE PLANTS & BEE
1. Discuss making the block.
2. Discuss how to trim blocks to size and using a window template.
3. Talk about borders. Have students draw a portion of a border so they know they can do it.
4. Review assembly and finishing the quilt.
5. Schedule reunion to showcase finished tops.

GALLERY

STUDENTS'

Flower Wreath Variations

MARILYN ECKERT
60" x 60", New Bloomfield, PA

POLLINATION

*T*he delicate shade of the fabric is the perfect background for the flowering wreaths. The sharply pieced triangles accent the brighter hues of the appliquéd blossoms. A close-up detail of one of Marilyn Eckert's wreaths and a Planning Chart for this quilt are presented in *Section Four* **DOGWOODS IN BLOOM** (pages 106–115).

Appliqué Basics: Flower Wreaths, Karen Kay Buckley

ELEANOR L. KARPER
67" x 81", Carlisle, PA

THROUGH THE WINDOW

*A*ttic Windows are used to showcase each of the nine flower wreaths and lets the viewer gaze upon an arrangement of flowers from all the blocks. The radiant sun gently beams down on the scene. A close-up detail of one of Eleanor Karper's wreaths and a Planning Chart for this quilt are presented in *Section Four* ORCHIDS & BLUEBELLS (pages 75–84).

LOIS HATLEBERG
38½" x 38½", Carlisle, PA

Flowers for the Season

Four different wreaths were framed with a pieced garden lattice sashing and border pattern creating the feeling of being in a beautiful manicured flower-garden. What attracts me most to Lois Hatleburg's quilts, aside from her excellent workmanship, is her use of soft pastel colors. The fragile flowers are gentle and elegant on this delicate background fabric which was used on both of her daughters' quilts.

LOIS HATLEBERG
45" x 45", Carlisle, PA

AROUND THE GARDEN

The swags and ribbon bows on the border create a soft frame around five of the wreath blocks. The pastel colors used in the flowers give this quilt a very serene feeling. Notice the beautiful butterflies gracefully floating around the center.

SUSAN WORLEY McCLAFFERTY
62" x 62", Mechanicsburg, PA

FLOWERS AND FRIENDS

A traditional sampler with all the right components: nine different appliquéd blocks, set with two-inch sashing strips and inner border, surrounded by a seven-inch wide outside border and corner blocks. Look closely at the finely quilted picket fence and radiating sun (see pg. 28 for pattern) and the nice way the crosshatch quilting showcases the colorful flower wreaths.

Appliqué Basics: Flower Wreaths, Karen Kay Buckley

CAROLYN S. RUTHERFORD
61" x 61", Dillsburg, PA
Quilted by Sandra Chambers

FLOWERS FOR MOTHER

*F*abulous scalloped edges complement the smooth curves of the appliqué, but it's the vibrant colors that Carolyn Rutherford used in her quilt that work so well on the black background. The small bouquets of orchids pull the design out into the corners, filling the border area. Outline-quilted around the wreaths, the quarter-inch double lines create a one-inch quilted lattice effect over the entire quilt.

Heard It Through the Grapevine

The vine and grape fabric Penny Sillery selected for the outer two-inch border complements the center wreath and enhances the overall theme. By repeating the dark fabric in the inner border and bias binding, a wonderful balance is achieved. I think the block looks striking with this double framed border! A close ¾" crosshatch quilting grid sets off the butterfly, flowers, grapes and leaves, and is perfectly proportioned for this small wallhanging.

RESOURCES & BIBLIOGRAPHY

RESOURCES

CALICO CORNERS
341 Barnstable Road
Carlisle, PA 17013
e-mail: Calicoquil@aol.com
– Almost every supply listed!

QUILTER'S GATHERING
5490 "C" Derry Street
Harrisburg, PA 17111
*– Thread, Templar, and basic sewing
supplies*

PRO CHEMICAL
P.O. Box 14
Somerset, MA 02726
– Retayne and Synthrapol

TWE/BEADS
P.O. Box 55
Hamburg, NJ 07419
Telephone: 973-209-1517
e-mail: info@twebeads.com
web: www.twebeads.com
– Beads

KAREN KAY BUCKLEY
1237 Holly Pike
Carlisle, PA 17013
*– Mylar washers – send a SASE
with $3.00*
– Bias press bars $5.00
– Teaching packet

BIBLIOGRAPHY

Oravecz, Cindy Zlotnik, *Into The Garden*, Quilters Fancy, Cortland, Ohio 1995.

Sienkiewicz, Elly, *Dimensional Applique*, C&T Publishing, Lafayette, CA. 1993.

Other AQS BOOKS

This is only a small selection of the books available from the American Quilter's Society. AQS books are known worldwide for timely topics, clear writing, beautiful color photos, and accurate illustrations and patterns. The following books are available from your bookseller, quilt shop, or public library.

Love to Quilt...
Petal by Petal
Appli-bond Flowers
$14.95
Joan Shay
#5013

Quilted Havens
CITY HOUSES, COUNTRY HOMES
$22.95
Susan Purney-Mark & Daphne Greig
#5336

Flower Patterns
To Appliqué, Paint, and Embroider
$19.95
JOAN SJUTS WALDMAN
#5238

Favorite REDWORK DESIGNS
$16.95
BETTY ALDERMAN
#5331

THREE-DIMENSIONAL APPLIQUÉ and **EMBROIDERY EMBELLISHMENT**
TECHNIQUES FOR TODAY'S ALBUM QUILT
$24.95
by Anita Shackelford
#3788

APPLIQUE MASTERPIECE
LITTLE BROWN BIRD Patterns
$21.95
Margaret Docherty
#5338

Blooms & Baskets
GEMS OF SUMMER
$24.95
Emily G. Senuta
#5175

Blossoms by the Sea
MAKING RIBBON FLOWERS FOR QUILTS
$24.95
Faye Labanaris
#4593

Love to Quilt... **Broderie Perse**
$14.95
The Elegant Quilt
#4833

Look for these books nationally or call **1-800-626-5420**

The Mortal Realms have been despoiled. Ravaged by the followers of the Chaos Gods, they stand on the brink of utter destruction.

The fortress-cities of Sigmar are islands of light in a sea of darkness. Constantly besieged, their walls are assailed by maniacal hordes and monstrous beasts. The bones of good men are littered thick outside the gates. These bulwarks of Order are embattled within as well as without, for the lure of Chaos beguiles the citizens with promises of power.

Still the champions of Order fight on. At the break of dawn, the Crusader's Bell rings and a new expedition departs. Storm-forged knights march shoulder to shoulder with resolute militia, stoic duardin and slender aelves. Bedecked in the splendour of war, the Dawnbringer Crusades venture out to found civilisations anew. These grim pioneers take with them the fires of hope. Yet they go forth into a hellish wasteland.

Out in the wilds, hardy colonists restore order to a crumbling world. Haunted eyes scan the horizon for tyrannical reavers as they build upon the bones of ancient empires, eking out a meagre existence from cursed soil and ice-cold seas. By their valour, the fate of the Mortal Realms will be decided.

The ravening terrors that prey upon these settlers take a thousand forms. Cannibal barbarians and deranged murderers crawl from hidden lairs. Martial hosts clad in black steel march from skull-strewn castles. The savage hordes of Destruction batter the frontier towns until no stone stands atop another. In the dead of night come howling throngs of the undead, hungry to feast upon the living.

Against such foes, courage is the truest defence and the most effective weapon. It is something that Sigmar's chosen do not lack. But they are not always strong enough to prevail, and even in victory, each new battle saps their souls a little more.

This is the time of turmoil. This is the era of war.

This is the Age of Sigmar.

CONTENTS

PRODUCED BY THE WARHAMMER STUDIO
With thanks to The Faithful for their additional playtesting services

Getting Started With Warhammer Age of Sigmar © Copyright Games Workshop Limited 2021. Getting Started With Warhammer Age of Sigmar, GW, Games Workshop, Warhammer, Warhammer Age of Sigmar, Battletome, Stormcast Eternals, and all associated logos, illustrations, images, names, creatures, races, vehicles, locations, weapons, characters, and the distinctive likenesses thereof, are either ® or TM, and/or © Games Workshop Limited, variably registered around the world. All Rights Reserved.

Games Workshop Ltd., Willow Road, Lenton, Nottingham, NG7 2WS, United Kingdom
warhammer.com

ASSEMBLE YOUR MINIATURES

1   STORMCAST ETERNALS VINDICTOR

2   KRULEBOYZ GUTRIPPA

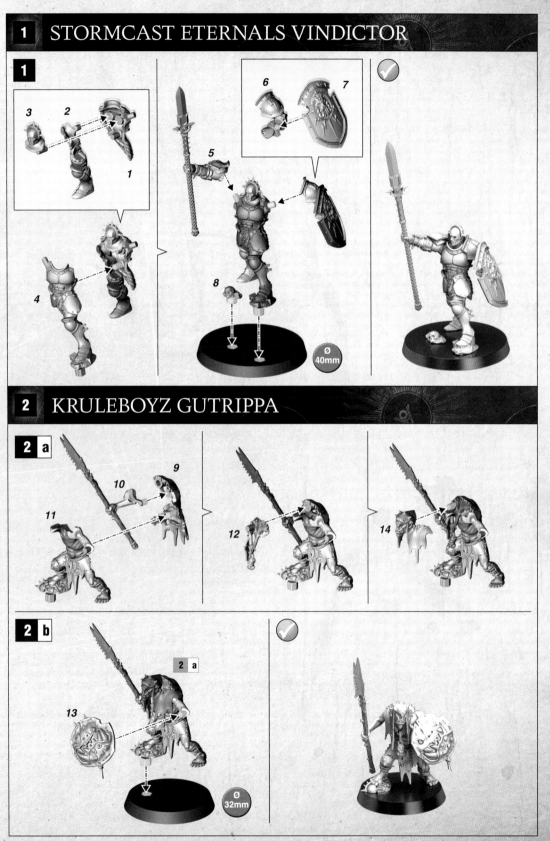

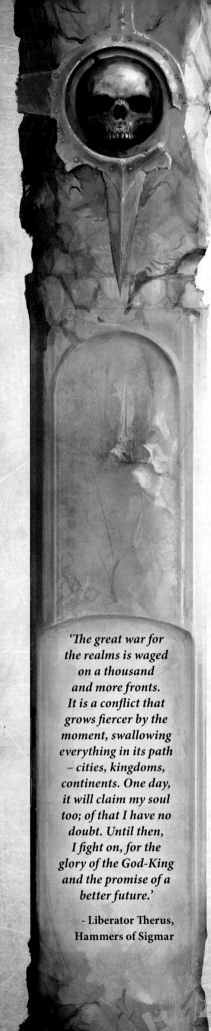

REALMS OF WAR

Welcome to the Age of Sigmar, an epic setting in which heroes, gods and monsters clash upon the fantastical battlefields of the Mortal Realms. This book is your gateway to a world of thrilling adventure and deadly peril, where the mighty champions of the God-King Sigmar fight to defend mortalkind against soul-hungering daemons, undead horrors and hordes of war-crazed brutes.

Warhammer Age of Sigmar tells the tale of the death-or-glory struggle for control over the Mortal Realms – eight elemental worlds, each with their own lethal hazards, monsters and long-buried secrets. For centuries, these lands languished under the dominion of Chaos Gods, primordial enemies of mortalkind. Their dominion lasted until Sigmar, the God-King of humanity, sent forth his heavenly hosts to conquer vast regions of the realms in a series of lightning crusades. Where Sigmar's armies triumphed, great cities were raised, and the roots of civilisation laid down. But the enemies of Order are legion, and they would see the flame of progress snuffed out forever.

The Stormcast Eternals are the God-King's greatest champions, heroes transformed into immortals, their souls and bodies bolstered by celestial lightning. It is well that each of their number is a masterful warrior outfitted with storm-forged weapons and armour, for arrayed against them is a fearsome assemblage of heathens, tyrants and monsters. First and foremost amongst the Stormcast Eternals' enemies are the twisted armies of Chaos – savage mortal warriors and daemons given unnatural gifts by the Dark Gods. Yet there are other great powers that would see Sigmar's nascent empire brought low. The undead hosts of the Great Necromancer are a constant menace to the living, and all the while the forces of Destruction rampage across the lands, smashing everything in their path to rubble.

The Age of Sigmar is an era of unending war. Though the God-King's armies have, through blood and toil, established many strongholds of civilisation, the vast majority of the Mortal Realms remains in the clutches of Chaos. To stray beyond the safety of high walls into the magic-ravaged wilds beyond is to risk corruption, mutation and an agonising death. Yet this is exactly what the champions of Order must do, if they are to spread the light of civilisation across a benighted realmscape.

This is the setting of the Warhammer Age of Sigmar hobby – a rich and ever-expanding saga that calls out for you to take up the warlord's mantle and decide the fate of the Mortal Realms. Will you choose to be the saviour of mortalkind, or its destroyer?

FORGING YOUR LEGEND

At its heart, the Warhammer Age of Sigmar hobby revolves around a vast range of beautifully sculpted and characterful Citadel Miniatures. From the heavily armoured Stormcast Eternals to the putrid daemons of Nurgle and the violent and cunning Kruleboyz, there are larger-than-life warriors and monsters of every description to choose from and collect. These miniatures are the means by which

'The great war for the realms is waged on a thousand and more fronts. It is a conflict that grows fiercer by the moment, swallowing everything in its path – cities, kingdoms, continents. One day, it will claim my soul too; of that I have no doubt. Until then, I fight on, for the glory of the God-King and the promise of a better future.'

- Liberator Therus, Hammers of Sigmar

you become both author and protagonist in the epic struggle for the Mortal Realms.

Your collection of Citadel Miniatures can be as expansive as you wish, drawing upon heroes, war engines and warriors from a dozen and more distinct factions. Alternatively, you may focus on a single element – such as a Warrior chamber of the Stormcast Eternals – building it up, unit by unit, into a mighty tabletop force. Along with a gorgeous collection of scenery pieces and even formidable 'endless spells', you have everything you need to bring the Mortal Realms to life right in your living room!

Even when your models are built and painted, your adventure is only just beginning. The warring factions of the Age of Sigmar are the focus of an ever-expanding library of battletomes and supplementary campaign books, which provide in-depth accounts of each race's origins, heroes and motivations.

After you have learned about the rich history of the Mortal Realms and the apocalyptic battles that have been fought over them, you will be ready to write the next chapter in this gripping saga yourself. The engaging and simple-to-follow rules provided in this book allow you to stage

your own grand battles on the tabletop in a variety of scenarios, and because no two battles are ever the same, there are no limits to the stories you can tell – so let your imagination run wild!

Warhammer Age of Sigmar offers rich tales of glorious heroism and nefarious villainy, whether you wish to wield the sword of righteousness to forge a brighter future for the peoples of the realms, or prefer to subjugate your foes through terror and brutality. Once you have set foot in this vibrant world, with its endless opportunities for adventure, you will want to return again and again!

The ravaged frontier settlement of Amberstone Watch is the site of a ferocious battle, as the noble Hammers of Sigmar face off against the malicious fen-stalkers known as the Kruleboyz.

Having lured them into the sucking swamps of Thondia, the Kruleboyz launch a vicious ambush on the Hammers of Sigmar. With enough spite and kunnin', even the mightiest champions can be felled.

If the God-King's mighty Stormcast Eternals are a vision of glory and celestial splendour, then the orruks of the Kruleboyz are their mirror opposite – spiteful, back-stabbing killers who will employ every underhanded trick at their disposal in order to torment and destroy their foes.

SENTINELS OF ORDER

The forces of Order are the bulwark against the darkness, the battered but resolute shield that keeps the terrors of the realms from preying upon mortals. For them, each day is not only a battle for survival, but also to reclaim what was lost over centuries of bloodshed and horror.

Of all the great alliances battling for control of the realms, the forces of Order are perhaps the most disparate. Not united by religion, species or even creed, the only thing these factions can agree on is that the goal of bringing civilisation back to the realms is preferable to endless, mindless violence, worship of the Dark Gods or slavery to an undead tyrant. What form that civilisation takes is, of course, never entirely agreed upon, for each faction naturally considers its own ways to be supreme. The armies of Order are composed of determined human soldiery, industrious and stubborn duardin, fey and mystical aelves and stranger beings besides. They believe in the power of the many over the few, and of whole societies turned towards a common goal; their ingenuity, determination and faith in the gods means they are capable of rising to – and overcoming – the myriad challenges they face clawing out an existence in the Mortal Realms.

Though the preachers and propagandists of Azyr claim that all stand together as a united front against the darkness, it would be a mistake to assume the armies of Order are universally noble. Over a century after the dawn of the Age of Sigmar, even the most honourable of their number are less than the paragons they once were. Plenty are malicious by human standards, or so unnatural in their morality that would-be allies have little chance of ever comprehending them. Tensions fester between many of the great

powers of Order, egos and desires clashing with often violent results. Their commitment to defending the civilisations of their allies lasts only as long as there is a threat bedevilling them all or some other benefit they can garner from the partnership. On many occasions the armies of Order have even drawn blades against one another, whether in pursuit of resources and land or to satisfy long-standing grudges.

But although many forces of Order are far from benevolent, it is also the growing nations of Order that produce many of the true heroes of the Mortal Realms. Be they human, duardin, aelf or otherwise, these champions recall the glory of elder days, and know that only by working together do they stand a chance of recovering that which they have lost. Many have been forced to undergo tormenting ordeals or make terrible choices in the wars for the realms, yet throughout they have held on to their essential nobility. Along with the brave warriors under their command, they carry the torch of civilisation into the dark places, putting their lives and very souls on the line for the chance to forge a brighter tomorrow for their people.

With the exception of the reptilian Seraphon, all the peoples of Order claim allegiance to a member of Sigmar's Pantheon. From the duardin's ancestor gods to the wise aelven deities, these beings were responsible for shaping the grand empires that arose during the Age of Myth. Their legacy can still be seen throughout the realms, preserved in the cultures of their followers and the forlorn ruins that dot the wastelands.

The Pantheon of Order was shattered in the Age of Chaos, likely never to be rebuilt. Still, the God-King and his allies stand firm against those who would undo their works. With Grungni returned and Alarielle accepting that isolation is no longer an option, there is a flicker of old times in the halls of Azyrheim once more; a sense that despite the many evils still to be vanquished, meaningful progress towards restoring civilisation is possible.

The greatest hope of Order is found in the huge metropolises and ever-expanding frontiers of the Sigmarite nations. For some these are true beachheads of light amidst the darkness; for others they are simply useful targets to absorb the fury of their enemies, or even resources to callously exploit in order to fuel their own ascension. The ramparts of these burgeoning settlements are manned by courageous mortal soldiery and the mighty Stormcast Eternals, aided by myriad allies old and new.

Out in the wilds, the various factions of Order seek prosperity and dominion in their own ways:

the Kharadron Overlords ply the skyways, Idoneth Deepkin raid from the seas, while the cold-blooded Seraphon weave the cosmic pattern to align with their mysterious Great Plan. Each morning, new hosts march out to the tolling of the Dawnbringer bells, striking out into hell to beat back the shadow of ruin. The scale of the task is lost on none. All know that each day can bring a new form of horror and see their gains crumble to naught. But mortal hopes are difficult to extinguish entirely, and so long as one warrior of Order stands fast, the forces of ruin and corruption will be denied their final victory.

Mere mortals they may be, but the bold warriors of the Cities of Sigmar face down the most hellish monsters in the realms with nothing more than swords, muskets and their faith in the God-King.

STORMCAST ETERNALS

The Stormcast Eternals are Sigmar's favoured champions, mighty warriors who wield the tempest's fury as a weapon and who return from death to continue the God-King's wars. Their Stormhosts have become famed across Sigmar's empire, and yet even these blessed champions possess their own, dark secrets.

In the throne rooms of Chaos Dreadholds, around the flickering fires of orruk war-camps and at the heart of morbid sepulchres, the forces of misrule whisper in fear of the God-King's holy knights. It is said that they ride to war upon bolts of lightning, that the rumble of the storm heralds their coming, and that even death cannot prevent them from returning to exact justice. The enemies of Sigmar are right to be afraid, for these knights are real. They are the hammer of the heavens, wielded both in vengeance for countless fallen civilisations and to forge the future. They are the Stormcast Eternals, and they are the God-King's fury made manifest.

Every Stormcast Eternal was chosen by Sigmar himself. Each was invested with the might of twelve mortals and charged with returning hope to the realms. Their armies descend from Azyr with comet-like force to lay low the most terrible of foes and triumph over the most unforgiving of odds. An existence of constant combat and strife asks much of the Stormcasts. Some have even come to view their ability to be Reforged upon death as more of a curse than a boon, as the flaws in the process begin to take their toll. Yet the Stormcasts have thus far proved equal to their mammoth task.

Through the sacrifice of the Stormcasts were the Realmgate Wars prosecuted and the Seeds of Hope first raised. They saw a thousand tyrants cast down and the banners of Order flown high to reclaim once mighty civilisations. Yet the Stormcasts are capable of inspiring as much fear as awe. In the past, their dedication to law

has been taken to extreme and bloody ends. The populations of Excelsis and Vindicarum, still shell-shocked in the wake of the Great Purges, are the best examples of the consequences of the Stormcasts' heavy-handed retribution, but uneasy rumblings have spread far beyond their walls. Now, Chaos cults use the reputation for retributive violence garnered by hardline Stormhosts as a means of stirring up dissent, while ambitious nobles plot to remove those Stormcasts who would curb their designs – via an assassin's dagger, if need be.

But to those who march in the Dawnbringer Crusades, opinion is very different. They have seen the might of Sigmar's chosen unleashed against their enemies, witnessed the storm-forged power of their warriors and the courage they display standing against the direst of odds. In turn, the Stormcasts bear those burdens that even the most determined of mortals could not; with their divine strength, celestial blessings and hard-won strategic acumen, they are the bane of even the most tenacious of evils.

Every Stormcast Eternal was once a mortal man or woman, taken from their former lives and remade into the weapons Sigmar needed. During the dark days following the closure of the Gates of Azyr, the God-King knew that he would require a new army to fight back against the triumphant forces of Chaos – an army specially forged for the wars to come. So did he cast his gaze across the realms, searching for those champions who stood firm against the armies of ruin. Those he deemed worthy

were snatched away from the precipice of death, carried to Azyr in blasts of celestial lightning. Not all chosen in this way were born warriors; some were physicians, blacksmiths and scholars, their only point of commonality being their heroic defiance of Chaos.

Nor was it only the living that Sigmar sought. He also took the most warlike spirits from the underworlds of Shyish, an act that saw him named thief and betrayer by Nagash. For all these interventions, there was a cost. Shorn of their greatest champions, many civilisations were overcome by Chaos, their people ground down through slaughter and misery. Hallost and Ossia were particularly stripped of their mightiest spirits, and those that remain believe that the God-King's theft was a prime cause of their near-total conquest by the armies of Khorne and Nurgle. Sigmar is not a god given to contrition, however, and considered all this to be a necessary evil; the fight against the Dark Gods was everything, and he would brook no compromise, no matter how dire the consequences.

Once transported to Azyr, a chosen soul undergoes the process known as Reforging. Few know even scant details concerning this sacred rite, for the Stormcasts do not speak of it to outsiders – and only rarely to each other. An aspirant soul must pass through the Cairns of Tempering, before being blasted apart and reconstituted through divine power upon the Anvil of Apotheosis. Not all are capable of surviving this ordeal: some simply discorporate into wisps of

Jerron Ghyrstrike had died in a marsh like this one. He hadn't intended to catch a god's eye, then, only to buy time for his family to flee the horde of beastkin. In that he had been profoundly unsuccessful, but Sigmar had chosen him anyway.

The Knight-Questor saw several reeds poking from the bog's surface twitch, before the orruks using them to breathe emerged waving cruel, spiked polearms. Jerron's face remained stoic as he parried. His blade, wreathed in a corposant halo, cleaved necks. One by one the greenskins fell, their wounds smoking.

The last dropped to its knees as its arm was severed. It looked up at him and gnashed its teeth, chuckling.

'Bet you want to know where we took your mates, hum—'

Jerron's blade fell, the only answer the greenskin would ever receive.

LET YOUR SOUL BURN BRIGHT

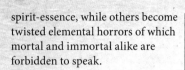

spirit-essence, while others become twisted elemental horrors of which mortal and immortal alike are forbidden to speak.

Nevertheless, those who endure earn the right to name themselves Stormcast Eternals. They are trained in the Gladiatorium, a colossal magical arena gifted to Sigmar by the Shadow King Malerion, and granted weapons forged with as much wondrous artifice as themselves. For these mighty heroes, death is not the end. It was the God-King's design that, upon being slain, they would explode into bright heavenly novas before their souls blasted back to Azyr. The celestial energy unleashed by this violent discorporation can devastate the enemy in scouring flares of purity. Upon returning to the heavenly realm the souls would undergo the Reforging once more, reborn through the skill of the Six Smiths – demigod servants of Grungni – before being hurled

yet again into the tumultuous cauldron of war. It has been known for some Stormcasts to be slain at the beginning of a gruelling siege, only to be agonisingly Reforged and return to fight at that same engagement's conclusion.

Reforging, however, carries its own dire cost. Each time a Stormcast is reborn upon the Anvil of Apotheosis, they return changed. For some, this alteration is in body; their voice becomes the boom of thunder, and when wounded lightning spills forth in place of blood. Far more commonly, however, it is their minds that are affected. Memories of past lives begin to fade, replaced with an endless cycle of bloodshed and death – a Lord-Celestant may learn the name of each foul tyrant she slays, yet forget the face of her son or the sight of the morning's first light rising over her ancestral homelands. Their morality grows more binary, to the point that they lose their ability to see in

anything but the most totalitarian terms. Those so affected may burn a village to the ground to stave off even the potential of Nurglite infection, or condemn a thief stealing bread to feed their starving family to the same harsh punishment they would a serial murderer.

Many Stormcasts dread this fate above all others. Though none would admit it openly, some have even come to believe that there can be no final victory for them – that even should they succeed in their dreams of reconquest, their souls and minds will be too degraded from enduring countless deaths and Reforgings to derive any joy from it. Many of their number now cling onto their half-remembered pasts all the more aggressively to counteract this slippage of memory, immersing themselves in their often long-dead former cultures and giving voice to battle cries not heard for centuries as they vent their fury upon the foe.

The greatest foes of the Stormcast Eternals are those who have let the foul corruption of Chaos into their souls, including the foetid, disease-spreading warriors known as the Maggotkin of Nurgle.

HOSTS OF THE GOD-KING

Every Stormcast belongs to a Stormhost, a gathering of hundreds or thousands of warriors united by heraldry, temperament, culture and tactical preference. Many Stormhosts have come into being since the days of the First Striking, and the basilica-cathedrals of the free cities echo with hymnals in praise of the most noble: the Hammers of Sigmar, golden champions who fight at the bleeding edge of the God-King's wars, and the Hallowed Knights, pious defenders who clad themselves in the bones of saints. Yet there are Stormhosts possessed of a more tempestuous mien, and the devotions lathered upon them are underpinned by a current of fear. The raging Celestial Vindicators, uncompromising Knights Excelsior and sinister Sons of Mallus all exemplify a darker side to the God-King's armies.

Though members of a Stormhost often take great pains to maintain relics and traditions from their former lives, they will also bond with their Reforged brothers and sisters through customs that have developed amongst their warrior societies. Though all adhere to the broad strokes of Sigmar's commandments, many Stormhosts possess their own rituals, titles and fraternities that embody their values. Some amongst the Celestial Vindicators, for instance, pay homage to a mysterious entity known as the Father of Blades – said to be formed from the conjoined animus of twelve legendary swords – while the patricians of the Tempest Lords place great stock upon making at least twelve kills in each battle, otherwise known as 'making the twelve-tally'. With every passing year the Stormhosts become more culturally divergent, and as the Stormcasts undergo repeated Reforgings, these new traditions have begun to supplant the memories of their past existences.

So vast are the Stormhosts that they rarely fight as a single entity. Instead, chambers and brotherhoods – the term applied to cross-conclave formations of Stormcast Eternals assembled for specific missions – are dispatched to garrison settlements, fight in the Dawnbringer Crusades and seek out Sigmar's enemies. For most of the Stormhosts' existence, their chambers have been divided into various specialisations. The warriors of the Strike chambers form the core of many brotherhoods, shields locked against the enemy's advance. The Vanguard auxiliary chambers are made up of cunning hunters and rangers accustomed to running down the enemies of Azyr by launching precise strikes. Those of the Sacrosanct chambers are warrior mages, channelling the power of the heavens into their weapons or through blasts of holy lightning.

Arguably the most fearsome of all Stormcasts are those of the Extremis chambers, the mailed fist of the God-King. These warriors ride to battle atop the celestial children of Dracothion, reptilian beasts who are endowed with the power of the cosmos and the storm. When their mounted echelons take to battle in great number, even the largest hordes are broken by their line-shattering charges.

Chambers are, in turn, comprised of retinues. Many different retinues make up the Stormhosts, but each can be classified as belonging to a conclave. The Redeemer conclaves, for example, are comprised of indomitable Stormcasts who anchor a battleline, such as Liberators and Vindictors, while the scarred veterans who fill out Annihilator and Retributor retinues are counted amongst the elite Paladin conclaves. At their head march the lords and knights who are entrusted with chamber command or who originate from temples devoted to a particular role, such as the morbid priests of the Relictor temple or wise seers of the Valedictor temple.

Though the hyper-specialised nature of the original Stormcast chambers made each incredibly effective in their particular brand of warfare, years of gruelling battle have forced the need to adapt to myriad new foes and challenges. Since Grungni's return, many chambers have begun to combine different types of conclave in hitherto unforeseen fashion – creating armies that are better able to adapt to a wide array of circumstances, and allow the Stormcasts to operate away from their strongholds for extended periods.

It is well that the Stormcasts have adapted, for rarely has their task ever seemed more insurmountable. The Era of the Beast has begun with a roar of terrible savagery, and even the realms themselves have been stoked into a frenzy. Simply to defend those gains already made would be a daunting proposition; to actively expand the frontiers of the Sigmarite nations is an order of magnitude greater still.

The Stormcast Eternals are an integral element of the Dawnbringer Crusades, often advancing at the fore of the column so that they will be the first to encounter the most terrible of horrors. Their commanders strategise alongside the leaders of mortal soldiery – sometimes from a position of brotherhood and nobility, at others dictating their orders in cold and clipped fashion – and along with the holy blood and prayers of consecration of the Devoted of Sigmar, they turn their own divine energies to the sanctification of the lands. Still, for all their might the Stormhosts nevertheless contend with realms transformed into veritable hellscapes, and even they cannot win every battle.

Once, all those Stormcast Eternals slain in the crusades would have blasted straight back to Azyr, there to be Reforged and dispatched to join the war once more. This, however, is no longer a sure thing. The machinations of the daemon Be'lakor have birthed what have become known as the 'cursed skies', localised but insidious arcane phenomena in which the upper vaults of the realms are polluted by raw Chaotic essence. So thick are these layers of corruption that they are capable of preventing the souls of many slain Stormcasts from returning to the Celestial Realm; only the most potent are able to penetrate the cursed skies, and many do not survive the attempt, cursed to be torn asunder by hungering daemons or devolve into shrieking lightning gheists. This severance from blessed Azyr is the worst fear of many Stormcasts realised, and for a time was even believed to put the lie to their supposed immortality. The Stormkeeps have thus become even more critical strongpoints, for they are now the only true fortresses many of Sigmar's armies can trust in, and their connections to their client cities are now stronger than ever.

The Cursed Skies could well have proved the bane of the Stormcasts, but hope remains in the form of Grungni. The Great Maker has at last returned to the smithies of Azyr, eyes aflame with the light of a thousand forges and hammer tolling endlessly against the Anvil of Apotheosis. Through his heroic toil the Stormhosts have been reinforced with a new martial masterpiece: thunderstrike armour. Only those Stormcasts who prove themselves to possess the worthiest souls are entrusted with this divinely wrought plate. Through the arcane maker's mark worked into each suit, these Thunderstrike Stormcast Eternals – as they are known – are capable of harnessing the fulminating energies within

them as never before. They descend from the heavens with a swiftness and force hitherto unseen, emerging from columns of celestial brilliance and to the approving crash of thunder to lay about the foe. The blaze of light that heralds their descent blinds their adversaries with its purity, while every blow they land crackles with the barely contained fury of the tempest. Should one of these champions fall, their thunderstrike armour channels and releases the energies unleashed at the moment of their demise with redoubled force – a final, blazing act of sacrifice and vengeance before their soul ascends to Azyr for Reforging.

The Thunderstrike Stormcasts are Sigmar's response to the changing nature of war in the realms, and unlike the potent but sometimes unwieldy hammer-blow formations of yesteryear, they are organised to operate autonomously for extended periods – for with the Sigmarite strongpoints constantly imperilled, the Stormcasts must become warriors of all the realms once more, not solely Azyr.

Exemplifying this is the Stormcasts' opposition of the Kruleboyz. Through the murky swamplands and across the primordial savannahs of Ghur they have fought these raiders, repelling them from the Sigmarite strongpoints and exacting retribution for those who have suffered at the hands of the greenskins. Sigmar has dispatched Yndrasta – one of the near-mythical lords of Azyr forged by the God-King's own hands – to combat these raiders and their raging god-monstrosity Kragnos, for the destruction spread in his wake cannot be allowed to reach the heartlands of the Sigmarite nations. It is an onerous challenge, but the Stormcasts will meet it with valour and determination – as they always have.

Many are the terrible battles fought between Order and Chaos, cataclysmic encounters that shake the earth and boil the skies. On such occasions, the full fury of the Extremis Chambers is unleashed, and Dracoth-riding Stormcast knights charge forth to crush the heathen hordes.

SENTINELS OF ORDER

The disparate factions of Order are united neither by religion, creed nor even species, but all agree that the goal of bringing civilisation back to the Mortal Realms is preferable to endless, mindless violence.

Vindictor
Stormcast Eternals

Knight-Arcanum
Stormcast Eternals

Praetor
Stormcast Eternals

Melusai Ironscale
Daughters of Khaine

Witch Aelf
Daughters of Khaine

Namarti Thrall
Idoneth Deepkin

Lotann, Warden of the Soul Ledgers
Idoneth Deepkin

Aether-Khemist
Kharadron Overlords

Endrinmaster
Kharadron Overlords

Grimwrath Berzerker
Fyreslayers

Hearthguard
Fyreslayers

Truestone Seneschal
Lumineth Realm-lords

Vanari Auralan Sentinel
Lumineth Realm-lords

Tree-Revenant
Sylvaneth

Arch-Revenant
Sylvaneth

Saurus Oldblood
Seraphon

Skink Starpriest
Seraphon

Freeguild Handgunner
Cities of Sigmar

Battlemage
Cities of Sigmar

In the battle for the Mortal Realms, mortal and immortal must stand as one. Sigmar's vision will only be made manifest through a great sacrifice in lives – and in that, perhaps he and the Dark Gods he opposes are not so different after all.

HARBINGERS OF DESTRUCTION

From out of the wildlands, the tribes and clans of Destruction come howling and stomping, the earth cracking beneath the violence of their primeval onslaught. With the realm-soul of Ghur stoked to a frenzy and ancient terrors on the march, these bestial hordes find themselves in the ascendant – to the misfortune of any caught in their warpath.

Since the earliest days of the Mortal Realms the hordes of Destruction have been smashing and bashing their way across the face of creation. The rowdy beasts and belligerent monsters that comprise their armies – orruks, ogors, grots, troggoths, gargants and more besides – relish any chance to 'duff up' those they consider to be 'soft gits', whether through excessive physical violence or spiteful cunning and backstabbing. For centuries they have been a threat to all others who would claim dominion of the Mortal Realms; now, however, the dawning of the Era of the Beast has seen this wild and barbarous threat rise to new, explosively belligerent heights.

It is becoming ever more clear that the hordes of Destruction may pose an even greater threat than the corrupt disciples of Chaos or malignant hosts of Death. Their lust for carnage makes them akin to a monstrous force of nature given full rein; they are almost impossible to reason with, and even those among them who do understand concepts such as negotiation and bartering are liable to disregard such agreements as soon as the mood strikes, in favour of good old-fashioned fighting. As many developing Sigmarite strongpoints have found to their cost, when the bestial hordes are stoked to the greatest heights of battle-lust, there is no wall, phalanx or sorcerous ruse that can hope to stop the ensuing onslaught.

All these disparate hordes are united through reverence for Gorkamorka, the two-headed god of destruction. This fealty is not expressed through conventional worship; indeed, it is unlikely that most who consider themselves children of Gorkamorka can even spell the word. Rather, they seek to impress their elemental god through committing the greatest feats of cunning and violence. Though Gorkamorka does not grant his faithful boons in the manner as the Ruinous Powers, his rumbling approval can still be felt in the manic energy that overcomes an army of Destruction on the warpath.

Like a great many gods of the realms, Gorkamorka is worshipped in different ways by the different cultures under his sway; Gutbuster ogors, for example, honour him in the form of the Gulping God, while the zealous Bonesplitterz view him as the supreme predator. Alongside him stands a crude pantheon of other near-mythical beings including the gibbering Bad Moon, scuttling Spider God and, most tangible and perhaps most terrifying, the recently unleashed earthquake deity known as Kragnos, End of Empires.

Broadly speaking, the instinctive desire of all beings sworn to Destruction is to reduce the realms to a more primal, natural state – to cast down the weakling trappings of civilisation and install in their place a bestial regime where might makes right. Of course, the disparate clans and creatures of Gorkamorka's favoured all have differing beliefs on what they consider to be 'natural'; while the Kruleboyz favour cloying and hag-light haunted swamplands, the brutish Ironjawz are most at home on the bone-strewn savannahs of Ghur, and the Beastclaw Raiders thrive in those lands plunged into perpetual, mystical winter. These varying opinions have sparked plenty of internecine conflict – or, at least, have provided a good excuse for a punch-up. Destruction factions tend towards being nomadic in nature. Many display a tendency for accumulating a crude form of culture as they follow their wanderlust, and so it is common to see orruk warclans or ogor mawtribes with wildly distinct beliefs and iconography of their own – though all focus around fighting in some form.

Such fractious tendencies have, in the past, been the only thing keeping the hobnailed boot of Destruction from the collective throat of the realms; not since the mythical days of the First Great Waaagh! have the tribes come together in any significant number. But all things change. The era of the Broken Realms saw the forces of Destruction mass with a conviction unseen for centuries, drawn to the heart of Ghur by a primal sensation known as the Great Stomp and united behind Kragnos and his grudging ally, the mighty orruk warlord Gordrakk. Now, spearheaded by the conniving Kruleboyz – who see the growing but often-isolated strongholds of Order as rich pickings for their cruel culture of domination – they are a storm ready to break with apocalyptic force. Even the realms themselves have been stoked into a frenzy by the machinations of the gods and the scars of war. The shamans of Destruction look to the mustering of the hordes and the furious wrath that exudes from the realm of Ghur, and see only one explanation. The greatest fight of all time is beginning – and from the runtiest orruk yoof to the mightiest Mega-Gargant, everyone wants to be at the forefront.

Strong enough to kick down a castle wall and massive enough to squash a warhorse underfoot, the Sons of Behemat are titanic, dull-witted thugs who revel in feats of brutish destruction.

ORRUK WARCLANS

When the orruk warclans are on the rampage, reality quakes. These green-skinned brutes are obsessed with fighting, and firmly believe that they are the 'ardest creatures in all the Mortal Realms. Led by their mighty warlords and bosses, they crush their foes through sheer bloody belligerence.

Orruks live for war. Many forces make such a boast, but none so completely exemplify the notion as do these brutal marauders. Battle is, for them, an end in itself; every moment that passes without their choppas carving through flesh is a moment wasted. Their warclans – the name given to the belligerent hordes of like-minded orruks who charge about the realms looking for a worthy scrap – are happy to fight just about anyone, as evidenced by the mountains of bodies left in their wake. They are a near-elemental force, practically impossible to reason with and just as difficult to resist. Everything that stands before them is soon stomped flat, the screams of the dying drowned out by the booming war cries and guttural laughter of the greenskins.

Orruks are the foremost children of Gorkamorka. In the Age of Myth they gleefully fought alongside him in his mission to cleanse the realms of monsters, and when the Twin-Headed God suddenly turned upon his fellow Pantheon deities, they joined in his rampage across reality. Whenever Gorkamorka has a particularly violent falling out with himself, he splits into two separate beings – Gork (who is brutal but kunnin') and Mork (who is kunnin' but brutal). Different warclans tend to gravitate towards one particular aspect of their god, though in truth all orruks are war-hungry maniacs who will happily bash their best mate to a pulp just for a laugh. It is the job of the shamans of the orruk race to divine the will of Gork (or possibly Mork) and direct the hordes to battle, as well as channel his energy into furious displays of spell-flinging.

Whichever aspect of the Twin-Headed God they favour, all orruks find themselves overcome with the same primal energy when war calls. Known as the Waaagh! – a term that can only be pronounced at ear-splitting volume – it rattles around in their thick skulls, intensifying with every moment. For some orruks the Waaagh! is akin to a sudden surge of energy that can be expended in one horrendous outpouring of destruction. For others the Waaagh! acts as a kind of savage dynamo, filling them with an irrepressible need to run down the foe, or sees their minds spin with spiteful schemes that can catch even a seasoned Freeguild officer off-guard. In all cases, however, the call of the Waaagh! cannot be ignored. Spurred on by this maddening impetus, the orruks charge forward at the vanguard of Destruction's unstoppable advance, minds aflame with the need to vent this volatile energy in acts of brutal carnage.

BUILT FOR FIGHTIN'

Orruks are universally green of skin. They are muscly brutes with small, beady red eyes, protruding tusks, sloped foreheads and a truly awful stink. Most orruks stand broader and taller than the average 'humie', and the more that they fight the larger they grow. It is for this reason that their warlords are invariably the biggest and strongest of the warclan. Their speech is uncomplicated and, just like the greenskins themselves, in most cases incredibly direct. There is little 'mukkin' about' when it comes to the orruks, and while many of them do relish

in the opportunity to pull a cunning trick on their foe, all are inevitably connected to violence in some manner.

This is not to say, however, that orruks are stupid. Rather, they simply do not concern themselves with any dilemmas that do not contribute to their immediate desires – most often finding a smaller greenskin to push around or enemies to hack apart. To them life is largely binary; either they are possessed of sufficient strength and cunning to 'krump' their rivals, or they will be krumped in turn. All orruks are unified by an instinctual contempt for the trappings of civilisation. They hate anything that grants false or unearned strength, be it a sturdy city wall, grimoire of forbidden lore, or the latest death-dealing innovations of the Ironweld guilds. Many have sneeringly described the orruks as the embodiment of brute force and ignorance, and while the rise of the Kruleboyz has put the lie to this claim, there is something to be said for their primal ferocity in the face of the ruses and snares of their enemies. When a proper Waaagh! gets going, the raw bloody-mindedness of the orruks is a weapon in itself – a weapon that, if left unchecked, could crush the Sigmarite nations to dust.

IRONJAWZ – FISTS OF GORKAMORKA

The Ironjawz embody the Gorkish side of the Gorkamorka divide. They are muscle-bound monsters clad in the thickest armour – the jagged metal plates of which are battered into shape by the pounding fists of the orruks – and wielding crude weapons that are as lethal as they are wildly oversized. To the Ironjawz, there is no problem worth tackling that can't be resolved with some good old-fashioned carnage. They view anything even resembling a complex battle-plan with suspicion, and any Ironjaw boss who decides to try anything so daring as a flanking manoeuvre, pincer attack or – most controversial of all – feigned retreat better have the muscle to back it up. The Ironjawz carry this straightforward approach into the make-up of their clans. Five mobs form a Fist – five being the highest number most Ironjawz can count to before getting bored – while five Fists make a Brawl. These formations (a loose term at best) are filled out by waves of bellowing orruks: hulking Brutes, eager Ardboys and stampeding Gore-gruntas – Ironjawz who have somehow managed to clamber atop huge porcine monsters and thus become a brutally efficient, if occasionally unpredictable, form of shock cavalry.

Ironjawz consider themselves to be the embodiment of 'proper orrukiness'. In fairness, if 'proper orrukiness' means solving every problem with gnarled green fists, they're probably right. Their fixation on raw strength stems from their origins upon the Ghurish plains, where only the mightiest can survive amongst the hunting grounds of gargantuan predatory monsters and deposits of concentrated, primeval magic. Most Ironjawz simply don't understand the Kruleboyz' conniving ways, and only grudgingly acknowledge them as true greenskins – in part because the swamp-dwellers seemed to emerge en masse a short time after Kragnos, a being possessed of such titanic might that many Ironjawz now consider him second only to Gorkamorka.

Ironjawz Brutes are the biggest and meanest orruks around, muscle-bound greenskins who delight in a life of endless, skull-smashing violence.

Ironjawz are boisterous and ostentatious, natural bullies who love showing off. They typically wear brightly coloured armour, the better to draw fights to them, and give their warclans aggressive names such as the Bloodtoofs, Stoneskulls and Facerippas. Nomadic by nature, Ironjawz are not typically ones for building anything grander than crude effigies of Gorkamorka assembled from lashed-together dung, rocks and scrap. Still, it is easy to tell where their warclans have been, judging by the trampled lands and unthinking vandalism left in their wake.

Ironjawz warleaders are known as Megabosses, scarred and hulking monsters that can dwarf even a Stormcast for sheer brawn. Nothing makes a Megaboss happier than the crush of the melee, where they exhibit a savage glee while hacking down swathes of foes. Might makes right for the orruks, and many courageous or overconfident Megabosses (not that there's always a difference) prove their strength by riding atop the reptilian immensities known as Maw-krushas – one of the few breeds of beast as ill-tempered as the orruks themselves, so much so that it is said they can achieve flight only because gravity has no desire to countermand them.

Though Megabosses are in their own way conduits of Gorkamorka's rage, they cannot direct it outside of unleashing deafening and fury-stoking battle cries. As such, they are commonly surrounded by gibbering Weirdnob Shamans and Warchanters – orruks who have become consumed by the Waaagh! and use the shattered armour and broken bodies of their enemies to drum a thumping tattoo of war. Greatest of all Megabosses is Gordrakk, who aspires to one day crush every realm to dust and best even the gods with his twin choppas Smasha and Kunnin'.

BONESPLITTERZ – TOUCHED BY THE WAAAGH!

Even other greenskins think there is something weird about the Bonesplitterz. There would have to be for an orruk to discard concepts such as metal weapons or armour in favour of charging about in little more than warpaint while waving crude flint blades. Though they are savages even by the standards of Destruction, the Bonesplitterz are not to be underestimated. Their wild warclans consider it their Gorkamorka-given duty to hunt down the mightiest monsters – and then promptly duff them up. In doing so, and by driving the looted bones through their scarred green flesh, they believe that they inherit some measure of Gorkamorka's primal strength. The mightier and more foul-tempered the beast, the more potent the released spirit-energy. The savage animus that surrounds a Bonesplitterz warclan on the move is undeniable: this aura of primeval mania sees animals tear at one another, trees violently uproot themselves and rocks tremble with the fury of the Waaagh!.

No orruk starts life as a Bonesplitter. The impetus to join this strange cult sparks when the thumping drumbeat of the Waaagh! lingers in a greenskin's mind even after battle. This invariably serves to send the afflicted orruk mad, or at least, madder than usual. Following strange portents – blood splattering in eye-catching fashion or clouds that look a little like boars if you squint are common motivators – they leave their former warclans behind to seek out other Bonesplitterz. Should they survive this deranged odyssey, they will be marked with sacred warpaint by the greenskin spell-flingers. These designs are daubed on using the crushed organs of their monstrous prey along with other weird ingredients, and though it defies easy explanation, they really do seem to protect the orruks from harm. Whether filling the skies with storms of primitive arrows, riding atop crazed war-boars or carrying huge spears known as Gorkteef, mobs of Bonesplitterz charge fearlessly into battle, shrugging off even the bullseye shots of Freeguild marksmen along the way.

Unusually for orruks, Bonesplitterz warclans are led by shamans rather than warriors. These Wurrgog Prophets and their Wardokk disciples are deeply connected to the bestial energies of Ghur – they have long preached that every realm has its own beast-soul, and the return of Kragnos has, in their own minds, proved them entirely correct. Though considered gibbering and frothing loonies by anyone that isn't a Bonesplitter, these shamans are capable of unleashing impressive displays of Waaagh! magic, imbuing their orruks with the fury of the bestial spirits or conjuring great calloused fists to crush the foe. Because of this, even greenskins who aren't Bonesplitterz are willing to follow them to war when the circumstances are right, though the wisest keep a fair distance between themselves and the spell-flingers – the better to avoid their often offensive scent and penchant for detonating in a burst of howling green magic at inopportune moments.

KRULEBOYZ – KUNNIN' RAIDERS

From out of the ancient bogs and stinking fens of the Mortal Realms, the Kruleboy orruks emerge into this new era of carnage. These marauders are the result of Morkish kunnin' taken to its natural extreme. They do not charge forward as a single howling tide, nor trust in brute strength to win the day, though when pressed

they can and will tear a human's arms off just for the fun of it. Rather, the Kruleboyz fight smart – and worse still, they fight dirty. The cruelly ingenious nature of their tactics has already garnered a dark reputation, for it stands quite opposed to conventional orruk behaviour. With each passing day tales spread of atrocities committed, and the ire of both the Grand Conclaves and the Stormhosts at such rampant predation of Sigmar's people is stoked ever hotter. The Kruleboyz themselves could not care less for such condemnation; indeed, they take a mean-spirited satisfaction in it. After many long years of skulking in the shadows, forced to watch the rampages of their more belligerent kin, they know that this is their hour – and already they are making up for lost time.

Long ago, the first Kruleboyz made their way into the deep swamps of the Mortal Realms, particularly those in the wilds of Ghur. Doubtless they went in looking for a fight, but what they found was very different. In these places, raw strength counts for little; muscle cannot protect a warrior from being smothered by mire-djinns formed of choking swamp gases, or the sentient marshes that hungrily drag armoured warriors beneath the surface. But for all their hooliganism, all breeds of orruk are incredibly determined. Refusing to be beaten, over time they adapted to their new homes. Their bodies grew rangier, better able to navigate the treacherous bogs, and they crafted spiked armour and terrifying scareshields to ward off the monsters that bedevilled them. Most importantly, the Kruleboyz grew kunnin'. They learned to use particularly filthy swamp-water as an ingredient in strange potions and broths, and could reflect upon past mistakes to a level unthinkable for most greenskins. Displays of devious intellect became an end in themselves for

the Kruleboyz; the oral legends of their clans are filled with tales of devilish deeds and unscrupulous trickery that saw the greenskins outfox their foes and leave them ripe for slaughter.

Kruleboyz find the notion of honour laughable; so long as victory can be achieved, the particulars are of secondary importance. Indeed, many would argue that the more sneaky and underhanded the tactic used to win, the more 'Morky' the victor is. As such, they see no issue in preying on those weaker than they are. Their raids are often launched with the intent of entrapping other creatures through spiteful but ingenious methods – indeed, this shared focus is often all that keeps the swamp-dwelling greenskins from each other's throats. Many are the schemes they employ to achieve this, from poisoning water supplies to weaken a Sigmarite strongpoint's garrison, to summoning clouds of sentient swamp-gas that eat away at a fortress's mortar and reduce its walls to rubble.

Kruleboyz take great satisfaction not only in dominating other beings, but also the landscape, transforming it through the strange magics of their spell-flingers to reflect their marshy homes. Here they construct gangly keeps and crooked watchtowers, and it is to here that their captives are dragged off, their fates unknown but no doubt ghoulish. The cruelty of the 'Snatchers' has seen them strike out at a great many Sigmarite strongpoints, and with every successful raid they grow bolder. Armed with their spiteful, innovative minds and endless capacity for malice, the Kruleboyz slink from the swamps in ever greater numbers to challenge man, duardin and aelf for control of the lands. If they can outfox and humble Sigmar's gleaming Stormcasts in the process, then so much the better.

HARBINGERS OF DESTRUCTION

From out of the wildlands, the tribes and clans of Destruction come howling and stomping, the earth cracking beneath the violence of their primeval onslaught.

Gutrippaz
Orruk Warclans

Hobgrot Slittaz
Orruk Warclans

Brute
Orruk Warclans

Wurrgog Prophet
Orruk Warclans

Arrowboy
Orruk Warclans

Loonboss
Gloomspite Gitz

Shroomancer
Gloomspite Gitz

Tyrant
Ogor Mawtribes

Warstomper Mega-Gargant
Sons of Behemat

AGENTS OF CHAOS

From beyond the veil, the Chaos Gods watch with hungry eyes. Created from the very sins of mortalkind, they desire to turn the realms into reflections of their own depraved natures. At their command march hordes of twisted mutants and mortal madmen granted unholy powers, as well as the daemon legions – shards of each god's malignant essence.

Chaos is the dark mirror of the soul, a blot upon reality that can only exist thanks to the flawed nature of mortals. From the Realm of Chaos, an unnatural hellscape that exists beyond the boundaries of space and time, the Ruinous Powers hold court over fields of bone and castles of flesh. Each of these dread entities is the reflection of a passion or emotion taken to the extreme. To understand the true nature of Chaos would drive the strongest of wills to madness, and even those in its thrall often have wildly different views on what exactly they pay homage to. Some say that there are many facets and minor deities of Chaos, others that the Ruinous Powers are but shadows cast by a singular, all-encompassing avatar of evil. Most agree, however, that there are five Dark Gods that comprise the pantheon of Chaos – Khorne, Tzeentch, Nurgle, Slaanesh and the Great Horned Rat.

Chaos is inherently corrupting. Many have tried to use the reality-warping potential it offers for noble purposes, to take its power without paying the terrible cost. All such efforts are doomed to fail. Just as the Dark Gods are formed from the most negative and destructive emotions coalesced and given divine personification, those they choose to receive their boons are inevitably compelled to let the darkest elements of their personality overtake them – to eventually lose themselves to their own sins, no matter how hard they resist. With that said,

the might offered by Chaos is undeniable, and in the dangerous wilds of the realms it is not hard to understand why so many would wish to possess such might. Skill at war, arcane might, forbidden knowledge, even immortality – all of these and more can be granted by the Dark Pantheon to their most devoted, and most successful, followers. Still, the gods give nothing for free. To truly excel amongst the hordes of Chaos one must not only give praise to the gods, but actively seek to advance their ruinous agendas by standing in opposition to all rival gods. Even then, plenty of would-be champions have been suddenly discarded by their callous deity, all to facilitate the rise of warlords deemed more worthy. A single misstep along the path to ascension, or even the whim of an uncaring god, can see one who commanded a dark empire on one day consigned to the gutter or the corpse-heap the next.

Humans are the most common species found in thrall to Chaos, but they are not alone amongst the armies of misrule. Aelves, duardin and stranger beings besides have sworn themselves to the Ruinous Powers over the long and bloody years. In the forests lurk the Beasts of Chaos, a race as old as the realms and filled with a loathing of civilisation. Though many do not consider themselves true servants of the gods, their ruinous aims align enough that common cause has been reached. The Great Horned Rat, meanwhile, is served by the skaven – a race of malicious and treacherous ratmen constantly conspiring to achieve dominance over all others. Ever underestimated by rivals and temporary allies alike, the clans of the skaven number in the billions, and should they have their way even the other gods of Chaos will ultimately be laid low. Only the ratmen's empire of ruination will remain.

Most terrifying of all the servants of the Ruinous Powers are the daemons. Each of these infernal beings is a shard of a Chaos God given sentience and sent forth to do their bidding. At the dawn of the Age of Chaos it was the daemonic legions who put a thousand empires to the sword, and numberless are the mortals they have butchered or turned to the service of the Brothers in Darkness. Though they cannot exist in the Mortal Realms indefinitely, daemons are also near impossible to destroy – in most cases they will simply be banished, waiting for the chance to return and exact revenge. Their powers are strange and unsettling, and rarely do they fight for recognisable mortal aims – instead, they make war to please the monstrous appetites and obsessive desires of their patron gods. When the mortal and daemonic servants of Chaos march in step, there is little that can stand before them, a truism made manifest when the Age of Myth perished in blood and fire.

Once, the powers of Chaos claimed dominion over almost all the Mortal Realms. That time will come again. The resurgence of civilisation is but a temporary setback to the designs of the Dark Gods, for wherever mortals go, their secret evils will follow them with a grim inevitability. Great swathes of the realms remain under the dominion of Chaos, and the armies of the Ruinous Powers constantly hurl themselves at the boundaries of the Sigmarite nations, probing them for any weakness to exploit. Should they ever succeed, then the realms themselves will be utterly consumed in a tide of madness, twisted and remade for the amusement of deranged deities and their fanatical disciples.

Fierce and eternal is the rivalry between the Blood God Khorne and Slaanesh, Lord of Excess. The daemons of these two warring gods wage a ceaseless battle across the Realm of Chaos.

AGENTS OF CHAOS

From beyond the veil, the Chaos Gods watch with hungry eyes. At their command march hordes of twisted mutants and mortal madmen granted unholy powers, as well as the dreaded daemon legions.

Bloodmaster
Blades of Khorne

Exalted Deathbringer
Blades of Khorne

Slaughterpriest
Blades of Khorne

Blue Horror
Disciples of Tzeentch

Tzaangor
Disciples of Tzeentch

Kairic Acolytes
Disciples of Tzeentch

Warlock Bombardier
Skaven

Skryre Acolyte
Skaven

Chaos Warrior
Slaves to Darkness

Darkoath Warqueen
Slaves to Darkness

Spoilpox Scrivener
Maggotkin of Nurgle

Sloppity Bilepiper
Maggotkin of Nurgle

Plagueridden
Maggotkin of Nurgle

Myrmidesh Painbringer
Hedonites of Slaanesh

Lord of Pain
Hedonites of Slaanesh

Blissbarb Archer
Hedonites of Slaanesh

Allurer
Hedonites of Slaanesh

When the legions of the Ruinous Powers march in step, scarce are the foes who can stand against them. In their wake, reality itself burns. Even the enlightened and majestic lands of Hysh crumble at their coming.

31

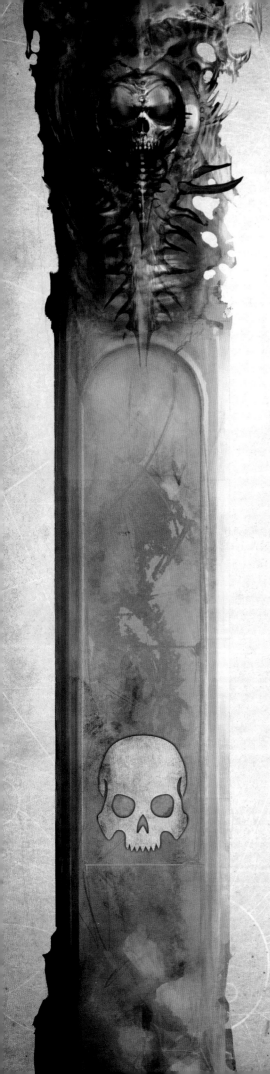

BRINGERS OF DEATH

The dead do not rest easy in the Mortal Realms. The fell winds of Shyish sweep across the lands, and where they pass, mouldering corpses and unquiet spirits stir. By harnessing this font of necromancy, the champions of Death are able to raise entire legions to assail the living. They, in turn, must serve the inviolable will of their master – Nagash, the Great Necromancer.

Nagash is the Supreme Lord of the Undead, the self-proclaimed master of Shyish. Thousands of years before the demise of the World-that-Was, he had mastered the dark art of necromancy – indeed, there are those who say that Nagash is the progenitor of that morbid craft. Ultimately, every creature of the grave that haunts the Mortal Realms is Nagash's to control, whether they wish it or otherwise. Once, this power was nominally employed in service to the Pantheon of Order, though even then the Great Necromancer schemed for sole dominion of the realms. Now the armies of the dead are set intractably against the living, Nagash's ambition writ large in the atrocities committed by his minions.

From the sepulchral citadel of Nagashizzar, located at the bottom of the soul-sucking void known as the Shyish Nadir, Nagash and his favoured champions, the legendary Mortarchs, plot to cast down the nations of the living. In their place, they would raise an unchanging empire solely under the control of the Great Necromancer, a 'necrotopia' in which concepts such as free will and emotion would be forgotten. In doing so, Nagash would starve his fellow deities of worship, leaving him the sole power in the cosmos. To achieve this, the Great Necromancer has myriad servants to call upon. The vampiric Soulblight warlords and their endless resurrected legions, the spectral terror-troops of the Nighthaunt processions, the deranged cannibals of the Flesh-eater Courts, the disciplined hosts of the Ossiarch Bonereapers – all of these forces march at the command of Nagash and his Mortarchs. Though the majority of these revenants are not individually as skilled as the living foes they face, they invariably attack in vast numbers beneath the cover of unnatural darkness. Worse still, their generals are suffused with necromantic power that sees their warriors rise again and again no matter how many times they are struck down. Few mortals can resist the relentless will of the dead indefinitely, and many a city and kingdom has been ground down by constant war against such abominations.

Of course, Nagash and his champions cannot be everywhere at once. The curse of undeath has spread far beyond Shyish to grasp at every corner of the cosmos. In the depths of Golvaria, vampires and Necromancers lurk amidst crumbling castles, calling on the seemingly endless dead of that land to serve in their war against the hordes of the Daemon Prince Zarthonax. In Ymetrica, mordants crawl throughout the Vertiginous Peaks, believing themselves to be noble knights on a quest for glory. Even in Ghur, the Ossiarch Bonereapers of the Ivory Host continue to strive for dominance over that bestial realm, though the savagery embedded in their bones may prove their undoing.

Though not all beings risen through the magic of Shyish are necessarily evil – in the free cities, songs are still sung of the Heldenhammer Crusade and the alliance struck between the Stormcasts and Celemnis, Banshee Queen of Elixia – these are more the exception than the rule. Whether jealous of life or determined to prove the supremacy of undeath, many of Nagash's cadaverous servants share their master's hatred of all that breathes, and they would think nothing of butchering an entire city simply to replenish the ranks of their necromantic hosts.

Nagash's machinations have been behind some of the most devastating conflicts in the realms' recent history. It was his command that saw vast quantities of grave-sand moved to the centre of the Realm of Death, inverting the magical polarity of that realm and creating the Shyish Nadir. The Necroquake – the magical calamity that stirred countless shrieking gheists into unlife across the realms – was a result of his millennia-spanning schemes, and the Soul Wars were his campaign to strike down those who would steal his rightful bounty of spirit-essence, Sigmar and the aelven

gods foremost among them. In this, Nagash was ultimately defeated: undone by the stratagems of Teclis, his corporeal form was destroyed by the aelementor spirits of Hysh. But the Great Necromancer has been destroyed in body many times before, and always he has returned to wreak terrible vengeance. Even now, his spirit gathers power in Shyish, coalescing and making plans for retribution. A time is coming when a field of fresh corpses will smother the realms once more. When it does, all should fear the wrath of the Undying King and his favoured champions.

The Ossiarch Bonereapers care not whom they slaughter; they simply require more bone with which to forge new undead soldiers. The bloody remains of Chaos-worshippers serve just as well as any.

BRINGERS OF DEATH

By harnessing the power of necromancy, the champions of Death are able to raise entire legions of undead to assail the living. They, in turn, must serve the inviolable will of their master – Nagash, the Great Necromancer.

Deadwalker Zombies
Soulblight Gravelords

Deathrattle Skeleton
Soulblight Gravelords

Vampire Lord
Soulblight Gravelords

Mortek Guard
Ossiarch Bonereapers

Vokmortian, Master of the Bone-tithe
Ossiarch Bonereapers

Mortisan Boneshaper
Ossiarch Bonereapers

Abhorrant Ghoul King
Flesh-eater Courts

Abhorrant Archregent
Flesh-eater Courts

Bladegheist Revenant
Nighthaunt

Tomb Banshee
Nighthaunt

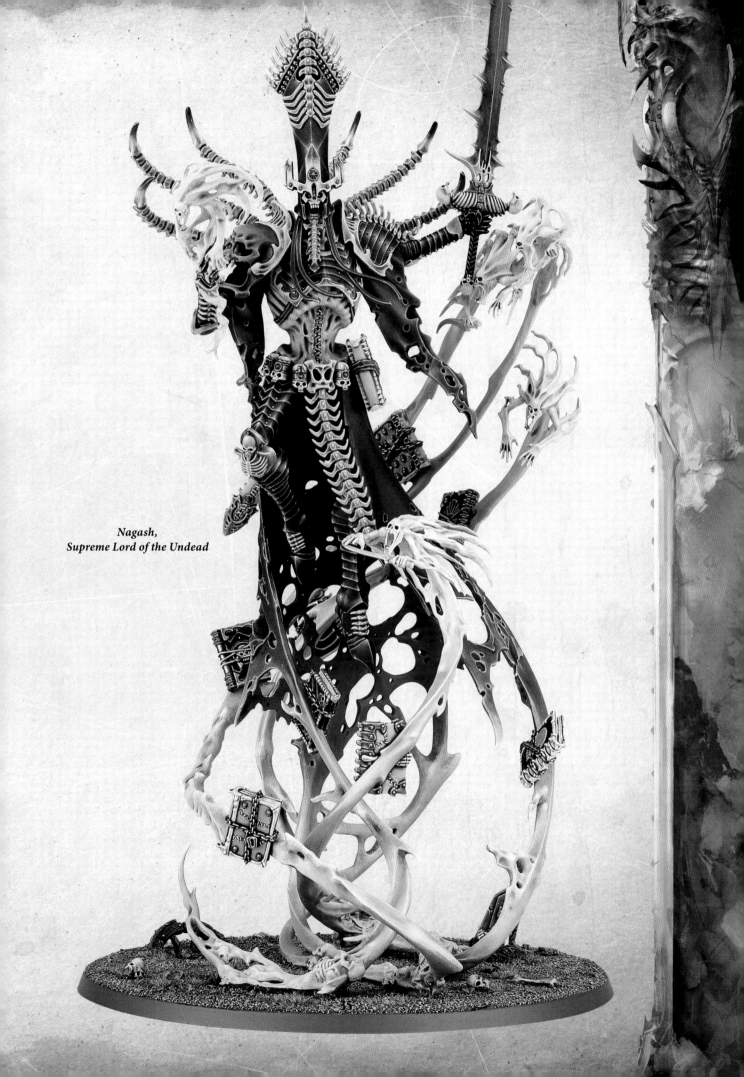

Nagash,
Supreme Lord of the Undead

THE MORTAL REALMS

The Mortal Realms are the bedrock of reality, the backdrop against which tales of carnage and infamy are told. Each is a creation of crystallised magic, a land of wonder and horror in equal measure. They are beyond the understanding of any mortal, though each has been saturated with the blood of those who would claim them.

If one was to observe them from without, the Mortal Realms would appear as eight glittering baubles set against the velvet blackness of the void. Each is a vast multi-hued sphere, a concentration of the raw and elemental stuff of creation. This magical energy, unleashed in the destruction of the World-that-Was, crystallised over many years into lands of incomparable scope and grandeur.

Formed from magic they may be, but the Mortal Realms are most assuredly habitable. At the centre of each realm, its arcane energy is least volatile and spread most thinly. Here, at least, mortals can farm the foods and find the resources they need to survive, though their surroundings are still as harsh as they are majestic. It is in these places that the great powers of the realms establish their empires and most often wage their endless wars. The further one journeys from a realm's core, however, the more bizarre things become. To travel towards a realm's edge is to pass into places where reality is charged to bursting with magic. In the space of a single heartbeat, a man may find that his flesh has turned inside out, that his body has aged or regressed by decades, or that he can unleash a burning crescent of witchfire that travels unimpeded for miles with but a careless sweep of the arm. All that is to say nothing of the many protean monstrosities and arcane constructs that haunt these magic-blasted regions. It would take decades at the very least to travel on foot from a realm's core to its edge, and few are foolish enough to make the attempt.

Though all are contained within the bounds of magical realmspheres, not all Mortal Realms appear the same. While many take the form of a flat disc made up of huge continents, others are akin to a shifting collection of sub-planes or appear as a nebula of shimmering magic when seen from afar. Equally, the terrain of each realm is variable in the extreme. Grassland, desert, ocean, rainforest, tundra: all of these landscapes and more can be found throughout each realmsphere, though the trees may glitter with the onset of oxidation in some and the snow may scald to the touch in others. Since the Age of Chaos, many of the lands of the realms have themselves become corrupt and eagerly vent their pain on unfortunate travellers.

One cannot simply walk from one realm to another. One must instead travel through mystical portals known as realmgates, and since the earliest days, these mysterious pathways have been points of great strategic value. Though some realmgates look like traditional stone gateways, others appear as waterfalls, shimmering veils of light, chasms that seem bottomless and stranger forms besides. They may grant passage within a single realm or allow one to traverse the cosmos in the blink of an eye. Many have been corrupted over the bloody centuries, with some even capable of diverting unlucky travellers to the hellish Realm of Chaos. The greatest realmgates, those capable of transporting entire armies, are the Arcways; there is but one Arcway per realm, and each connects to the interstitial sub-realm known as the Eightpoints, a land conquered long ago by the armies of Archaon.

DOMINION OF SHADRAC

THE PRIME INNERLANDS

THE EVERSPRING SWATHE

AZYR

YMETRICAN GEOSEGMENT

GHYRAN

GHURISH HEARTLANDS

GHUR

THE GREAT PARCH

CHAMON

THE SPIRAL CRUX

AQSHY

THE REALMSPHERES

The realms are vast, functionally if not literally infinite, and each is defined by the magic bound into its very being. Within the limits of each realmsphere can be found a mind-bogglingly colossal array of peoples, creatures and landscapes, though all are influenced by the magical essence infused into their home realms.

GHUR THE MONSTROUS

It is a common maxim that in Ghur, all things are predator or prey. There is a savage literalism to this claim: rivers hungrily devour the land, living mountains grind across the plains in search of prey, and even the continental plates are locked in constant tectonic battle. Jagged peaks spear the horizon while the bones of ancient megafauna litter the savannah. Beasts of all kinds populate Ghur, and plenty are hunters themselves. Even in the Age of Myth, the Realm of Beasts was a violent place, its nomadic tribes forced to battle both the monsters of the wilds and one another for survival. Unsurprisingly, Ghur is the spiritual home of all the bestial clans of Destruction, for in these primeval vistas, their creed of 'might makes right' is demonstrated most brutally.

AQSHY THE BRIGHT

A land of arid plains, choking ash clouds and sweltering rainforests, Aqshy gives rise to tempers that burn as hot as magma. Amongst the inhabitants of the Realm of Fire, passion and simmering aggression hold sway over cool-headed deliberation. Aqshy suffered greatly during the Age of Chaos; in some of its lands, so much blood has been spilt that the earth has begun to crack and scab over. But from the ashes of fallen empires, new civilisation has arisen. Aqshy's Great Parch has been a key battleground in Sigmar's war of reclamation, though even that is still largely controlled by bloodthirsty Chaos worshippers. Men, aelves and duardin fight furiously to reconquer the splintered lands and forge a worthy existence in this unforgiving, volatile realm.

SHYISH THE GRIM

Shyish is unlike any other realm. Its continents, known as underworlds, are birthed through the strength of mortal belief. As the concept of an afterlife spreads throughout a living society, a fitting underworld will come into being at Shyish's edge; when a member of such a society dies, their soul will pass to the relevant underworld. Some are places of toil and torment, whilst others are idyllic paradises – though few are free from the scars of war. The living exist in Shyish too, sometimes coexisting with the dead, sometimes in thrall to them. At Shyish's heart, there exists a raging black void known as the Shyish Nadir; this abyss is suffused with death magic, and more than one underworld has been completely undone and devoured by its grasping pull.

GHYRAN THE VERDANT

Often known as the Jade Kingdoms, Ghyran is a realm forever in growth. Thick forest canopies grasp towards the sky, and the air seems to burgeon with the raw potential of life. Ghyran is a realm of seasons and cycles, where it was once believed that all things were held in balance. Yet its inhabitants have suffered greatly for such presumption. Corruption and plague dominate the Realm of Life, for the damned hosts of Chaos delight in seeing all that is natural become twisted and foul. Forests and jungles have devolved into miasmic mulch while bogs and lakes seep with thick, cloying slime. Despair has long held sway in Ghyran, but the resurgence of the goddess Alarielle and her Sylvaneth children has granted a reprieve. In time, Ghyran may yet begin to heal.

CHAMON THE BURNISHED

In Chamon, the only constants are transience and flux. Unlike many of its siblings, the Realm of Metal is no simple flat disc but an array of sub-realms that hang in the firmament like the apparatus of some cosmic alchemist. The people of Chamon have long been renowned for their technology and metalcraft. Once, it was the favoured domain of Grungni the Maker, whose divine hand fashioned many of the realm's isles. But the warping power of Chaos has taken a firm grasp on this realm, and now Chamon's lands are bent and twisted. Daemons formed of raw mutability caper across the pulsating plains, and the abundant natural ores and magical resources of the Realm of Metal can only be claimed through steel and sorcery.

HYSH THE RADIANT

Hysh is a realm of not only physical light but also spiritual and mental enlightenment. It forms the gleaming sun of the other realms, forever orbiting its sister-sphere of Ulgu, and brightness and radiance are ever present. The Ten Paradises that comprise the Realm of Light are havens of symmetry, symbolism and clear thought. Excellence has long been their prime export, and the scholars, tutors and artisans of Hysh are famed across the realms as numbering amongst the most skilled of their breed. Yet the brightest lights cast the longest shadows. Arrogance, rigidity and obsession are often the darkened mirror to brilliance, and the Hyshians have paid dearly for these sins. Those who remain now fight a desperate war to atone for the failings of their past.

ULGU THE SHROUDED

Of all the realms, the least is known about Ulgu. This is as it should be, for the Realm of Shadows is formed from the very stuff of lies and illusion. In Ulgu, gloom is pervasive and constant; it spins in concert with Hysh, and when it reaches its apogee, night falls over the other realms. To live in Ulgu is to be adaptable and to trust in senses beyond sight; in the Grey Realm, one's surroundings can shift in moments and honesty is but the punchline of many a cruel joke. Hidden things stalk the darkness, and shadows skulk and move of their own accord. Death in Ulgu comes quick and unseen, and many who walk the foggy moors or dark forests of this realm are simply never seen again.

COLLECTING CITADEL MINIATURES

The worlds of Warhammer Age of Sigmar offer unlimited possibilities for the avid miniatures collector. With a huge range of miniatures to choose from and constantly evolving lore to fuel your imagination, you will never run out of inspiration when it comes to assembling your own heroic band of warriors.

The Warhammer Age of Sigmar hobby is centred around collecting and assembling Citadel Miniatures, the most beautifully sculpted fantasy models in the world. These intricately designed miniatures represent the heroes and villains of the Warhammer universe, along with the ranks of hard-bitten warriors and warbeasts they lead into battle. There are over twenty factions to which you can pledge your allegiance, from hulking, green-skinned orruks in search of a good punch-up to sleek, sea-dwelling aelves who would steal away your soul as soon as look at you. Even the architecture and magical phenomena of the Age of Sigmar are represented; gorgeous scenery kits allow you to recreate the ancient splendour of the Mortal Realms, while arcane manifestations known as endless spells bring wild and untamed sorcery to life in front of your eyes.

With such an array of incredible miniatures to choose from, how do you settle on which army, faction or characters to collect first? On the following pages you will find three core approaches that might help you decide – namely collecting for display, theming your collection around a narrative, or assembling an army to dominate the battlefield at tournaments and gaming events.

These are by no means hard and fast distinctions. Many hobbyists fall somewhere in the middle of these categories, and others are driven by entirely unique inspirations. The most important aspect of the Warhammer hobby is having fun, and you should feel free to approach assembling your collection of Citadel Miniatures in any way that brings you joy!

The Stormcast Eternals are immortal warriors destined to do battle with the enemies of civilisation until the end of time. These shining champions are just one of the many factions available for Warhammer Age of Sigmar.

COLLECTING FOR DISPLAY

Whether they prefer to paint individual warriors to a glorious standard, or delight in creating unique dioramas depicting climactic battles and heroic last stands, the Age of Sigmar provides endless challenges for creative hobbyists who wish to showcase their talents.

There are few better feelings for a hobbyist than adding the finishing touches to a lovingly painted collection of miniatures and then putting your work on display for all to see. For many, this is the simplest and most rewarding way to collect Citadel Miniatures – choosing those models that appeal to you and painting them to the best of your ability. This method offers the greatest variety and freedom for those hobbyists whose main enjoyment comes from the act of building and painting their miniatures, coming up with eye-catching colour schemes and lavishing their full attention on every inch of every model. Without any restrictions to consider, you can pick and choose those models that most appeal to you, regardless of their affiliation in the background of Warhammer Age of Sigmar, and get started on the rewarding process of painting them up.

It is quite common for such collectors to arrange their creations on a shelf or in a cabinet, formed up on parade with just as much care as they were assembled and painted. Over time, such collections become ever more sprawling and ambitious, as the hobbyist lavishes many hours over increasingly more ambitious centrepieces.

As you develop your painting and modelling skills, you may even wish to enter your latest creations into one of the many community painting competitions that are held in Warhammer stores and gaming clubs around the world. Perhaps, one day, you might even enter the prestigious Golden Demon, Games Workshop's ultimate painting competition!

Dankhold Troggoth by Maxime Penaud
Slayer Sword Winner – Golden Demon 2019

CHOOSING A FACTION

Rather than choosing from the vast range of Citadel Miniatures, some hobbyists fall in love with a single faction, and choose to make that army the focus of their Age of Sigmar experience. In this way, the techniques for painting models from that faction soon become second nature to these collectors.

While it can be extremely rewarding to make full use of the incredible diversity of the Age of Sigmar range, many hobbyists get just as much enjoyment from immersing themselves in the lore of a single faction. Perhaps they fall in love with an aspect of one faction's aesthetic, such as the twisting roots and branches of the Sylvaneth or the insane war-machines of the Skaven. Perhaps they simply find themselves attached to a particular faction's inimitable character – the ruthless profiteering of the Kharadron Overlords, for example, or the fungus-addled lunacy of the Gloomspite Gitz. Sometimes, the particular contours and textures of a faction's common design elements happen to complement a collector's painting style.

Whatever the reason behind their original inspiration, something has triggered a deep connection between these hobbyists and a particular range of miniatures. With dedication and great attention to detail, these collectors raise vast armies from their chosen faction. Over time they will build up a truly impressive host that will allow them to carry the flag of their allegiance in gaming events or simply in the comfort of their home.

Each of our factions consists of a large range of varied model kits, so whichever army happens to capture a hobbyist's imagination, they can rest assured there will be plenty to keep them entertained. In fact, digging deep into the background of a certain faction can bring its own rewards; there are many hobbyists who choose to create their own Stormcast Eternal Stormhost, for example, following the detailed guidance provided in that faction's battletome in order to create unique heraldry for their army. One might even choose to give every single warrior in their collection a name and a list of glorious past deeds!

Warhammer World Studio Manager James Karch has been collecting Stormcast Eternals since the very first edition of Warhammer Age of Sigmar. His Astral Templars army has reached truly gigantic proportions!

This Nighthaunt army belongs to Ben Johnson, Warhammer Age of Sigmar Product Developer. Ben is a keen gamer and the proud owner of multiple armies, which he regularly takes to events such as tournaments.

COLLECTING FOR GAMING

The thrill of battlefield command is what truly drives the collections of some hobbyists. These warlords assemble armies built for playing games; each unit will be chosen because of its particular strengths and abilities, and all of them will combine to form a devastating force upon the tabletop.

For many, the Warhammer Age of Sigmar hobby is all about gaming, playing exciting tabletop battles with their models using the rules system detailed later in this book. Rather than picking miniatures that appeal for aesthetic or thematic reasons, these collectors will more often look for inspiration in the rules for the different factions and the units they are able to field, choosing to assemble an army capable of dominating that of their opponent.

These savvy commanders will sift through the rules for their models, looking for abilities that complement their favoured strategy. Some might seek to assemble a fast and hard-hitting force that can secure an early win, while others might instead prize the ability to outlast their foes and hold objectives over several rounds of battle. Whatever the aim, the rules provide near-limitless tactical opportunities, and there are always new tricks to discover.

Often, these hobbyists come together at gaming tournaments, eager to test their armies upon the field of battle in a good-natured yet competitive environment. Tabletop battles should always be friendly affairs, but at the same time, there's nothing wrong with a healthy desire to win! Many gamers build and paint multiple armies, each with their own strengths and weaknesses, and might even assemble a new host for each tournament.

STARTER SETS

The Warhammer Age of Sigmar Starter Sets include everything you need to fight battles in the Mortal Realms. In each box you will find two starter armies, a guidebook containing in-depth background and rules, and all the tools you need to take to the battlefield in search of glorious victory!

The Mortal Realms suffer under the stranglehold of Chaos, but there is yet hope for a better dawn. The thunder of Sigmar's wrath still rolls across the skies, columns of lightning dispatching his Stormcast Eternals to wreak vengeance on the myriad fiends and barbarians who threaten civilisation. Under the protection of these immortal champions, new settlements are raised upon every frontier. Yet the ominous boom of war drums echoes as a new foe rises to meet the God-King's chosen, for the numberless orruk warclans are on the march.

EXTREMIS EDITION STARTER SET

A fantastic introduction to the war-torn Mortal Realms, the Extremis Edition Starter Set contains 32 push-fit Citadel Miniatures representing two fantastical armies: the God-King's avenging Stormcast Eternals and the spiteful, swamp-dwelling Kruleboyz. It also contains everything you need to begin playing games of Warhammer Age of Sigmar, including guidebooks, gaming tools and warscroll cards, as well as a fold-out gaming board and a set of Citadel scenery pieces.

HARBINGER EDITION STARTER SET

The Harbinger Edition is a great-value starter set for Warhammer Age of Sigmar. It includes 32 push-fit Citadel Miniatures representing the Stormcast Eternals and the orruk Kruleboyz, as well as guidebooks, essential gaming tools, a fold-out gaming board and a flat-pack terrain feature.

WARRIOR EDITION STARTER SET

Ideal for those new to Warhammer Age of Sigmar and the wider hobby experience of collecting, building and painting Citadel Miniatures, the Warrior Edition is a starter set that contains 18 push-fit Citadel Miniatures as well as all the rules and accessories a budding warlord needs to play games with their models!

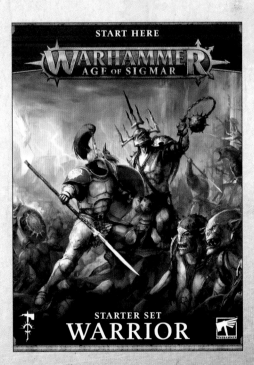

BATTLETOMES

Battletomes are the ultimate guide to the factions of the Mortal Realms. Each contains detailed lore, breathtaking miniatures showcases and a host of rules you'll need to use your army in games of Warhammer Age of Sigmar. Below are just some of the battletomes available; for the full range, visit warhammer.com.

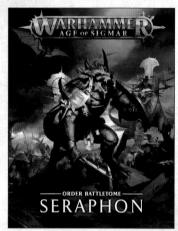

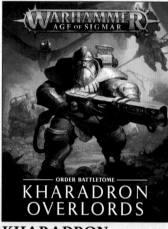

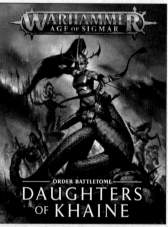

SERAPHON

For aeons the reptilian Seraphon have protected the cosmos from the predations of the Dark Gods, waging war with celestial magic, cold-blooded ruthlessness and primal savagery.

KHARADRON OVERLORDS

To the Kharadron, profit is all. These sky-faring duardin seek fortune at every opportunity, aided by their mastery of aether-gold technology and their vast fleets of advanced, heavily armed skyvessels.

DAUGHTERS OF KHAINE

The Daughters of Khaine are a faction of bloodthirsty aelves who make war with quicksilver speed and ferocious zeal. Each foe they slay is a sacred offering to their murderous deity.

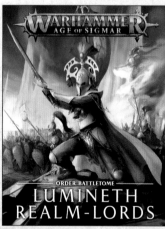

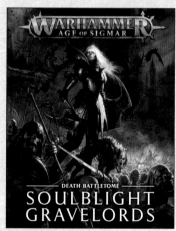

LUMINETH REALM-LORDS

Graceful and wise, the Lumineth Realm-lords are the aelven denizens of Hysh. Aided by powerful aelementor spirits, their shining armies fight to save the realms from Chaos – no matter the cost.

FLESH-EATER COURTS

In their delusion, the abhorrants and mordants of the Flesh-eater Courts believe themselves to be noble knights and men-at-arms, when in truth they are a flesheating, cannibalistic blight upon the realms.

SOULBLIGHT GRAVELORDS

The blood-drinking Soulblight vampires are amongst the most terrible of all undead. Their horrifying armies are filled with the risen dead, empowered by necromantic sorcery to grind their foes to dust.

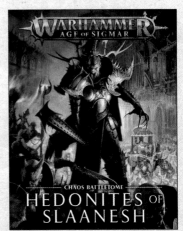

HEDONITES OF SLAANESH

The Hedonites of Slaanesh have devoted themselves to an existence of wild excess, and delight in inflicting the most unimaginable torments upon their victims.

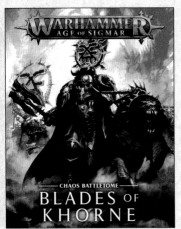

BLADES OF KHORNE

Khorne's brutal followers have ravaged the Mortal Realms for generations, drowning the lands in violence and terror in their quest to sate their god's lust for battle, blood and skulls.

SLAVES TO DARKNESS

Across the Mortal Realms, countless mortal tribes have pledged themselves to the Chaos Gods. When their hordes march, led by mighty god-touched champions, the realms themselves are left broken and corrupted.

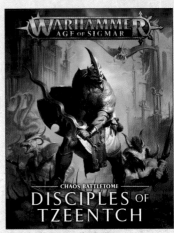

DISCIPLES OF TZEENTCH

Servants of the Change God, the Disciples of Tzeentch are scheming masters of magic. Those who face them are soon undone by deception and overwhelmed in storms of kaleidoscopic witchfire.

BEASTS OF CHAOS

Eternal foes of civilisation and order, the Beasts of Chaos surge forth from the darkest corners of the wilds, bellowing primal war cries as they gore, tear and trample their prey in a savage, hate-fuelled frenzy.

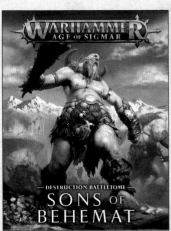

SONS OF BEHEMAT

Mightier makes Rightier! To the gargants of the Sons of Behemat, anything smaller than them deserves to be squashed. When these titans band together, the carnage that follows is truly terrifying to behold.

START COLLECTING!

If you're looking to build a new Warhammer Age of Sigmar army or expand an existing force, look no further than the 'Start Collecting!' sets. In each of these great-value boxes you'll find core troops, elite warriors and a powerful hero. Most factions have their own Start Collecting! set, so start planning your all-conquering army today!

SERAPHON
Seraphon are star-spawned saurian warriors from another age who wage an eternal battle against Chaos.

SYLVANETH
From the darkest forests come the Sylvaneth, deadly foes of all who would corrupt the wild places of the realms.

DAUGHTERS OF KHAINE
The ferocious Daughters of Khaine make war with quicksilver speed, every slain foe an offering to the Bloody-Handed God.

KHARADRON OVERLORDS
The mercantile Kharadron Overlords dominate the skies with swift airships, advanced technology and overwhelming firepower.

BEASTCLAW RAIDERS
Among the Ogor Mawtribes, the Beastclaw Raiders are known for their massive warbeasts and the freezing Everwinter that follows in their wake.

FLESH-EATER COURTS
The abhorrants of the Flesh-eater Courts are bestial vampires who believe themselves to be noble lords surrounded by loyal vassals, who themselves are, in truth, deranged cannibals.

SLAVES TO DARKNESS

The cursed and damned mortals who revere the Dark Gods are granted daemonic boons and unnatural power in exchange for profane worship.

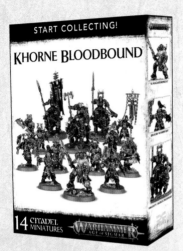

KHORNE BLOODBOUND

The Khorne Bloodbound seek to honour their rage-filled deity with mountains of worthy skulls and rivers of gore.

DAEMONS OF KHORNE

Servants of the wrathful Lord of Skulls, the daemons of Khorne care only for the fury of battle and the spilling of blood.

DAEMONS OF TZEENTCH

The daemons of Tzeentch are embodiments of anarchic madness who lay waste to their foes with torrents of flesh-melting sorcery.

DAEMONS OF SLAANESH

As darkly graceful as they are lethal, the daemons of Slaanesh delight in tormenting and eviscerating their hapless mortal victims.

BEASTS OF CHAOS

The vile and bestial destroyers known as the Beasts of Chaos bray with bloodthirsty delight as they bring anarchy and ruin to the civilised races.

BUILDING AND PAINTING YOUR MINIATURES

The first steps into the Warhammer Age of Sigmar hobby usually involve building and painting your first model. It takes time to perfect your creative skills, but before long you will be able to bring to life a vast host of fantastical warriors of which you can be rightly proud!

One of the great joys of collecting Citadel Miniatures is the process of assembling and painting your models, transforming grey plastic components into vibrant recreations of the heroes, monsters and magic of the Mortal Realms. There are few better feelings than seeing your fully painted army arrayed in all its splendour, perhaps arranged before a custom-made backdrop or set up in a glass display case to be admired by all. Your miniatures can also be a great way to express yourself – those you collect and the way you decide to assemble and paint them has the potential to say something about you as an individual. Once a miniature is removed from the box, assembled and painted, it takes on something of its creator and becomes something wonderfully unique.

PAINTING GUIDES

The Warhammer YouTube channel is a fantastic source of inspiration and advice for budding hobbyists. It offers a range of painting guides for different armies and colour schemes and explains a lot of the more commonly used painting techniques.

You can find all of the paints and tools you need to bring your miniatures to life at warhammer.com and in your local Warhammer store. There are also many independent retailers who stock our products.

Citadel Miniatures do not come already assembled, but putting these kits together is both easy and rewarding. Your models will come on a number of plastic frames (1), with each individual component clearly marked. All you need to build them is a pair of clippers and some glue (2), both of which can be found in any Warhammer store. Then, simply follow the instructions in the construction booklet provided in the box with your models (3). In time, you might even find yourself experimenting with more ambitious methods, such as combining components from different kits in order to create something unique to your collection – this is a great way of putting your stamp upon your army!

When your models have been built, you can begin the satisfying process of bringing them to life with your paintbrush. Whatever your skill level, painted miniatures look great whether arranged on a cabinet shelf or charging across a tabletop battlefield, and the sense of achievement from painting them just can't be beaten. It always pays to take your time choosing the right colour scheme for your army; this will help to imbue your models with character, and define who they are. Once you're ready to begin, Games Workshop offers a huge range of paints and brushes, along with all the information, advice and guides you'll need to go from beginner to accomplished painter in no time.

Using the Citadel Colour System, you can follow an easy three-step process to quickly get your warriors looking 'Battle Ready'. After priming your miniatures with spray paint, you will first apply some flat colour using Base paints (1). Then, an application of Shade paints (2) will add depth to the detail. Finally, you will use Layer paints (3) to pick out the raised surfaces and add some highlights. Achieving great results with your painting really is that simple!

If you want to get your army painted as fast as possible, then Contrast paints are for you. When used over special Contrast primer spray, they provide both depth and vibrancy in one application, allowing you to get your miniatures Battle Ready in no time. The Gutrippa on the right was painted using just one paint for each colour!

THE CITADEL COLOUR SYSTEM

Over the following pages, you will find step-by-step guides to painting your assembled miniatures in the colours of their faction, as well as an introduction to the easy-to-follow Citadel Colour System. With an array of essential tips and hints to follow, you'll soon have your army of mighty heroes arrayed in all their fantastical glory!

Painting your assembled collection of miniatures is one of the most satisfying and appealing parts of the hobby for many collectors. It's the stage of the army-building process where your force really begins to come alive, and all the personal touches and creative flourishes you have lovingly added to each miniature are brought to vibrant life.

With the enormous range of Citadel paints at your disposal, there are limitless options when it comes to choosing a paint scheme for your army. Some collectors might opt for colour combinations that suit their army's intended backstory. For example, a hobbyist creating a dour host of Stormcast Eternals hailing from the Realm of Death might opt for funereal blacks and purples that radiate a sombre, gothic splendour. Likewise, a tribe of feral orruks

hailing from Aqshy, the Realm of Fire, might smear themselves with red and orange warpaint and daub skull-masks on their faces with white ash. Effects like these are easy to achieve if you follow a few, simple guidelines.

These essential tips and tricks are presented over the following pages in a simple stage-by-stage process. You'll swiftly master the basic techniques required to get your models looking fantastic either on the tabletop or in your display case.

And remember, the paint schemes suggested are simply recommended options for those new to the hobby. Should you wish to try something a bit different, the same basic principles can be applied to whichever colour combination you choose. Embrace your creative side!

PAINTING HANDLE

Designed for painters by painters, the Citadel Painting Handle makes it much, much easier to hold your miniatures securely while painting them, allowing you to find the perfect angle from which to access the fiddly bits and avoid the inevitable hand cramps that come from holding a base for a long time.

PAINTING TECHNIQUES

TECHNIQUE 1: BASECOATING

The foundation upon which the entire paint system is based, a well-applied basecoat gives your model a smooth starting point for later stages. Basecoats use Citadel Base paints, which have high pigment content and excellent coverage (pg 56).

TECHNIQUE 2: SHADING

Shading is a technique that brings out all of the subtle details and textures on your model using Citadel Shade paints. Formulated to flow into recesses, these paints provide natural, effective shading that gives definition to your miniatures (pg 57).

TECHNIQUE 3: DRYBRUSHING

Drybrushing is an excellent technique for capturing raised features and creating natural highlights on models, especially those with a lot of small details or sharp edges. Citadel Dry paints are designed to make this much-loved method of painting as straightforward as possible (pg 58).

TECHNIQUE 4: LAYERING

Citadel Layer paints have a lighter pigment count than Base paints, meaning they can be applied in multiple layers to help bring out extra detail on your miniatures. They're particularly great for edge highlighting (pg 59).

CONTRAST PAINTS

The Citadel Contrast paint range provides a revolutionary way to make beautiful painting simple and fast. Each Contrast paint, when applied over a light Contrast undercoat, gives you a vivid basecoat and realistic shading all in a single application (pg 60).

TECHNICAL PAINTS

Technical paints are designed to help you achieve a range of special effects, from metallic verdigris and foetid slurry to grisly gore and spectral auras.

BASING

A miniature is never truly finished until it has been based. Fortunately, the Citadel Technical paint range includes many paints for creating spectacular bases (pg 61). The use of textured Technical paints is the perfect way to ensure all the bases in your army have brilliant, consistent finishes. Once the paint is dry, you can either leave the base as it is or shade and highlight it like any other part of the model. You can even add grass tufts for a finishing touch.

BRUSHES

The Citadel range of brushes has been designed from the ground up by our Studio painters, specifically for use with the Citadel Colour System. Each brush works best for a particular technique, allowing you to get the best results on all of your miniatures.

BASE

Base brushes have tough-wearing bristles designed to survive the rigours of basecoating your models. There are four sizes (S, M, L and XL) to help you tackle any painting challenge. You'll notice the larger brushes have a broad, flat head with a fine, pointed edge; this allows you to both ensure your basecoat covers your models and paint those tricky-to-reach areas.

DRY

Drybrushing can be quite hard on your brushes, so the brushes in the Dry range are made to be especially rugged and durable.

LAYER

With fine heads and soft bristles, Layer brushes are perfect for precise layering, while the Artificer Layer brushes are ideal for picking out the smallest details on your miniatures.

CARE TIPS

1. Wash your brush regularly. Keep a pot of clean, cold water on standby to wash your brush with. Swirl the brush vigorously in the water to clean it but don't grind the bristles against the edge or bottom. You should wash your brush often: any time you notice a change in the flow of paint as you are working and whenever you change colours.

2. Never let paint reach the ferrule (the metal area of the brush just past the bristles). Never dip your brush so far into the paint that it touches this; otherwise, when it dries, your bristles will splay out. If you get some paint on there by accident, wash the brush thoroughly.

3. Always use the largest brush suitable for the job. You will be surprised how, with a little practice, you can use a much larger brush than you expected to get the same result. Using a larger brush speeds up the process nicely and helps ensure smooth results.

4. Keep a sharp point. Maintain the point on your brush by twisting the bristles softly against your palette. Check out our painting tutorials online for examples.

CHOOSE YOUR WEAPONS!

Taken as a whole, the wide range of Citadel brushes available could seem daunting to a beginner, but fear not! Just like collecting an army or building up your palette of paints, you can start with the basics and work up from there.

The best place to begin is with a small (S) Layer brush and a medium (M) Base brush. With these two finely crafted painting implements at your disposal, you will have a great start to your brush collection and you can attempt all of the techniques detailed on the following pages with confidence.

Of course, there's nothing like using the right tool for the right job, and as your confidence and skill grows, you will want to look into all the other sorts of Citadel brushes. As a good foundation to build upon, however, these two brushes are the choice of the professionals!

SHADE

Citadel Shade brushes come in two sizes: M and L. Both have bristles designed to hold the maximum amount of Shade paint, improving the flow as you draw the brush over your models. For most tasks, you'll want to use the M Shade brush, as the sharp point allows you to apply Shade paints with accuracy. The L brush is for particularly large models.

GLAZE

Glazing tends to be quite precise, so the Glaze brush has synthetic bristles to keep its point while you work.

TEXTURE

The M Texture tool is a spreader for applying textured Technical paints to your models and their bases. Use the large end to scoop the paint from the pot and the narrow end to spread it across the surface.

SCENERY

Citadel Scenery brushes are extra-large brushes with coarse bristles – ideal for quickly getting a lot of coverage on boards and scenery pieces.

UNDERCOATING

Undercoating helps paint adhere to your models and helps prevent it from flaking off. Most people use an undercoat spray that matches the main colours they intend to use on their Citadel Miniatures, enabling them to undercoat whole units quickly and neatly.

There are a number of spray paints in the Citadel range, from Chaos Black and Corax White to Retributor Armour and Leadbelcher. If you're new to using spray paints, make sure you read the instructions on the can carefully before you start.

When undercoating models, do it outside in a well-ventilated area and well away from things you value (such as your car or pets). We recommend using a spray stick (see bottom-right) to hold your models, so you can spray the models from every angle without having to touch them while they are still wet.

Before spraying, shake the spray can for at least two minutes so that the paint and propellant mix properly.

Shake it less than this and you could end up with streaky paint, a cloudy finish or, worse, a totally ruined model. It's worth reiterating: two minutes, no less! Always keep the spray can upright, too, otherwise the spray mix may come out inconsistently.

Sometimes, such as when it's cold outside, you may want to undercoat a model by hand. For this, you'll need a pot of Abaddon Black and the largest Base brush you can use for the task. Simply apply the paint as you would a basecoat (pg 56).

When spraying your models, a quick burst from the spray can (less than a second) from around 8-12 inches away is more effective

than a prolonged barrage at closer range, since the latter can obscure the details of your models and leave them dripping with paint. Work around the model, undercoating it in short, quick blasts until the whole miniature is evenly undercoated. Again, a spray stick is handy for this as it helps you to economise on paint and enables you to turn the models around without having to handle them, which would risk smudging the undercoat.

Lastly, when you've finished undercoating your models, clean out the nozzle of the spray can by turning it upside down and spraying until only gas comes out. This prevents the nozzle from clogging and ruining the can.

A coloured undercoat is great for models that will display large areas of that colour. A Chaos Black undercoat is ideal for darker miniatures, and provides deeper shading. The model in the middle has been coated with Retributor Armour – perfect for the gold worn by the Hammers of Sigmar. The model on the right has been undercoated with Corax White, ready for a deep all-over shade to fill recesses and add texture.

For our spray sticks, we use a piece of wood about two feet long. Stick a strip of double-sided tape along the top and gently attach your models to it, leaving a little space between them. Secured in this way, the spray stick can be held at any angle so you can spray every part of the models. We recommend wearing a latex glove on the hand holding the stick to avoid accidentally undercoating your fingers.

BASECOATING

A basecoat provides the first layer of paint you apply to a model after the undercoat and forms the foundation of every other colour on the model – indeed, the foundation of the entire paint job itself. Read on for the essentials and a few top tips from the masters.

Basecoating is the first painting technique you'll apply to your miniatures and, if done well, will make painting your models much easier and more enjoyable. Many painting frustrations can be alleviated with a neat, smooth basecoat right from the start.

There are four Base brushes in the Citadel brush range. Always use the largest one you can for the job; not only does it make painting easier, it also makes it much faster. The Vindictor shown below was painted using an L Base brush and took only a couple of minutes to basecoat. Once the main basecoat has been applied, you can carefully begin to fill in the details of your miniature with different paint colours and smaller Base brushes.

While there is a temptation to use the paint straight out of the pot, always water it down. Firstly, this stops you applying the paint too thickly. Two thin coats of paint are better than one thick one – a mantra you will come across often in Games Workshop painting guides and tutorials. Remember, you can always put more paint on a model, but you can't take it off. Secondly, a dab of water stops the paint from drying out on the palette, which can make it go thick and tacky, leading to a lumpy, uneven basecoat.

1 When getting paint out of the pot, use your brush to take a small amount from the lid rather than dunking the brush into the pot itself.

2 Put the paint on a palette and mix in about half as much water as there is paint. Pulling the brush towards you, coat the bristles in paint.

3 As mentioned in the Brushes section (pg 54), never get paint on the ferrule. An even application halfway up the bristles is easily enough paint.

4 Using the flat of the brush, apply the basecoat (in this case Retributor Armour) to the model in smooth, even coats.

5 Don't worry about being a little messy with your first basecoat colour as this will cover the majority of the model; you can always tidy up with subsequent basecoats.

6 When you begin to fill in the details on your basecoated miniature, use a smaller Base brush. This will give you greater control and accuracy.

SHADING

Shading your models with Citadel Shade paints creates areas of rich, darker colour that accentuate the natural shadows on the miniature, making them perfect for capturing all that detail and creating a sense of depth across the model.

Citadel Shade paints are specially formulated to flow into the recesses and around the details on your Citadel Miniatures. The perfect follow-up to a good basecoat, shading provides your miniatures with effortless, natural depth. Shading is a very simple technique and provides fantastic results on almost any model, from the largest monsters and war machines to the tiniest Clanrat or Nurgling.

Typically, you will apply a Shade paint before you begin layering or drybrushing your model, as it helps to bring out the details on your models. Sometimes, you

might use a Shade paint later on in the painting process, which can be useful for staining the layers of paint below. Either way, there are three main shading techniques: all-over shading, section shading and recess shading. The first covers the whole model, the second covers large areas, and the third focuses on neatly applying the Shade paint to the model's recesses only.

Citadel Shade brushes have bristles specifically designed to hold plenty of liquid, so you can apply the Shade paint simply by adding it straight to your miniature. As you press your brush against the

model, the Shade paint will flow out, and you can use your brush to move the Shade paint around the model to where you need it.

Because Shade paints are much thinner than other paints, they will take a bit longer to dry. Factor this in when you are painting – once you've applied your Shade paints, set the model to one side for half an hour or so. While this model dries, you can be painting another. Don't be tempted to use a hair dryer to speed things up, since this can change the way the Shade paint dries or even push it out of the recesses.

Before you use any Citadel Shade paint, make sure the lid is firmly closed and shake it vigorously to ensure the paint is well mixed.

Use your M Shade brush to take paint from the pot and transfer it to your palette. Citadel Shade paints do not need to be watered down.

When you apply Citadel Shade paints, your brush should not be overloaded – aim for the saturation level shown in this example.

Apply the Shade paint to your model in a smooth motion, using the brush to ensure it flows where you want it to.

Sometimes you only want to shade the recesses of a model. In these cases, use a smaller brush such as an S Layer brush to paint more precisely.

Once you have applied the Shade paint, give it plenty of time to dry. As it dries, it leaves rich colours within all the crevices, adding depth to your model.

DRYBRUSHING

Drybrushing is a fantastic technique for quickly capturing all the raised details on a model and providing subtle and effective highlights. Here, we show you the essentials and how the Studio army painters use drybrushing to take their own paint jobs to the next level.

Drybrushing is a technique beloved by painters everywhere, useful for everything from highlighting the scales of towering Stardrakes and Carnosaurs to skaven fur and chainmail armour. Essentially, the technique consists of rapidly brushing your Dry brush against the model to capture all the raised details through a light dusting of paint.

Drybrushing is very simple, as you can see in the stages below. Having loaded your brush with

Dry paint, you proceed to wipe off the excess on a piece of tissue or paper towel. This leaves you with a small amount of very 'dry' paint on the bristles.

As you brush the bristles against the model, you'll see the paint transfer. The longer you brush, the heavier the coverage will be. When it seems like you are running low on paint on your bristles, simply reload your brush with more paint, carefully wipe off the excess, and carry on.

The beauty of drybrushing is that the results are instant. You can gauge the effect as you go along and decide if the coverage is sufficient and the highlight light enough or if you want to continue building up the colour. Because of this, drybrushing is often the stage where you can most clearly see the paint job coming to fruition – highlights appear on the edges over areas of deep colour and the model nears completion. This gradual improvement is incredibly satisfying to witness.

First, load some Dry paint onto your brush directly from the pot. There's no need to take too much paint – just use a little bit at a time.

Wipe off the excess paint from your brush onto a piece of tissue or paper towel. You should remove almost all of the paint, as shown here.

With the paint removed, your brush should look like this. You can see a little paint remaining in the bristles – this is enough for drybrushing.

Next, gently brush the bristles against your model in a quick back-and-forth motion to transfer the paint to your model. Try to catch the edges of the detail to accentuate its shape.

Drybrushing is a fantastic technique for use on textured areas like this scale mail. Simply brush against the grain of the detail to catch all the edges.

When drybrushing smaller details like this Vindictor's kneepad, use an S Dry brush and careful motions to avoid getting paint on other areas of the miniature.

LAYERING

Layering is a painting technique designed to bring life and realism to your miniatures by accentuating the raised areas of a model. Done well, the end result is a beautifully painted model with natural-looking highlights that really stands out on the battlefield.

There are two main techniques to layering: the solid layer and the highlight. A solid layer is designed to cover a whole section of a model while leaving the basecoat and shade visible only in the recesses. This has the dramatic effect of changing the colour of a model. Because Layer paints have a thinner consistency than Base paints, layering in this way may require several coats of paint to cover the darker colours beneath. Just like basecoating, a few thin layers are better than one thick layer – take your time, apply your layers neatly, and you'll get a smooth, even finish. As with any painting technique, it's easier to add more paint than it is to clean up an overloaded miniature.

Highlighting is another form of layering, designed to simulate the effect of light catching the raised edges of your miniatures. Light naturally catches the most prominent edges of an object, which is why highlights are only applied sparingly to a miniature and normally only to raised areas. A final highlight to a sword or face is often the last process to be applied to a miniature, the finishing touch to all your hard work and a moment to be relished.

Gently rotate the brush when drawing paint from your palette. This will help you keep the tip of the brush as fine and pointed as possible.

Ensure there's not too much paint on your Layer brush. It should be evenly distributed across the bristles and never cover so much as to reach the ferrule.

When layering over large areas, always try to keep the brush strokes going in the same direction to minimise streaks, lines and patchy sections.

When applying highlights along the edge of a detail, use the edge of an S Layer brush, as it will give you better control than the tip. This is often called edge highlighting.

Be sure to wash your Layer brush regularly to prevent the paint drying on the bristles and ruining the precision of the brush.

Apply multiple highlights, using increasingly lighter colours, to the most prominent edges of the model. This simulates light falling naturally on the model.

CONTRAST PAINTS

Citadel Contrast paints have been designed to achieve great results in one application of colour. These paints will appear darker where they settle in the recesses and will remain lighter and more vibrant on the raised detail. Contrast paints are ideal if you want to get your miniatures Battle Ready as quickly as possible.

As with any Citadel Miniature, you will need an undercoat. Wraithbone and Grey Seer sprays provide the perfect undercoat for Contrast paints, or, if you prefer, you can undercoat your model by hand.

Before starting, shake your Contrast paint pot well to make sure that any settled pigment is mixed and ready for use.

Use an M Shade brush and a palette to apply your Contrast paints; you don't want to overload the brush as this could result in pooling. The palette allows you to control how much paint you put on the brush.

Being careful not to add too much at once, apply the Contrast paint to your chosen area as precisely as possible. One coat of Contrast paint should suffice. Leave this to dry fully before proceeding.

Tidy up any messy areas or overspill using a pot of your chosen undercoat colour. This will make sure that the Contrast paint colour does not show through on the wrong areas.

When you start painting finer details or more difficult-to-reach areas, use a smaller brush for added control. Remember to be as neat as you can when applying each Contrast paint.

TECHNICAL PAINTS

Technical paints are special formulations of paint that are designed to achieve a variety of special effects, such as blood splatter, rust, snow and slime. There are quite a few Technical paints that are intended to add texture to a model's base in one application, and which simulate the look of rough ground.

CRACKING PAINTS

Some Technical paints, such as Agrellan Earth, are used to create realistic cracked-earth bases. To achieve this effect, load up an M Base brush with a large glob of one of these thick paints and apply it liberally to your model's base, being careful to avoid its feet. Leave the model to dry – overnight is best – to allow the paint to crack. If you paint a layer of PVA glue on the model's base first, let it dry, then apply the cracking paint, the cracks will be even bigger!

BASING WITH TECHNICAL PAINTS

It's really easy to decorate a model's base using a Technical paint such as Stirland Mud, which you can see in the guide below. Once the paint is dry, you can enhance it even further by shading it and drybrushing it with a lighter colour. Finally, if you glue some rocks and grass tufts to the base too, you'll take the look of your miniature to the next level!

Use the broad head of your M Texture tool to scoop out a glob of textured Technical paint.

Spread the paint over the base with your M Texture tool until it covers the entire surface.

Once the paint has fully dried (this can take around 45 minutes), apply a Shade paint to emphasise all the textures.

Finally, once the Shade paint is dry, give the surface a drybrush to complete the look, then apply a basecoat to the base's rim.

PAINTING STORMCAST ETERNALS: CLASSIC METHOD – BATTLE READY

First, apply Retributor Armour spray all over your Vindictor to achieve a rich gold basecoat. Try to get as even a covering as possible. Alternatively, you can apply a basecoat using a pot of Retributor Armour.

Next, apply Kantor Blue to the pauldrons and the field of the shield; apply Leadbelcher to the spearhead, scale mail and belt buckle; and add Corax White to the pauldron and shield detailing.

Shade the gold areas on the model with Agrax Earthshade, being careful not to get the Shade paint on any other areas.

Add Screamer Pink to the weapon haft and Mechanicus Standard Grey to the rocks. Apply Abaddon Black to the leather, undersuit and base. Add a basecoat of Morghast Bone to the skull.

Shade the silver metal, weapon haft, rocks and rivets on the pauldrons with Nuln Oil. Shade the skull with Seraphim Sepia.

Once all of the paint has dried, apply a coat of Stirland Mud Technical paint to the bare earth areas of the Vindictor's base using an M Texture tool.

PAINTING STORMCAST ETERNALS: CONTRAST METHOD – BATTLE READY

First, spray your Vindictor with Wraithbone, following the instructions on the can. You can undercoat the model using a pot of Wraithbone, if you prefer.

Apply Nazdreg Yellow to the areas of gold armour. Once this is dry, you can tidy up any messy areas with Wraithbone Base paint.

Apply Leviadon Blue to the pauldrons and the field of the shield; paint the spearhead, scale mail, belt buckle and rocks with Basilicanum Grey; and add Skeleton Horde to the skull.

Add Apothecary White to the pauldron and shield detailing, then apply Volupus Pink to the weapon haft. Paint the leather and the undersuit with Black Templar.

Apply Stirland Mud Technical paint to the bare earth areas of the Vindictor's base using an M Texture tool. Finally, paint the base rim with Abaddon Black.

TOP TIP

As Contrast paints are quite thin, it is a good idea to protect your models from the wear and tear of battle with a coat of Stormshield or Munitorum Varnish. This will seal the colour, and prevent the paint from rubbing away on the harder edges after being repeatedly handled.

When spraying your models with varnish, always make sure the area that you are spraying in is free of dust and dander, and anything else that might adhere to the varnish as it dries. No one wants to see an errant bit of fluff stick to their fresh paint job!

63

PAINTING KRULEBOYZ: CLASSIC METHOD – BATTLE READY

First, undercoat your Gutrippa with Chaos Black spray. Try to get as even a covering as possible.

Next, apply a basecoat of Orruk Flesh to the model's skin.

Paint the field of the shield with Mephiston Red; apply Steel Legion Drab to the cloth and wooden spear haft; and paint the spearhead and armour with Leadbelcher.

Add Mournfang Brown to the binding and Mechanicus Standard Grey to the necklace totem. Paint the Stormcast helmet and the teeth and eyes on the shield with Retributor Armour.

Apply a shade of Agrax Earthshade carefully over the whole model. Be careful not to overload the brush as you don't want the paint to pool.

Once all of the paint has dried, use the narrow end of an M Texture tool to apply Stirland Mud Technical paint to the Gutrippa's base.

PAINTING KRULEBOYZ: CONTRAST METHOD – BATTLE READY

First, undercoat your Gutrippa with Wraithbone spray or, if you prefer, you can use a pot of Wraithbone to undercoat by hand.

Apply a coat of Plaguebearer Flesh to the model's skin. Once this is dry, you can tidy up any messy areas with Wraithbone Base paint.

Paint the field of the shield with Blood Angels Red. Apply Snakebite Leather to the cloth and the teeth and eyes on the shield.

Apply Wyldwood to the binding, wooden spear haft and the model's teeth and eyes. Paint the armour with Basilicanum Grey and add a coat of Nazdreg Yellow to the Stormcast helmet.

Once all of the paint has dried, use the narrow end of an M Texture tool to apply Stirland Mud Technical paint to the Gutrippa's base. Finally, apply a few coats of Abaddon Black to the base rim.

TOP TIP

It's important to be as neat as you can with Contrast paints. However, if you get some Contrast paint on an area already painted in another colour, you can mix a small amount of the undercoat colour – in this case, Grey Seer – with the Contrast paint that had previously been applied and paint over the problem area. This can take a little trial and error, but it works as a way to fix mistakes.

PAINTING STORMCAST ETERNALS: CLASSIC METHOD – PARADE READY

Apply a couple of thin coats of Auric Armour Gold to the gold armour in order bring some lustre back, ensuring that you avoid the recesses.

To finish off the gold armour, use an S Layer brush to add a layer of Liberator Gold to the most raised elements and pick out the edges of the armour panels.

Edge highlight the blue armour with Calgar Blue. This will really help to accentuate the crisp edges of the Vindictor's pauldrons.

Shade the white elements with a 1:1 mix of Drakenhof Nightshade and Lahmian Medium. Then apply a highlight of White Scar to the white detailing.

For any areas of silver metal, such as the spearhead, use an S Layer brush to carefully edge highlight with Stormhost Silver.

For the binding on the spear haft, apply a careful drybrush of Changeling Pink using an S Dry brush.

PARADE READY

Once your miniatures are Battle Ready, your games will look really spectacular! However, you don't need to stop there. Many hobbyists continue to add further painted detail to their models, such as highlights to add even more depth and additional layers of colour to restore vibrancy to areas that may have been dulled down at previous stages. This standard is what we call 'Parade Ready'.

Drybrush the base (including the rocks and the skull) with Tyrant Skull and add Middenland Tufts to finish.

PAINTING STORMCAST ETERNALS: CONTRAST METHOD – PARADE READY

For the gold armour, we want to create the impression of a shiny, metallic finish. This can be achieved by using the tip of an S Layer brush to add an edge highlight of Screaming Skull.

Using the very tip of your brush, apply a fine highlight of Ulthuan Grey to the edges of the silver metal areas, such as the spearhead.

Carefully edge highlight the blue armour with Calgar Blue using an S Layer brush, being as neat as possible.

Highlight the white detailing with White Scar. This will really help to make the white look cleaner.

For the binding on the Vindictor's spear haft, apply a careful drybrush of Changeling Pink using an S Dry brush.

Drybrush the base (including the rocks and the skull) with Tyrant Skull and add Middenland Tufts to finish.

PAINTING KRULEBOYZ:
CLASSIC METHOD – PARADE READY

Apply a layer of Orruk Flesh to the Gutrippa's skin, ensuring that the recesses remain dark to provide a sense of depth.

Using an S Layer brush, dot the eyes with Evil Sunz Scarlet and paint the teeth with Screaming Skull.

TOP TIP

Getting your miniatures to a Parade Ready standard usually involves picking out the finer details, such as eyes and teeth. Don't worry if your brush control isn't great on your first few attempts – as they say, 'practice makes perfect'. Having the right tool for the job really helps – in this case, an S or XS Artificer Layer brush. Many hobbyists reserve a fine brush specifically for these tiny areas, as keeping the brush tip in good condition is key to achieving a good result.

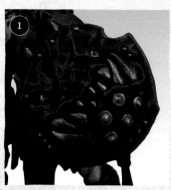

Highlight the edges and ridges of the shield with Evil Sunz Scarlet using an S Layer brush.

Add a layer of Canoptek Alloy to the teeth and eyes, ensuring the recesses remain dark. Highlight the string with Sons of Horus Green.

Drybrush the base (including the Stormcast helmet) with Tyrant Skull and add Middenland Tufts to finish.

With an S Layer brush, apply a highlight of Stormhost Silver to all of the metallic elements on the model. Feel free to add some small dashes to add to the effect of worn metal.

Highlight all of the cloth areas with Baneblade Brown using your S Layer brush. Finally, if you want to add an extra level of detail, pick out all of the stitchwork with the same paint.

PAINTING KRULEBOYZ: CONTRAST METHOD – PARADE READY

Using an S Layer brush, apply a highlight of Krieg Khaki to the most raised areas of the Gutrippa's skin.

Using an S Layer brush, dot the eyes with Evil Sunz Scarlet and paint the teeth with Screaming Skull.

Apply an edge highlight of Fire Dragon Bright to the edges and ridges of the shield.

Highlight the cloth areas and the teeth and eyes on the shield with Balor Brown.

Drybrush the base (including the Stormcast helmet) with Tyrant Skull and add Middenland Tufts to finish.

Using the very tip of your brush, apply a fine highlight of Ulthuan Grey to the edges of the silver metal areas, such as the spearhead and armour.

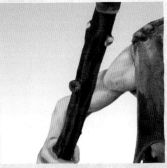

Drybrush the wooden spear haft with Golgfag Brown, being careful not to get paint on any other areas.

PLAYING THE GAME

The Mortal Realms are replete with tales of mighty heroes, bloodshed and betrayal, but you need not solely enjoy them through reading the narrative in our books. By using your collection of Citadel Miniatures in games of Warhammer Age of Sigmar, you can tell epic stories of your own upon the tabletop battlefield.

The rules on pages 76-113 provide you with a framework to craft your own saga set in the Mortal Realms, and to fight glorious battles with your collection of Citadel Miniatures. Whatever your goal – whether to pitch yourself against an opponent in an evenly balanced contest, or to see just what happens when Nagash, Archaon and Alarielle come up against one another in battle – these rules allow you to play out one exciting tale of conflict after another. Each new encounter will generate spectacular war stories that you will remember for years to come.

The rules for Warhammer Age of Sigmar are split into the core rules and the open play, narrative play and matched play rules. The core rules explain the fundamentals of using your collection of Citadel Miniatures to fight battles set in the Mortal Realms. They explain how to organise an army, set up the battlefield, move and fight with the warriors under your command, and what you need to do to lead your army to ultimate victory!

The core rules are common principles that are used in all games of Warhammer Age of Sigmar, but within that framework there are many different ways to play a game. To this end, the core rules are followed by three sections that describe the most popular ways in which games are played. These 'three ways to play' are called open play, narrative play and matched play, and they are described in more detail on the following pages. Together with the core rules, these sections of the book provide you with a gaming toolbox that will enable you to find the way of playing games with your collection of Citadel Miniatures that suits you best.

OPEN PLAY

Open play is the default setting for games of Warhammer Age of Sigmar. It allows you to set up and play a game with the minimum amount of fuss and preparation, while providing you with almost limitless options and flexibility as to what you can include in your army.

The essence of open play is to allow players to use any miniatures in their collection in a game. Often, this means that the players will choose their armies based purely on what looks great on the battlefield. In open play, there are no restrictions on which models you can include in your army. For example, you can field a force consisting entirely of giant monsters or elite heroes.

This freedom of choice makes open play the ideal play style if the main appeal of the hobby for you is the simple joy of collecting Citadel Miniatures, as you can field any of your models in the same army on the battlefield. The beauty of the open play format is that it is limited only by your imagination. It allows you explore the near-infinite wonders of the Mortal Realms on the tabletop, and collect any of the amazing miniatures in the Warhammer Age of Sigmar range that you desire.

Open play games are similar to 'exhibition matches' in some sports. The players aren't there to climb the ranks; everyone just wants to show off their miniatures, roll some dice and have a great time to boot!

NARRATIVE PLAY

With a cast of indomitable heroes and fearsome villains, plots of conquest, zealous loyalty and ruthless betrayal, and a near-endless array of spectacular locations, Warhammer Age of Sigmar is replete with exciting stories. Narrative play is about forging a legend for your miniatures on the tabletop.

Narrative play games centre around telling stories with your Citadel Miniatures. This can be as simple as devising a reason for two armies to battle each other, such as a deep-seated rivalry, a contested territory, or a vital objective that must be secured before it falls into the wrong hands. Narrative play games can be based on a story you have read in any Warhammer Age of Sigmar book, or one you have written yourself after having been inspired by reading about the Mortal Realms. There are a number of narrative play battleplans available in our books that are based on important events that have occurred throughout the history of the Mortal Realms, and which are ready to pick up and play straight away.

By linking the battles you fight with a continuous narrative, you can grow the seed of a story into a sprawling saga in which the characters in your army are the main protagonists. Each subsequent battle may continue or conclude the tale begun in the first – a warlord casts down a would-be usurper, an invasion is defeated, or a lost artefact of great power is recovered. In no time, your warriors will be taking part in an epic legend that will be retold by troubadours and chroniclers the realms over for time immemorial – though whether they are lauded as heroes or cursed as monsters is up to you!

Here we see a narrative game in action, based around a great story – Teclis and his Lumineth Realmlords must defend a realmgate from the Slaves to Darkness. Can they hold them off until the game ends?

Matched play is all about playing games that have been balanced to give no particular advantage to either player. For this reason, it is the most common play style used in events such as competitive tournaments.

MATCHED PLAY

People play Warhammer Age of Sigmar for all kinds of reasons. Many want to play games that test their skill as the commander of an army, in as evenly balanced a competition as possible. If you like the thought of games like this, then matched play games will be just right for you.

There are countless benefits to matched play games. While narrative play games allow you to use your army to tell a story, and open play games enable you to include any models you like, matched play games give you the option to fight battles with forces that are a test of your skills as a general.

The first challenge in matched play is how to select the units in your army. Do you take mostly high-powered models and risk being overrun by a larger force of individually weaker units? Or do you build a more versatile fighting force that is capable of taking on a variety of army compositions, though at the risk of becoming a 'jack of all trades but master of none'?

Normally in matched play games you will be required to stick with one faction, so your knowledge of the units available to you will be pivotal in this selection process. Similarly, knowledge of your opponent's force is just as vital, as well as the aspects of different 'match-ups', the ways in battles between two specific factions commonly – though certainly not always – play out.

But however fascinating and enjoyable it is to design the perfect army, a true general will only be satisfied after their force has sallied forth and proven its worth on the battlefield. One of the benefits to matched play games is that once you have settled on an army to use, you essentially have a pick-up-and-play force that you can bring to any table and against any opponent. This makes matched play ideal for tournaments and leagues, as it provides clear guidelines on the size and strength of the armies taking part, as well as ensuring that all battles are as fair as they can be.

THE RULES

This section explains how to play games of Warhammer Age of Sigmar with your collection of Citadel Miniatures. It also includes the Player's Code, a handy set of guidelines that will help you and your opponent get the most out of your games.

THE WARHAMMER AGE OF SIGMAR PLAYER'S CODE

There is a famous adage that goes, 'It matters not if you win or lose, it's how you play the game.'

We believe that Warhammer Age of Sigmar is a game best played in this spirit, and to help with this, we've put together a set of guidelines that we call the 'Player's Code', which you can see opposite.

The cardinal rules of the Player's Code are all you really need to follow, as the principles that come below them are really just examples of the cardinal rules in practice. If you follow the Player's Code, you'll find yourself having more fun, and what's more, you'll be playing Warhammer Age of Sigmar as it's meant to be played – as an enjoyable pastime played in a spirit of friendly rivalry.

THE CORE RULES

The core rules are the foundation of playing games of Warhammer Age of Sigmar. These rules show you how your models move, cast magic spells, shoot their missile weapons, charge into battle and fight with their close-range weapons – basically everything you need to start waging war with your Citadel Miniatures! The core rules provide you with the key mechanics that govern how everything works – from battle-hardened infantry to gigantic monsters – allowing you to quickly build up from your first few simple games to grand spectacles of large-scale conflict.

THE PLAYER'S CODE

CARDINAL RULES
- Always be polite and respectful.
- Always tell the truth and never cheat.

PRINCIPLES

- Arrive on time with all of the things you need to play the game.

- Make a respectful gesture to your opponent before and after the game, such as offering a handshake, wishing them good luck, etc.

- Avoid using language your opponent might find offensive.

- Ask your opponent's permission if you wish to use unpainted models or substitute models.

- Offer your opponent a chance to examine your army roster before the battle starts.

- Answer any questions your opponent has about your army and the rules that apply to your army.

- Measure moves and distances carefully and accurately.

- Give your opponent the chance to examine your dice rolls before picking up the dice.

- Ask permission before touching any of your opponent's miniatures.

- Remind your opponent about rules they may have forgotten to use or that they have used incorrectly, especially when doing so is to your opponent's advantage rather than your own.

- Never deliberately waste time during a game.

- Avoid distracting an opponent when they are trying to concentrate, and be careful to respect their personal space.

- Never complain about your bad luck or your opponent's good luck.

- Never fix the outcome of a game.

THE CORE RULES

The following rules explain how to use your collection of Citadel Miniatures to play a game of Warhammer Age of Sigmar.

1.0 CORE CONCEPTS

This section of the core rules contains important principles that are used in all games of Warhammer Age of Sigmar.

1.1 FACTIONS, BATTLETOMES AND BATTLEPACKS

To play a game of Warhammer Age of Sigmar, first you must pick the **factions** you wish to include in your **army** (see 1.4). Each faction has its own **battletome**, which contains the **warscrolls** (see 1.3.1), **Pitched Battle profiles** (see 25.0) and **allegiance abilities** (see 27.0) for that faction. Then, you and your opponent must agree upon a **battlepack** to use (see 28.0). The battlepack contains instructions on how to pick your army, set up the battlefield (see 2.0), and what you need to do in order to win the battle.

1.2 MODELS

The Citadel Miniatures that make up your army are referred to as **models**. Most models have a plastic **base** that allows them to be stood on the battlefield and that are used when measuring distances to or from the model (see 1.5.1). The base is considered to be part of the model for rules purposes. A model cannot be set up or end a move on top of another model, either wholly or partially.

1.2.1 FRIENDLY AND ENEMY MODELS

Models from your army are referred to as **friendly** models, and models from your opponent's army are referred to as **enemy** models. If a rule states that it affects models without specifying whether they are friendly or enemy, then it affects friendly *and* enemy models.

1.2.2 REMOVED FROM PLAY

Sometimes models will be **removed from play**, most commonly if they are **slain** (see 14.2) or **flee** (see 15.1) or to make their unit **coherent** (see 1.3.3). Place models that have been removed from play to one side, so they are no longer on the battlefield. They are no longer part of your army.

1.3 UNITS

Models are organised into **units**. A unit is a group of one or more models that use the same warscroll (see 1.3.1). The number of models in a unit is shown on its Pitched Battle profile (see 25.0). A unit is destroyed when the last model in the unit is removed from play.

1.3.1 WARSCROLLS

Every unit has a **warscroll**, which provides information that is needed to use it in a game. You can find out more about warscrolls in section 22.0. Warscrolls are also provided for endless spells (see 19.3), invocations (see 20.3) and faction terrain features (see 23.0).

Some words appear in **rules bold***. This indicates that these are important terms that are used throughout the rules for Warhammer Age of Sigmar.*

The title for each core rule has a section number. These will help you quickly find a rule that is referenced elsewhere in the core rules. For example '(see 2.0)' means that you should refer to section 2.0 – The Battlefield.

Citadel Miniatures are also used to represent terrain features (see 17.0), endless spells (see 19.3) and invocations (see 20.3). However, only the Citadel Miniatures that represent the warriors in your army are considered to be 'models' for rules purposes.

A model with a base.

1.3.2 KEYWORDS

Every warscroll includes a list of **keywords** that apply to all of the models in a unit that uses that warscroll. Keywords appear in **KEYWORD BOLD** in the rules and are used to identify one or more units. For example, a rule might say that it applies to **STORMCAST ETERNALS** units. This means that the rule would apply to all units that have the **STORMCAST ETERNALS** keyword on their warscroll.

1.3.3 UNIT COHERENCY

Units must be set up and finish every move as a single **coherent** group. A unit with _2 to 5 models_ is coherent if each model in the unit is within 1" horizontally and 6" vertically of at least 1 other model in the unit. A unit with _more than 5 models_ is coherent if each model in the unit is within 1" horizontally and 6" vertically of at least 2 other models in the unit. If a friendly unit is not coherent at the end of a turn or after you set it up, you must remove models in the unit from play, one at a time, until it is coherent.

1.4 ARMIES

Each player in a game of Warhammer Age of Sigmar is the **commander** of an **army**. All of the units in your army must be from the factions you picked for your army (see 1.1). The battlepack you are using will explain how to pick the units in your army (see 28.0). An **army roster** that can be used to record the units in your army is included at the end of the rules.

1.4.1 ENDLESS SPELLS, INVOCATIONS AND FACTION TERRAIN

Your army can include 1 **endless spell** (see 19.3) for each **WIZARD** in your army and 1 **invocation** (see 20.3) for each **PRIEST** in your army. In addition, your army can include 1 **faction terrain feature** (see 23.0).

1.4.2 YOUR GENERAL

After you have picked your army, you must pick 1 model in your army to be your **general**. Generals are used to generate **command points** (see 6.0).

The singular and plural forms of a keyword are synonymous for rules purposes. For example, a 'BLOODLETTER unit' means the same as a 'BLOODLETTERS unit'.

Units that are set up in a location other than on the battlefield, for example, reserve units (see 3.1), are always considered to be set up in a coherent group.

A warscroll

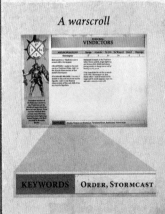

| KEYWORDS | ORDER, STORMCAST |

Each model in the Vindictors unit must be within 1" of at least 1 other model in the unit. Each model in the Gutrippaz unit must be within 1" of at least 2 other models in the unit (see 1.3.3).

*Sometimes a rule will say that a model or unit needs to be **wholly within** a distance of something else. A __model__ is wholly within a certain distance of something if every part of its base is within the stated distance. A __unit__ is wholly within a certain distance of something if every part of the bases of all of the models in the unit are within the stated distance.*

1.5 TOOLS OF WAR

In order to play a game of Warhammer Age of Sigmar, you will need some six-sided dice and a ruler or tape measure marked in inches (").

1.5.1 MEASURING DISTANCES

Distances in Warhammer Age of Sigmar are measured in inches ("). The distance between two models is measured between the closest points on the bases of the models. If a model does not have a base, measure to and from the closest point on the model instead. You can measure distances whenever you wish.

When measuring the distance between units, always measure between the closest models from each unit. For example, a unit is within 12" of another unit as long as at least one model in one of the units is 12" or less from at least one model in the other unit.

Sometimes a rule will require you to draw a straight line between two models or two points on the battlefield. When this is the case, the line is an imaginary one and is assumed to be 1mm wide.

1.5.2 DICE

Warhammer Age of Sigmar uses six-sided dice (sometimes abbreviated to **D6**). Often when a dice is rolled, a **target number** must be equalled or exceeded for the roll to be a **success**. A target number is usually written as a number followed by a plus sign. For example, if a roll requires a roll of 3 or more to be a success, the target number would be '3+'.

Some rules refer to 2D6, 3D6, and so on. These are referred to collectively as **xD6** rolls. When making an xD6 roll, roll a number of dice equal to 'x' and add them together. A **double** is a 2D6 roll where the dice used to make the roll show the same number before modifiers are applied. If a rule requires you to roll a **D3**, roll a dice and halve the total, rounding up.

1.5.3 ROLLING OFF

Sometimes a rule may require the players to **roll off**. To roll off, each player rolls a dice, and whoever rolls highest wins. If a roll-off is tied, roll off again. You cannot re-roll or modify the dice when you roll off.

1.5.4 RE-ROLLS

Some rules refer to **re-rolls**. To make a re-roll, roll the dice used for the roll again. You cannot re-roll a dice roll more than once. If a rule allows you to re-roll an xD6 roll, you must re-roll all of the dice used for the roll.

In most cases, modifiers are cumulative. However, some dice rolls, such as hit and wound rolls, will specify that the roll cannot be modified by more than +1 or -1. When this is the case, add up all the modifiers that apply, and if the total is more than +1 or -1, treat it as being either +1 or -1 as appropriate.

1.5.5 DICE ROLL MODIFIERS

Sometimes a **modifier** will apply to a dice roll. Modifiers are applied after re-rolls. Rules that refer to an **unmodified** roll are referring to the dice roll after re-rolls have been made but before modifiers are applied. If a rule instructs you to pick or change a roll, do so after re-rolls are made but before modifiers are applied.

1.6 ABILITIES AND EFFECTS

Every warscroll includes **abilities**, each of which has an **effect**. When an ability is used, its effect is applied. In addition, most effects have **restrictions**. Abilities can also be found in sets of allegiance abilities (see 27.0) and in the rules for battalions (see 26.0). An example ability is shown below:

> **Hawk of the Celestial Skies:** *The sight of Yndrasta's seraphic form soaring overhead inspires her warriors with immeasurable resolve.*
>
> Do not take battleshock tests for friendly STORMCAST ETERNALS and CITIES OF SIGMAR units wholly within 12" of this unit.

1.6.1 ABILITIES AND PHASES

Most abilities are used in one of the phases of a turn (see 5.0). Abilities can only be used in the phase specified in their rules.

An ability may say that it is used at the **start of the phase** or at the **end of the phase**. If it does not specify, then it is used **during the phase**. Abilities that are used at the start of a phase are used before anything else happens in the phase, while abilities used at the end of the phase are used after anything else happens in the phase. Abilities that are used during a phase can be used at any time in the phase, as long as they are used after abilities that are used at the start of the phase and before abilities that are used at the end of the phase.

1.6.2 SIMULTANEOUS EFFECTS

If the effects of two or more abilities would be applied at the same time in a turn, the player whose turn is taking place applies the effects of their abilities first, one at a time, in the order they desire. Their opponent then does the same.

If the effects of two or more abilities would be applied at the same time other than during a turn, the players roll off and the winner applies the effects of their abilities first, one at a time, in the order they desire. Their opponent then does the same.

1.6.3 CONTRADICTORY EFFECTS

When the effects of two or more abilities are contradictory, the last one that was applied takes precedence.

1.6.4 TRIGGERED EFFECTS

The effects of some abilities are applied when a dice roll **triggers** them. For example, the effect of an ability might be triggered if the unmodified hit roll for an attack is 6. A triggered effect is applied immediately after the roll that triggered it. If two or more effects are triggered by the same roll, only one of those effects can be applied. The player who made the roll must pick which effect is applied.

1.6.5 SHOOTING OR FIGHTING MORE THAN ONCE

The effects of some abilities allow a unit to shoot (see 10.1) or fight (see 12.1.1) more than once in the same phase. However, the effect of an ability cannot allow a unit to shoot or fight more than twice in the same phase (this is an exception to the principle that the effects of abilities take precedence over core rules).

If the effect of an ability contradicts a core rule, then the effect takes precedence.

The effect of the 'Hawk of the Celestial Skies' ability is that the player commanding the unit with the ability does not take battleshock tests for the listed units; the restriction is that the effect only applies to those units if they are wholly within 12" of the unit with the ability.

Effects that allow a unit to fight at the start or end of the combat phase are called **strike-first effects** *and* **strike-last effects** *respectively. Special rules apply to when units with these effects attack (see 12.4).*

When something is **affected** *by an ability, it means that the effect of that ability is applied to the thing in question.*

If the effect of an ability modifies a core rule, then all restrictions that apply to the core rule still apply unless the effect specifically notes otherwise.

Some abilities have an area of effect. For example, Yndrasta's 'Hawk of the Celestial Skies' ability affects all friendly STORMCAST ETERNALS *and* CITIES OF SIGMAR *units wholly within 12" of her. In such cases, the effect of the ability is considered to be applied as soon as the affected unit is within the specified distance, not necessarily when it benefits from the effect.*

If the players agree, they can use a battlefield that has been modelled to include hills and slopes. When this is the case, the hills and slopes are considered to be open ground.

Reserve units are picked as part of your army before the battle begins, while summoned units are units added to your army once the battle is underway. Models that have been removed from play can be used as part of a summoned unit.

2.0 THE BATTLEFIELD

The **battlefield** is a flat surface upon which the models can stand, such as a dining table or the floor. The size of the battlefield will be determined by the battlepack you have decided to use (see 28.0). The terrain on the battlefield is represented by scenery pieces from the Warhammer Age of Sigmar range, which are called **terrain features** in the rules (see 17.0). The battlepack you are using will tell you how to set up the terrain features (see 28.2.3). The rest of the battlefield is **open ground**.

3.0 DEPLOYMENT

After the battlefield has been prepared, you and your opponent must **deploy** your armies. The battlepack you are using will explain how deployment takes place (see 28.2.4).

3.1 RESERVE UNITS AND SUMMONED UNITS

Sometimes a rule will allow you to set up a unit in a location other than the battlefield as a **reserve unit**. A unit that is added to your army once the battle is underway is called a **summoned unit**.

When you set up a reserve unit, either during deployment or once the battle is underway, you must tell your opponent that the unit is **in reserve** and keep it to one side instead of placing it on the battlefield. At the start of the fourth battle round, units that are still in reserve are destroyed. Units cannot cast spells or use abilities while they are in reserve unless the spell or ability specifically says it can be used by reserve units.

4.0 BATTLE ROUNDS

A battle is fought in a series of **battle rounds**. At the **start of the battle round**, the players make a **priority roll** and then each player takes 1 **turn**. Each turn is split into 6 **phases**. Once the second turn has finished, it is the **end of the battle round** and then a new one begins.

4.1 THE PRIORITY ROLL

At the start of each battle round, the players must roll off. This is called the **priority roll**. The winner has **priority** in that battle round and must decide who will take the first turn and who will take the second turn.

In the event of a tied priority roll, do not roll off again. Instead, if it is the first battle round, the player who finished deploying their army first has priority. Otherwise, the player who went first in the previous battle round has priority.

4.1.1 STARTING COMMAND POINTS

After determining who will take which turn, the player who will take the first turn receives 1 **command point** (see 6.0) and the player who will take the second turn receives 2 command points.

5.0 TURN SEQUENCE

When it is your turn, you must carry out the phases in your turn in the following **turn sequence**.

1   Hero Phase (see 7.0)
2   Movement Phase (see 8.0)
3   Shooting Phase (see 10.0)
4   Charge Phase (see 11.0)
5   Combat Phase (see 12.0)
6   Battleshock Phase (see 15.0)

When a rule refers to one of your phases (for example, your hero phase), it means that phase in your turn.

When a rule refers to the or a phase (for example, the hero phase or a hero phase), it means that phase in either player's turn.

Command abilities that are used in the hero phase can be found on the next page. Those that are used in other phases appear later in the core rules.

6.0 COMMAND POINTS

Command points allow you to use **command abilities**. You receive command points at the start of the battle round after priority is determined (see 4.1). In addition, if your general is on the battlefield at the start of the hero phase, you receive 1 command point. At the end of the battle round (see 16.0), any command points that have not been used are lost.

6.1 USING COMMAND ABILITIES

To use a command ability, you must spend 1 command point, pick 1 friendly model to **issue** the command, and pick 1 friendly unit to **receive** the command. Unless noted otherwise, the models that can issue commands and the units they can issue them to are as follows:

- Unit champions can issue commands to their own unit (see 22.3.2).
- **HEROES** can issue commands to units that are wholly within 12" of them.
- Generals can issue commands to units that are wholly within 18" of them.
- **TOTEMS** can issue commands to units that are wholly within 18" of them.

Each command ability will say when it can be used and what effect it has on the unit that receives it. A model cannot issue more than 1 command in the same phase and a unit cannot receive more than 1 command in the same phase. In addition, you cannot use the same command ability more than once in the same phase (even for different units).

7.0 HERO PHASE

At the start of the **hero phase**, starting with the player whose turn is taking place, *each* player can pick 1 **HERO** to perform a heroic action (see 7.1), and *each* player receives 1 command point if their general is on the battlefield (see 6.0). In addition, in your hero phase, you can use friendly **WIZARDS** to attempt to cast spells (see 19.0), friendly **PRIESTS** to chant prayers and attempt to banish invocations (see 20.0), and both to attempt to dispel endless spells (19.3). In the enemy hero phase you can use friendly **WIZARDS** to attempt to unbind spells (see 19.2).

7.1 HEROES AND HEROIC ACTIONS

A unit with the **HERO** keyword on its warscroll is a **HERO**. At the start of the hero phase, you can carry out 1 **heroic action** from the table below with 1 friendly **HERO**. The effect of the heroic action is treated in the same way as the effect of an ability for rules purposes (see 1.6).

HEROIC ACTIONS

 Heroic Leadership: Pick 1 friendly **HERO** and roll a dice. Add 2 to the roll if your general has been slain. On a 4+, you receive 1 command point that can only be spent during that turn to allow that **HERO** to issue a command.

 **Heroic Willpower:** Pick 1 friendly **HERO** that is not a **WIZARD**. If it is the enemy hero phase, that **HERO** can attempt to unbind 1 spell in that phase as if they were a **WIZARD**. If it is your hero phase, that **HERO** can attempt to dispel 1 endless spell in that phase as if they were a **WIZARD** (you can still only attempt to unbind or dispel the same spell or endless spell once in the same phase).

 Their Finest Hour: Pick 1 friendly **HERO**. Add 1 to wound rolls for attacks made by that **HERO** until the end of that turn, and add 1 to save rolls for attacks that target that **HERO** until the end of that turn. You cannot carry out this heroic action with the same **HERO** more than once in the same battle.

 Heroic Recovery: Pick 1 friendly **HERO** and make a heroic recovery roll by rolling 2D6. If the roll is less than that **HERO**'s Bravery characteristic, you can heal up to D3 wounds allocated to that **HERO**. If the roll is equal to that **HERO**'s Bravery characteristic, you can heal 1 wound allocated to that **HERO**.

7.2 HERO PHASE COMMAND ABILITIES

You can use the following command ability in the hero phase (see 6.1):

Rally: *At a shouted command, injured warriors stagger back to their feet and prepare to fight once more.*

You can use this command ability at the start of the hero phase. The unit that receives the command must be more than 3" from all enemy units. Roll 1 dice for each slain model from that unit. For each 6, you can return 1 slain model to that unit.

8.0 MOVEMENT PHASE

In your **movement phase**, you can pick 1 friendly unit that is more than 3" from all enemy units and declare that it will make a **normal move** or that it will **run**, or you can pick 1 friendly unit that is within 3" of an enemy unit and declare that it will **retreat**.

Once you have moved the models in that unit, you can pick another friendly unit and declare that it will make a normal move, run or retreat, and so on, until as many units as you wish have either made a normal move, run or retreated. Once you have made a normal move, run or retreated with a unit, you cannot pick it again in that phase.

8.1 NORMAL MOVE

When you pick a unit to make a **normal move**, you can move each model in that unit a distance in inches equal to or less than the **Move** characteristic shown on the unit's warscroll. Units cannot move within 3" of enemy units when making a normal move.

8.2 RETREAT

When you pick a unit to **retreat**, you can move each model in that unit a distance in inches equal to or less than the Move characteristic shown on the unit's warscroll. The unit must end the move more than 3" from all enemy units. You cannot shoot or attempt a charge later in the turn with a unit that has retreated.

8.3 RUN

When you pick a unit to **run**, you must make a **run roll** for the unit by rolling a dice. Add the run roll to the Move characteristic of all models in the unit until the end of that phase. You can then move each model in that unit a distance in inches equal to or less than their modified Move characteristic. No part of a run can be within 3" of an enemy unit. You cannot shoot or attempt a charge later in the turn with a unit that has run.

8.4 MOVEMENT PHASE COMMAND ABILITIES

You can use the following command abilities in the movement phase (see 6.1):

At the Double: *Eager for battle, the warriors pick up their pace and surge towards the enemy.*

You can use this command ability after you declare that a friendly unit will run. That unit must receive the command. The run roll is not made for that unit. Instead, 6" is added to that unit's Move characteristic in that phase. The unit is still considered to have run.

Redeploy: *As the enemy draw close, battle-hardened warriors adjust their position to leave their foe at a disadvantage.*

You can use this command ability in the enemy movement phase after an enemy unit finishes a normal move, run or retreat. The unit that receives the command must be within 9" of that enemy unit and more than 3" from all enemy units. You can make a D6" move with the unit that receives the command, but it must finish the move more than 3" from all enemy units and cannot shoot later in the turn.

The rules that explain how to make a move with a model can be found on the next page.

You can either choose for a unit to run or choose for it to retreat. It cannot do both.

CORE RULES

9.0 MOVEMENT

You can change the position of a model on the battlefield by making a **move** with the model. Models can be moved in the movement phase (see 8.0), the charge phase (see 11.0) and the combat phase (see 12.0), and some abilities allow you to move a model at other times, such as in the hero phase.

To move a model, first trace a **path** over the surface of the battlefield showing the route the model will travel. You can trace the path in any direction or combination of directions, as long as it does not pass through other models or over the edge of the battlefield, and as long as the length of the path is not greater than the distance the model is allowed to move.

Then, move the model along the path to the new location. You can pivot the model freely as you move it along the path. No part of the model's base can pass across the base of another model or over the edge of the battlefield, and at the end of the move no part of the model's base can be further from its starting location than the distance the model is allowed to move.

9.1 UNIT COHERENCY

After you have moved all of the models in a unit, it must be coherent (see 1.3.3). If it is impossible for a unit to be coherent after it has moved, you cannot move that unit.

9.2 REMAINING STATIONARY

If you make a move with any models in a unit, all of the models in the unit are considered to have made a move in that phase. If you wish, instead of making a move with a unit, you can choose for it to remain **stationary**. If you do so, you cannot move any of the models in the unit in that phase, but none of the models in the unit are considered to have made a move in that phase.

Pick a model you wish to move.

Trace the path of the model's move. The path cannot be longer than the move distance (see 9.0).

Move the model along the path. No part of its base can end the move further from its starting location than the move distance (see 9.0).

9.3 TERRAIN

When you move a model, you can trace the path of its move over **terrain features** but not through them. When you move the model, it follows the path along the surfaces of the terrain features but its base is assumed to remain parallel to the surface of the battlefield as it does so.

9.3.1 JUMPING DOWN FROM TERRAIN FEATURES

When you move a model that is on a terrain feature, you can say it will jump down from the edge of the terrain feature to land on a lower part of the same or different terrain feature or to land on the battlefield. To do so, you must trace the path of the model's move to the edge of the terrain feature and then directly down to the surface below. The distance the model drops down counts towards the distance it has moved.

9.4 FLYING

If the warscroll used by a model says that it can **fly**, you can ignore other models and terrain features when you trace the path of its move across the battlefield (it flies over them). In addition, when a model that can fly starts or finishes a move on a terrain feature, instead of tracing its move across the battlefield, you can trace it 'through the air', as shown in the diagram below.

A flying model cannot finish a move on top of another model or finish a normal move, run or retreat within 3" of an enemy unit.

9.4.1 PASSING ACROSS

Some abilities require a model that can fly to **pass across** another model. For it to pass across another model, the path of the flying model's move must be traced across part of the other model's base.

The Vindictor on the left climbs the wall to the top of the ruin (see 9.3). The Praetor in the centre jumps down from the ruin to the ground below (see 9.3.1). Yndrasta flies from the ground to the top of the ruin (see 9.4). Even though the length of the path traced for each of the models is the same, Yndrasta has actually covered more distance because she is able to take a more direct route by flying through the air (see 9.4).

The rules for making an attack can be found in section 13.0.

A unit can shoot at an enemy unit that is within 3" of another friendly unit without penalty.

When shooting with a unit, you do not have to shoot with all of the models in the unit if you do not want to. This is different to when you are making combat attacks with a unit, in which case all of the models in the unit must attack if they are able to (see 12.3).

A unit cannot shoot if it ran or retreated earlier in the turn.

A unit cannot attempt a charge if it ran or retreated earlier in the turn or if it is within 3" of an enemy unit.

You do not have to pick a target for a charge attempt before making the charge roll.

10.0 SHOOTING PHASE

In your shooting phase, you can pick a friendly unit and **shoot** with it. When you shoot with a unit, you make **shooting attacks** with each model in the unit until you have shot with all the models you want to. You can then pick another friendly unit that has not shot and shoot with it, and so on, until you have shot with as many of your units as you wish.

10.1 SHOOTING ATTACKS

When you make **shooting attacks** with a model, it attacks with any of the missile weapons it is armed with (see 13.1.1).

10.1.1 SHOOTING NEAR ENEMY UNITS

A unit that is within 3" of any enemy units can only target enemy units that are within 3" of it.

10.1.2 LOOK OUT, SIR!

You must subtract 1 from the hit roll (see 13.3) for an attack made with a missile weapon if the target is an enemy **Hero** within 3" of an enemy unit that has 3 or more models. The **Look Out, Sir!** rule does not apply if the enemy **Hero** has a Wounds characteristic of 10 or more.

11.0 CHARGE PHASE

In your charge phase, you can pick a friendly unit that is within 12" of an enemy unit to **attempt a charge**. You can then pick another friendly unit within 12" of an enemy unit to attempt a charge, and so on, until you have attempted a charge with as many units as you wish. A unit cannot attempt a charge more than once in the same phase.

11.1 CHARGE MOVES

When you attempt a charge with a unit, make a **charge roll** for the unit by rolling 2D6. You can then make a **charge move** with each model in that unit by moving the model a distance in inches that is equal to or less than the charge roll. The first model you move in a unit attempting a charge must finish the move within ½" of an enemy unit. If this is impossible, no models in the unit can make a charge move.

11.2 CHARGE PHASE COMMAND ABILITIES

You can use the following command abilities in the charge phase (see 6.1):

Forward to Victory: *Nothing will stop these ferocious warriors from reaching combat.*

You can use this command ability after you make a charge roll for a friendly unit. That unit must receive the command. You can re-roll the charge roll for that unit.

Unleash Hell: *These warriors have prepared their missile weapons so they can unleash a devastating volley at the last possible moment.*

You can use this command ability after an enemy unit finishes a charge move. The unit that receives the command must be within 9" of that enemy unit and more than 3" from all other enemy units. The unit that receives the command can shoot in that phase, but when it does so, you must subtract 1 from hit rolls for its attacks and it can only target the unit that made the charge move.

12.0 COMBAT PHASE

In the combat phase, the players alternate picking a friendly unit to **fight**, starting with the player whose turn is taking place.

12.1 FIGHT SEQUENCE

When it is your go to pick a unit to fight, you must either pick 1 eligible friendly unit to **fight** or you must **pass**. A unit is eligible to fight if it is within 3" of an enemy unit and it has not fought in that phase, or if it made a charge move in the same turn and it has not fought in that phase. You cannot pass if there is a friendly unit that is eligible to fight.

12.1.1 FIGHT

When you pick a unit to **fight**, first you can make a pile-in move with each model in the unit (see 12.2) and then you must make combat attacks with the models in the unit (see 12.3). That unit has then fought.

12.1.2 PASS

If you **pass**, you do nothing and the option to fight or pass goes back to your opponent. If both players pass in succession, the combat phase ends unless there are any units with strike-last effects (see 12.4).

12.2 PILE IN

You can move a model making a **pile-in move** up to 3". When you make a pile-in move with a model, it must finish the move no further from the nearest enemy unit than it was at the start of the move.

12.3 COMBAT ATTACKS

After you have made all of the pile-in moves for a unit, you must make **combat attacks** with each model in the unit that is within range of an enemy model (see 13.1.2).

12.4 STRIKE-FIRST AND STRIKE-LAST EFFECTS

Some abilities have an effect that allows a unit to fight at either the start or the end of the combat phase. These effects are called **strike-first effects** and **strike-last effects** respectively. The rules in sections 1.6.1-1.6.3 do not apply to these effects: use the rules here instead.

If a strike-first effect applies to any units, those units fight before all other units fight. If a strike-last effect applies to any units, those units fight after all other units fight.

If a strike-first effect applies to units from both players' armies, the players alternate fighting with those units, starting with the player whose turn it is. Similarly, if a strike-last effect applies to units from both players' armies, the players alternate fighting with those units, starting with the player whose turn it is. If a strike-first effect and a strike-last effect apply to the same unit at the same time, then they cancel each other out and neither effect applies to that unit.

12.5 STRIKE-FIRST AND STRIKE-LAST SEQUENCING

1. Start of combat phase abilities are used
2. Units with strike-first effects attack
3. Units without strike-first/strike-last effects attack
4. Units with strike-last effects attack
5. End of combat phase abilities are used

Both sides fight in the combat phase.

A unit that is not within 3" of the enemy at the start of the combat phase is allowed to fight later during that combat phase if an enemy unit finishes a move within 3" of it later in that phase. This means that units with strike-first effects can still be picked to fight later in the phase even if they were not within 3" of an enemy unit at the start of the phase.

In the combat phase, you must pick a unit to fight with if you have any eligible to do so, and the models in the unit must attack with all of the weapons they are allowed to use that are within range of an enemy unit.

The rules for making an attack can be found on the next page.

Example: The player whose turn is taking place has two units with strike-first effects (units A and B) and one with a strike-last effect (unit C), while their opponent has one unit with a strike-first effect (unit D) and two units with no strike-first or strike-last effects (units E and F). The players alternate fighting with the strike-first units, starting with the player whose turn is taking place, so unit A fights, then unit D, and then unit B. Next, units with no strike-first or strike-last effects fight, so units E and F fight. Finally units with strike-last effects fight, so unit C fights.

CORE RULES

87

13.0 ATTACKING

When you shoot or fight with a unit, you make **attacks** with the **weapons** the models in the unit are **armed** with. The weapons that the models in a unit are armed with are listed on the unit's warscroll. **Missile weapons** are used when models make shooting attacks, and **melee weapons** are used when models make combat attacks.

13.1 PICKING TARGETS

When you shoot or fight with a unit, before you make any attacks, you must pick the **target** unit (or units) for all of the attacks that will be made by the models in the unit. Only enemy units can be picked as the target for an attack. Once the targets for the unit's attacks have been picked, you can make the attacks in the order you wish.

13.1.1 SHOOTING ATTACKS

When a friendly unit shoots, you can make **shooting attacks** with any of the missile weapons the models in the unit are armed with that they are allowed to use (including missile weapons used by mounts).

The target of a shooting attack must be within a number of inches of the attacking model equal to the **Range** characteristic of the weapon being used to make the attack. The range must be measured to the closest **visible** model in the target unit (if you are unsure whether a model is visible, stoop down and take a look from behind the shooting model). Models can see through other models in their unit.

Some missile weapons have a Range characteristic with a **minimum range** (e.g. 6"-48"). Units wholly within the minimum range cannot be targeted with these weapons.

13.1.2 COMBAT ATTACKS

When a friendly unit fights, you must make **combat attacks** with all of the melee weapons the models in the unit are armed with that they are allowed to use (including melee weapons used by the unit's mounts, if there are any).

The target of a combat attack must be within a number of inches of the attacking model equal to the Range characteristic of the weapon being used to make the attack (the target does not have to be visible).

13.2 NUMBER OF ATTACKS

The number of attacks you make with a weapon is equal to its **Attacks** characteristic. Make the attacks one at a time, unless you are making combined attacks (see 13.2.1). If a weapon has an Attacks characteristic of more than 1, you can split the attacks between target units.

Some models are armed with two of the same weapon (often referred to as paired weapons). When this is the case, the Attacks characteristic for the weapon will already take the extra weapon into account, or the model will have an ability to represent the model dual-wielding.

13.2.1 COMBINED ATTACKS

You can make **combined attacks** if all of the attacks are made by models from the same unit, with the same type of weapon, against the same target unit, and where the same re-rolls and modifiers apply to the attacks. If this is the case, make all of the hit rolls at the same time, then make all of the wound rolls, and finally make all of the save rolls.

A unit of Man-skewer Boltboyz prepares to loose some close-range shots at a unit of Annihilators.

13.3 ATTACK SEQUENCE

Use the following **attack sequence** for each attack made by a friendly model. In some cases, you can roll the dice for multiple attacks at the same time (see 13.2.1).

1. Hit Roll

Roll a dice. If the roll equals or beats the attacking weapon's **To Hit** characteristic, the attack scores a **hit** and you must make a **wound roll**. If not, the attack **fails** and the attack sequence ends. An unmodified hit roll of 1 always fails and an unmodified hit roll of 6 always hits. A hit roll cannot be modified by more than +1 or -1 (this is an exception to the principle that abilities take precedence over core rules).

Sometimes an ability will allow a single hit roll to score two or more hits. If this is the case, make all of the wound and save rolls for those hits at the same time.

2. Wound Roll

Roll a dice. If the roll equals or beats the attacking weapon's **To Wound** characteristic, the attack **wounds** the target and your opponent must make a **save roll**. If not, the attack **fails** and the attack sequence ends. An unmodified wound roll of 1 always fails and an unmodified wound roll of 6 always wounds. A wound roll cannot be modified by more than +1 or -1 (this is an exception to the principle that abilities take precedence over core rules).

3. Save Roll

Your opponent rolls a dice, modifying the roll by the attacking weapon's **Rend** characteristic. If the roll equals or beats the target unit's **Save** characteristic, the target is **saved** and the attack sequence ends. If not, the attack is **successful** and you must determine the **damage** that is inflicted on the target. An unmodified save roll of 1 always fails. A save roll cannot be modified by more than +1 (this is an exception to the principle that abilities take precedence over core rules).

Designer's Note: *Save rolls do not always succeed on an unmodified roll of 6, and they can be modified by more than -1.*

4. Damage

Each successful attack inflicts damage on the target unit equal to the **Damage** characteristic of the weapon used for the attack.

13.3.1 ALLOCATE WOUNDS

Once all of a friendly unit's attacks have been made, add up the damage that was inflicted on each target unit. The player commanding each target unit must **allocate** a number of wounds to that unit equal to the damage that was inflicted on it (see 14.1). Once all of the damage inflicted by a unit's attacks has been allocated, that unit's attacks have been **resolved**.

13.4 ATTACK COMMAND ABILITIES

You can use the following command abilities during an attack. Command abilities that affect an attack must be used before the attack sequence for that attack has started (this is an exception to the principle that abilities take precedence over core rules).

All-out Attack: *With a singular purpose, these warriors attack with all of their might.*

You can use this command ability when you pick a friendly unit to shoot in your shooting phase or fight in the combat phase. That unit must receive the command. Add 1 to hit rolls for attacks made by that unit until the end of that phase.

All-out Defence: *With consummate skill, these cunning warriors protect themselves from attack.*

You can use this command ability when a friendly unit is picked as the target of an attack in the shooting or combat phase. That unit must receive the command. Add 1 to save rolls for attacks that target that unit until the end of that phase.

14.0 WOUNDS

Units suffer **wounds** when damage is inflicted on them by attacks (see 13.0) and when **mortal wounds** are caused to them (see 14.5).

14.1 ALLOCATING WOUNDS

Wounds are **allocated** to the models in a unit 1 wound at a time. You can allocate the wounds caused to your units as you see fit. However, once you have allocated a wound to a model, you cannot allocate wounds to other models in the unit until that model is slain (see 14.2). If a unit is destroyed, all wounds that remain to be allocated to the unit are negated and have no effect.

14.2 SLAIN MODELS

Once the number of wounds allocated to a model equals its **Wounds** characteristic, the model is **slain** and you cannot allocate any more wounds to it. A slain model is removed from play (see 1.2.2) after all of the wounds caused to its unit have been allocated and all attacks that inflicted damage on the unit have been resolved.

14.2.1 RETURNING SLAIN MODELS

Some abilities allow you to return slain models to a unit. Set up the models, one at a time, within 1" of a model from their unit that was not returned to the unit earlier in the phase. Slain models can only be set up within 3" of an enemy unit if a model in the unit they are returning to that was not returned to the unit in the same phase is already within 3" of that enemy unit.

14.3 WARDS

Some abilities allow you to roll a dice to negate a wound before it is allocated to a model. Abilities of this type are referred to as **wards**, and the dice roll is referred to as a **ward roll**. Up to 1 ward roll can be made for each wound or mortal wound before it is allocated to the model in question. If the ward roll is successful, the wound or mortal wound is negated and has no effect on the model.

14.4 HEALING WOUNDS

Some abilities allow you to **heal** wounds that have been allocated to a model. For each wound that is healed, reduce the number of wounds allocated to the model by 1, to a minimum of 0. You cannot heal wounds on a model that is slain.

14.5 MORTAL WOUNDS

Some attacks, spells and abilities cause **mortal wounds**. Do not make hit, wound or save rolls for mortal wounds. Instead, the damage inflicted on the target is equal to the number of mortal wounds that were caused.

Mortal wounds caused while a unit is attacking are allocated at the same time as wounds caused by the unit's attacks: after all of the unit's attacks have been made. Mortal wounds caused at other times are allocated as soon as they are caused. Mortal wounds are allocated in the same way as wounds and are treated in the same manner as wounds for rules purposes.

One of these Praetors has been slain by the Killaboss. It is removed from play by being placed to one side.

15.0 BATTLESHOCK PHASE

In the **battleshock phase**, the players must take a **battleshock test** for each friendly unit that had models slain in that turn. The player whose turn is taking place takes all their battleshock tests first, followed by the other player.

15.1 BATTLESHOCK TESTS

You must make a **battleshock roll** for each friendly unit that has to take a battleshock test. To make a battleshock roll, roll a dice and add the number of models in the unit that were slain in that turn to the roll. If the battleshock roll is greater than the unit's **Bravery** characteristic, the battleshock test has been **failed**. If the test is failed, for each point by which the battleshock roll exceeds the unit's Bravery characteristic, 1 model in that unit must **flee**. You decide which models flee. A model that flees is removed from play.

15.2 SPLIT UNITS

If a friendly unit is not coherent at the end of a turn, you must remove models in the unit from play, one at a time, until it is coherent (see 1.3.3).

15.3 BATTLESHOCK PHASE COMMAND ABILITIES

You can use the following command abilities in the battleshock phase:

Inspiring Presence: *The stoic leaders of these mighty warriors never falter, inspiring their comrades to fight no matter the odds.*

You can use this command ability at the start of the battleshock phase. The unit that receives the command does not have to take battleshock tests in that phase.

16.0 END OF BATTLE ROUND

The **end of the battle round** is reached once the battleshock phase of the player taking the second turn has finished. The players must then check the battlepack they are using to see if the battle ends or if any special actions must be carried out. If the battle did not end, all command points that the players have remaining are lost and a new battle round begins.

If a slain model is returned to its unit in the same turn that it is slain, it still counts as having been slain in that battle round for the purposes of battleshock tests.

Two models from this unit of Gutrippaz, with a Bravery characteristic of 5, have been slain. A battleshock roll of 3 is made for the unit, and 2 is added to the roll. The modified roll is not greater than 5, so no models flee.

Terrain is represented by
scenery pieces, while the
warriors in your army are
represented by *models*. A
group of one or more scenery
pieces is a *terrain feature*, and
a group of one or more models
is a *unit*.

*Terrain that is too small to
have an effect on a battle, or
is otherwise inconsequential,
is called **scattered terrain**.
Its use is purely decorative,
and you can ignore it when
moving units, making attacks
or checking visibility.*

*A list of the scenery pieces we
make for Warhammer Age of
Sigmar and the scenery rules
that apply to them can be
found at warhammer.com.*

17.0 TERRAIN

The terrain over which a battle takes place is represented by
scenery pieces from the Warhammer Age of Sigmar range called
terrain features. The battlepack you are using will tell you how to set
up terrain features (see 28.0), and the rules for movement explain how
models can move over and onto terrain features (see 9.3). Terrain features
cannot be picked as the target of an attack unless noted otherwise.

17.0.1 WHOLLY ON TERRAIN

Sometimes a rule will require you to determine if a model is **wholly on**
a terrain feature. A model is wholly on a terrain feature if its base is
touching the terrain feature and no part of its base extends beyond the
edge of the terrain feature. If a model does not have a base, it is wholly
on a terrain feature if it is touching the terrain feature and no part of the
model extends beyond the edge of the terrain feature.

17.0.2 BEHIND TERRAIN

A target unit is considered to be **behind** a terrain feature if all of the
following criteria are met:

- The target unit is more than 3" from the attacking unit.
- All of the models in the target unit are within 1" of a terrain feature.
- It is impossible for the attacker to draw a straight line from the closest
  point of a model in the attacking unit to the closest point of a model in
  the target unit without that line passing across a terrain feature.

17.0.2 FACTION TERRAIN

Faction terrain is a special type of terrain that is taken as part of an army.
A **faction terrain feature** has a faction terrain warscroll (see 23.0), which
will tell you how it is set up and what additional rules apply to it.

17.1 SCENERY RULES

Terrain features have one or more **scenery rules**. The scenery rules
for a terrain feature are determined by its size and appearance as
described below.

17.1.1 COVER

A target unit is in **cover** if all of the models in the unit are wholly on a
terrain feature or behind a terrain feature. Add 1 to save rolls for attacks
that target a unit that is in cover. A unit that has a Wounds characteristic
of 10 or more or that has made a charge move in the same turn
does not receive the benefit of being in cover.

*The unit by the terrain feature is in cover from the
model in front of it but not from the model to its side.*

*The model on the left is not wholly on the terrain feature
because its base overlaps the edge of the terrain feature.*

17.1.2 DEFENSIBLE TERRAIN

Defensible terrain features are structures that it is possible for entire units to enter and defend, such as intact buildings or fortifications like towers or bastions. Defensible terrain features can be garrisoned (see 17.2). You cannot move models over a defensible terrain feature unless the model can fly, and you cannot move a model onto a defensible terrain feature (even if it can fly) unless it is garrisoning the terrain feature.

17.1.3 LARGE AND VERY LARGE TERRAIN

Terrain features that are extremely big are referred to as **large** or **very large** terrain features. A terrain feature that is more than 12" and up to 19" across at its widest point is a large terrain feature. A terrain feature that is more than 19" across at its widest point is a very large terrain feature.

Large and very large defensible terrain features can be garrisoned by more models than normal defensible terrain features (see 17.2). In addition, if the battlepack you are using for a battle specifies the number of terrain features that you can set up on the battlefield, then each large terrain feature counts as 2 terrain features towards the number of terrain features on the battlefield, and each very large terrain feature counts as 4 terrain features towards the number of terrain features on the battlefield.

17.1.4 WYLDWOOD TERRAIN

Forests and woods in games of Warhammer Age of Sigmar are called **wyldwoods**. Targets that lie within them are concealed from sight by thick foliage. If the scenery pieces that make up a wyldwood terrain feature are formed into a circle with an area of open ground inside the circle, then the area of open ground inside the circle is considered to be part of the wyldwood terrain feature.

Visibility between 2 models is blocked if a straight line 1mm wide drawn between the closest points of the 2 models passes across more than 3" of a wyldwood terrain feature. Visibility to or from models with a Wounds characteristic of 10 or more is not blocked by wyldwood terrain features.

This unit is wholly on the wyldwood because the open ground enclosed by the wyldwood scenery pieces is treated as being part of the terrain feature.

If restrictions preclude any of the models in a unit from garrisoning a defensible terrain feature, then that unit cannot garrison it.

A friendly unit can garrison a defensible terrain feature that is within 3" of an enemy model as long as the terrain feature is not being garrisoned by the enemy.

A model in a garrison can still do anything it could do if it were on the battlefield, apart from moving. For example, it can cast spells, issue commands, and so on. When it does so, measure the range and visibility from the terrain feature.

A defensible terrain feature that has been demolished is left on the battlefield. It can no longer be garrisoned but models can move onto and across it.

Most defensible terrain features include areas upon which models can stand. Garrisoning models can be placed on these areas but are treated as being in the garrison for rules purposes.

17.2 GARRISONS

Units can **garrison** defensible terrain features (see 17.1.2). Up to 60 models can garrison a very large terrain feature, up to 30 models can garrison a large terrain feature, and up to 15 models can garrison other defensible terrain features. Models with a Wounds characteristic of 10 or more cannot garrison terrain features. Units and models garrisoning a terrain feature are in that terrain feature's garrison.

17.2.1 JOINING A GARRISON

During deployment, a friendly unit can be set up in a defensible terrain feature's garrison if the terrain feature is wholly within an area in which friendly units can be set up. In addition, a friendly unit can garrison a defensible terrain feature instead of making a normal move if all of the models in the unit are within 6" of the terrain feature and no enemy models are in the terrain feature's garrison. Units that garrison a terrain feature are removed from the battlefield and are assumed to be 'inside' the terrain feature. Friendly units must treat terrain features that are being garrisoned by enemy units as if they were enemy models.

Subtract 1 from hit rolls and add 1 to save rolls for attacks that target a unit in a garrison. The range and visibility to and from models in the unit are determined using the terrain feature instead of the models themselves.

17.2.2 LEAVING A GARRISON

A friendly unit in a garrison can **leave** the garrison at the end of your movement phase. If it does so, set it up so that all models in the unit are within 6" of the terrain feature and more than 3" from all enemy units. A unit cannot join and leave a garrison in the same turn.

17.2.3 DEMOLISH

Sometimes a rule will allow you to **demolish** a defensible terrain feature. When a defensible terrain feature is demolished, all units garrisoning it must leave and it is no longer treated as defensible. If a defensible terrain feature is being garrisoned when it is demolished, roll a dice for each model in the garrison. On a 1, that model is slain. The surviving models from the garrison must then be set up within 6" of the terrain feature and more than 3" from all enemy units.

18.0 OBJECTIVES

Battles are fought to gain control of vitally important locations. These locations are called **objectives** and each is usually indicated with an **objective marker**.

18.1 OBJECTIVE MARKERS

The battleplan being used for a battle will show or explain how objectives are placed (see 28.2.3). When measuring distances to and from objectives, always measure to and from the centre of the objective marker. If an objective is placed on the border between two territories, it is considered to be within both of them.

18.1.1 OBJECTIVE MARKER CONTROL

After set-up is complete but before the first battle round begins, each player gains **control** of all objectives that are within 6" of any friendly models and more than 6" from all enemy models. In addition, at the end of each turn (after the battleshock phase), you must check to see if you have gained control of any objectives. To do so, you must count the number of friendly models that are **contesting** each objective (see 18.1.2). You gain control of an objective if there are more friendly models contesting it than enemy models. Once you gain control of an objective, it remains under your control until your opponent gains control of it.

18.1.2 CONTESTING OBJECTIVES

A model must be within 6" of an objective in order to contest it. If a friendly unit has models within 6" of two or more objectives, you must pick 1 of those objectives for the models from that unit to contest. Unless noted otherwise, each **MONSTER** counts as 5 models for the purposes of contesting objectives, and each model with a Wounds characteristic of 5 or more that is not a **MONSTER** counts as 2 models for the purposes of contesting objectives.

18.2 TERRAIN CONTROL

Sometimes a battleplan will require that you gain control of a terrain feature. Defensible terrain features are controlled by the player who has any units garrisoning them (if a defensible terrain feature is not being garrisoned, then neither player controls it). Other types of terrain feature are controlled in the same manner as an objective (see 18.1.1), except that friendly models must be within 3" of a part of the terrain feature to contest it, instead of needing to be within 6" of its centre.

The Stormcast Eternals control the objective. They count as having 12 models within 6" of the objective because the Lord-Celestant on Stardrake counts as 5 models and the Knight-Arcanum counts as 2 models.

An objective marker is simply an object, such as a coin or an appropriate miniature, that you use to mark the location of an objective on the battlefield. It is perfectly acceptable to move the marker to one side as long as you measure distances to the objective using the marker's original location.

If the way in which terrain features have been set up means that an objective has to be placed on a terrain feature, the objective marker is placed so that it stays in the indicated position horizontally but is as close to the battlefield as possible vertically. For example, if the location where you are required to place an objective is occupied by a multi-level ruin, the objective marker would need to be placed on the lowest level of that ruin.

*If a model has an ability that allows it to count as more than 1 model when contesting an objective, you must use that ability instead of counting it as 5 models if it is a **MONSTER** or 2 models if it is not a **MONSTER** but has a Wounds characteristic of 5 or more.*

Sometimes an ability will allow a model that is not a WIZARD to attempt to cast or unbind spells. These models do so using the following rules and are affected by abilities that modify casting and unbinding rolls, but they are not WIZARDS for other rules purposes.

19.0 WIZARDS

A unit with the WIZARD keyword on its warscroll is a WIZARD. You can use a friendly WIZARD to cast spells that they know in your hero phase and to unbind spells in the enemy hero phase. The number of spells you can attempt to cast or unbind with a WIZARD is noted on their warscroll (see 22.0). All WIZARDS know the Arcane Bolt and Mystic Shield spells (see 19.2). In addition, a WIZARD knows all of the spells on their warscroll and on the warscrolls of endless spells (see 19.3) in the same army as them.

19.1 CASTING SPELLS

In your hero phase, you can attempt to cast spells with friendly WIZARDS. You cannot attempt to cast the same spell more than once in the same hero phase, even with a different WIZARD. In order to attempt to cast a spell, pick a friendly WIZARD, say which of the spells that they know will be attempted, and then make a casting roll by rolling 2D6. If the casting roll is equal to or greater than the casting value of the spell, the spell is successfully cast.

19.1.1 MISCASTS

On an unmodified casting roll of 2, the spell is miscast. The spell is not successfully cast, the caster suffers D3 mortal wounds, and the caster cannot attempt to cast any more spells in that hero phase.

19.1.2 UNBINDING SPELLS

If a spell is successfully cast, your opponent can pick 1 of their WIZARDS that is within 30" of the caster to attempt to unbind the spell before its effects are applied. In order to attempt to unbind a spell, first say which WIZARD will attempt to unbind it. Then make an unbinding roll by rolling 2D6. If the unbinding roll is greater than the roll used to cast the spell, then the spell is unbound and its effects are not applied. The number of spells a WIZARD can attempt to unbind is noted on their warscroll. Only 1 unbinding attempt can be made for each spell.

19.2 SPELLS

The first sentence of a spell will always list the casting value of the spell. It will also list the range of the spell if it has one. The rest of the rule is the effect of the spell.

All spells have a casting value followed by an effect. In addition, a spell may have a range. The effect of the spell is treated in the same way as an effect of an ability for rules purposes (see 1.6).

The range of a spell is always measured from the caster.

Arcane Bolt: *The caster calls forth a ball of crackling arcane energy that hovers above their outstretched hand, ready to be hurled at a foe.*

Arcane Bolt is a spell that has a casting value of 5 and a range of 12". If successfully cast, at the start of any 1 phase before your next hero phase, you can pick 1 enemy unit within range and visible to the caster. That unit suffers 1 mortal wound. If that unit is within 3" of the caster, it suffers D3 mortal wounds instead of 1.

Mystic Shield: *The caster conjures up a shield of shimmering energy to protect themselves or an ally from harm.*

Mystic Shield is a spell that has a casting value of 5 and a range of 12". If successfully cast, pick 1 friendly unit wholly within range and visible to the caster. Add 1 to save rolls for attacks that target that unit until your next hero phase.

19.3 ENDLESS SPELLS

An **endless spell** is a magical entity that is **summoned** to the battlefield by casting the spell on its **endless spell warscroll** (see 24.0). Unless noted otherwise, an endless spell cannot be attacked or be affected by abilities. You can move models across or through an endless spell as if it were not there, but you cannot finish a model's move on an endless spell.

19.3.1 SUMMONING ENDLESS SPELLS

In your hero phase, you can attempt to **summon** 1 endless spell with each friendly **WIZARD**. When the spell used to summon an endless spell is successfully cast and not unbound, the endless spell is set up on the battlefield as described on its warscroll. If any restrictions make it impossible to set up the endless spell, the casting attempt is unsuccessful.

19.3.2 DISPELLING ENDLESS SPELLS

At the start of the hero phase, each player can attempt to **dispel** 1 endless spell with each friendly **WIZARD** and friendly **PRIEST**. The player whose turn is taking place makes all of their dispelling attempts first. If a **WIZARD** attempts to dispel an endless spell, they can attempt to cast or unbind 1 fewer spell in that hero phase. If a **PRIEST** attempts to dispel an endless spell, they can chant 1 fewer prayer in that hero phase. The same player cannot attempt to dispel the same endless spell more than once per phase.

To attempt to dispel an endless spell, pick 1 endless spell that is within 30" of a friendly **WIZARD** or friendly **PRIEST** and that is visible to them. Then make a **dispelling roll** by rolling 2D6. If the roll is greater than the casting value of that endless spell, it is **dispelled** and removed from play. An endless spell cannot be summoned again in the turn that it is removed from play.

19.3.3 REMOVING ENDLESS SPELLS

An endless spell remains in play until it is removed from play. An endless spell is removed from play if:

a) The endless spell is dispelled.
b) The endless spell touches the edge of the battlefield after it is moved.
c) A method on the endless spell's warscroll is used to remove it from play.

19.4 UNITS OF WIZARDS

WIZARDS are usually units consisting of a single model. If a unit with the **WIZARD** keyword has more than 1 model, it counts as a single **WIZARD** for rules purposes and you must pick 1 model in the unit with which to cast or unbind a spell before you attempt to cast or unbind it. Determine the range and visibility for the attempt using that model.

The battlepack you are using will tell you if you can include endless spells in your army. The endless spells you include in your army are not set up until they have been summoned.

*You cannot attempt to summon more than 1 endless spell with the same **WIZARD** in the same turn, even if they are allowed to attempt to cast more than 1 spell per hero phase.*

*The spell used to summon an endless spell is still a spell for rules purposes. It therefore counts as 1 of the spells a **WIZARD** is allowed to attempt to cast in your hero phase.*

After an endless spell is removed from play, it can be summoned again if the spell on its warscroll is successfully cast in a different hero phase (it cannot be set up on the turn it is removed).

The distance a predatory endless spell can move will be noted on its warscroll. Some predatory endless spells can fly; this too will be noted on its warscroll. An endless spell is moved in the same way as a model, unless noted otherwise.

19.5 PREDATORY ENDLESS SPELLS

Many endless spells are immobile, and once summoned, they remain in the same location. However, some can move across the battlefield. These are noted on their warscroll as being a **predatory endless spell**. Predatory endless spells are moved at the end of the hero phase. If either player has any abilities that can be used at the end of the hero phase, they must be used after all predatory endless spells have been moved.

19.5.1 PREDATORY ENDLESS SPELL CONTROL

Before moving predatory endless spells, you must first determine which are **controlled** and which are **wild**. A predatory endless spell within 30" of the model that summoned it is controlled by that model. A **WIZARD** can control 1 predatory endless spell per hero phase. If there is more than 1 predatory endless spell that a friendly **WIZARD** could control, you must pick which they will control. Predatory endless spells that are not controlled are wild.

19.5.2 MOVING PREDATORY ENDLESS SPELLS

After determining control of predatory endless spells, the player whose turn is taking place moves all of the predatory endless spells controlled by friendly **WIZARDS**. Their opponent then does the same. Once all controlled predatory endless spells have been moved, the players alternate picking 1 wild predatory endless spell to move, starting with the player whose turn is taking place, until all of the wild predatory endless spells have been moved. A player must pick a wild predatory endless spell to move if any are eligible to do so and cannot pick a wild predatory endless spell that has already moved in that phase.

When a player picks a predatory endless spell to move, they are considered to be the commanding player of that predatory endless spell until the start of the next hero phase. All other endless spells are under the command of the player that summoned them.

20.0 PRIESTS

A unit with the **PRIEST** keyword on its warscroll is a **PRIEST**. Each friendly **PRIEST** can **chant** 1 prayer that they **know** in your hero phase. All **PRIESTS** know the **Bless** and **Smite** prayers. In addition, a **PRIEST** knows all prayers on their warscroll and on the warscrolls of invocations (see 20.3) in the same army as them.

20.1 CHANTING PRAYERS

In your hero phase, you can **chant** prayers with friendly **PRIESTS**. You cannot chant the same prayer more than once in the same hero phase, even with a different **PRIEST**. In order to chant a prayer, pick a friendly **PRIEST**, say which of the prayers that they know will be chanted, and then make a **chanting roll** by rolling a dice. If the chanting roll is equal to or greater than the **answer value** of the prayer, the prayer is **answered**.

20.1.1 DIVINE WRATH

On an unmodified chanting roll of 1, the chanting **PRIEST** suffers **divine wrath**. The prayer is not answered and the chanting **PRIEST** suffers 1 mortal wound.

20.2 PRAYERS

All prayers have an **answer value** followed by an **effect**. In addition, a prayer may have a **range**. The effect of the prayer is treated in the same way as an effect of an ability for rules purposes (see 1.6).

Bless: *The priest calls upon the gods to protect the faithful.*

Bless is a prayer that has an answer value of 4 and a range of 12". If answered, pick 1 friendly unit wholly within range and visible to the chanter. Until the start of your next hero phase, that unit has a ward of 6+.

Smite: *The priest calls upon the gods to vanquish a heretic.*

Smite is a prayer that has an answer value of 2 and a range of 48". If answered, pick 1 enemy **PRIEST** within range and visible to the chanter. That enemy **PRIEST** suffers 1 mortal wound. If the chanting roll was 6 or more, that enemy **PRIEST** suffers D3 mortal wounds instead of 1.

20.3 INVOCATIONS

An **invocation** is a divine entity that is **summoned** to the battlefield by chanting the prayer on its **invocation warscroll** (see 24.0). Unless noted otherwise, an invocation cannot be attacked or be affected by abilities. You can move models across or through an invocation as if it were not there, but you cannot finish a model's move on an invocation. Invocations are under the command of the player who summoned them.

20.3.1 SUMMONING INVOCATIONS

In your hero phase, you can attempt to **summon** 1 invocation with each friendly **PRIEST**. When the prayer used to summon the invocation is answered, the invocation is set up on the battlefield as described on its warscroll. If any restrictions make it impossible to set up the invocation, then the prayer is not answered.

20.3.2 BANISHING INVOCATIONS

At the start of your hero phase, you can attempt to **banish** 1 invocation with each friendly **PRIEST** instead of chanting a prayer with that **PRIEST** in that hero phase. The same player cannot attempt to banish the same invocation more than once per phase.

To attempt to banish an invocation, pick 1 invocation within 48" of a friendly **PRIEST** that is visible to them. Then make a **banishment roll** by rolling a dice. If the roll is greater than the answer value of that invocation, it is **banished** and removed from play. An invocation cannot be summoned again in the turn that it is removed from play.

20.3.3 REMOVING INVOCATIONS

An invocation remains in play until it is removed from play. An invocation is removed from play if:

a) The invocation is banished.
b) The invocation touches the edge of the battlefield after it is moved.
c) A method on the invocation's warscroll or in an allegiance ability is used to remove it from play.

The range of a prayer is always measured from the chanter.

PRIESTS can attempt to dispel endless spells and banish invocations, but WIZARDS can only attempt to dispel endless spells.

21.0 MONSTERS

A unit with the **MONSTER** keyword on its warscroll is a **MONSTER**.

21.1 MONSTROUS RAMPAGE

At the end of the charge phase, each player can carry out 1 **monstrous rampage** from the table below with each friendly **MONSTER**. The player whose turn is taking place carries out all of their monstrous rampages first. The same player cannot carry out the same monstrous rampage more than once per phase. The effect of the monstrous rampage is treated in the same way as the effect of an ability for rules purposes (see 1.6).

*Because you cannot carry out the same monstrous rampage more than once in the same phase, this means that you can carry out a maximum of 4 monstrous rampages per phase (if you have enough **MONSTERS** in your army).*

MONSTROUS RAMPAGES

 Roar: Pick 1 enemy unit within 3" of this model and roll a dice. On a 3+, that unit cannot issue or receive commands in the following combat phase.

 Stomp: Pick 1 enemy unit within 3" of this model that is not a **MONSTER** and roll a dice. On a 2+, that unit suffers D3 mortal wounds.

 Titanic Duel: Pick 1 enemy **MONSTER** within 3" of this model. Add 1 to hit rolls for attacks made by this model that target that enemy **MONSTER** until the end of the following combat phase.

 Smash To Rubble: Pick 1 faction terrain feature or defensible terrain feature within 3" of this model and roll a dice. On a 3+, the terrain feature is demolished if it was defensible (see 17.2.3), and the scenery rules on its warscroll cannot be used for the rest of the battle if it was a faction terrain feature.

The Monstrous Rampage rules reflect the fact that the sheer mass of some creatures is a weapon in itself. Some of these Ungors will surely be trampled by this Bastiladon if it thunders into them!

22.0 WARSCROLLS

Every set of Citadel Miniatures in the Warhammer Age of Sigmar range has its own **warscroll**, which provides you with all of the information needed to use those miniatures as a unit in a game.

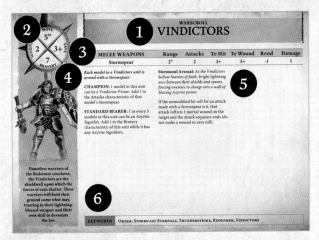

22.1 NAME AND TYPE

Every warscroll has a **name** at the top, which corresponds to the name of the models used to make up the unit. Units that use the same warscroll are all considered to be of the same **type**.

22.2 CHARACTERISTICS

Warscrolls contain a set of **characteristics** that are referred to in the rules and that determine how the model can be used in the game.

22.2.1 CHARACTERISTIC MODIFIERS

Modifiers can never reduce a characteristic to less than 0.

22.2.2 REND MODIFIERS

While most modifiers add to or subtract from a characteristic, the Rend characteristic is **improved** or **worsened**. Modifiers can never make the Rend characteristic worse than '-'.

22.2.3 SAVE OF '-'

A Save characteristic of '-' means that you must roll a 7 or more when making a save roll for the unit. In most cases this will be impossible, so no roll needs to be made, but sometimes modifiers will make a roll of 7 possible, in which case you can attempt to make the roll.

22.2.4 RANDOM CHARACTERISTICS

Sometimes, the Move, Range, Attacks or Damage characteristics on a warscroll will show a **random characteristic roll** instead of a fixed value. When this is the case, the value of the characteristic is generated each time you need to use the characteristic, as described below. If a modifier applies to a random characteristic, determine the value of the characteristic first and then apply the modifier to it.

Random Move: If you need to know the value of a random Move characteristic for a unit, make the random characteristic roll shown on the unit's warscroll. The roll is the Move characteristic for all models in that unit for the rest of that phase.

When we republish a warscroll, the new version takes precedence over all versions with an earlier publication date or no publication date.

1. Name
2. Characteristics (model)
3. Characteristics (weapons)
4. Description
5. Abilities
6. Keywords

If a characteristic says 'See below', the warscroll will include an ability that explains how to determine it or what to do instead of using that characteristic.

Example: A Rend characteristic of -1 that is improved by 1 becomes Rend -2. A Rend characteristic of -1 that is worsened by 1 becomes Rend '-'.

Apply modifiers that multiply or divide a value before applying modifiers that add to or subtract from a value.

Example: A unit's Move characteristic might be 2D6", or a weapon's Damage characteristic might be D3.

CORE RULES

If you are making multiple attacks with a random Attacks or Damage characteristic, generate the characteristics for each of the weapons separately and add them together.

Command models must be represented by the appropriate Citadel Miniatures. They are assumed to be armed with the same weapons as the other models in the unit unless noted otherwise, even if they are not shown on the model itself.

Wounds Suffered	Move
0-4	12"
5-8	11"
9-12	10"
13-16+	8"

Random Range: If you need to know the value of a random Range characteristic for a weapon being used by a unit, make the random characteristic roll shown on the unit's warscroll. The roll is the Range characteristic for all weapons of that type used by all models in that unit for the rest of that phase.

Random Attacks or Damage: If you need to know the value of a random Attacks or Damage characteristic for a weapon being used by a unit to make an attack, make the random characteristic roll shown on the unit's warscroll. The roll is the characteristic *for that attack*. If you need to know the value of a random Attacks or Damage characteristic for a weapon at a time other than when it is being used to make an attack, count it as having a value of 1.

22.3 DESCRIPTION
All warscrolls include a **description**, which will tell you what weapons the models in the unit are armed with. It may also include other important information, such as whether the unit is a **Wizard**.

22.3.1 MOUNTS, COMPANIONS AND CREW
Sometimes the description on a warscroll will say whether the models in the unit have **mounts**, **companions** or a **crew**. When a model attacks, its mount, companions and crew attack too, and when the model is removed from play, its mount, companions and crew are removed too. For rules purposes, companions and crew are treated in the same manner as mounts.

22.3.2 COMMAND MODELS
Some units can include uniquely named **champions**, **standard bearers** or **musicians**. These are known collectively as **command models** and the warscroll may include upgrades that apply only to them or abilities that can only be used if they are part of the unit.

22.3.3 WEAPON OPTIONS AND UPGRADES
Many warscrolls allow **weapon options** or **upgrades** to be taken by '1 in every x' models. When this is the case, if the unit has fewer than 'x' models, the weapon or upgrade cannot be taken.

22.4 ABILITIES
Most warscrolls include one or more **abilities** (see 1.6). You must use the rules on a unit's warscroll if the unit is part of your army. The abilities section will also include information about any command abilities or magic the unit can use.

22.5 DAMAGE TABLES
Some warscrolls have a **damage table** that is used to determine one or more values for a model, such as the characteristics of the model and the weapons it uses or the values for abilities on its warscroll. Look up the number of wounds that are currently allocated to the model to determine the value in question.

22.6 KEYWORDS
Every warscroll includes a list of **keywords** that apply to the unit the warscroll describes and to each of the models in the unit (see 1.3.2). Sometimes you will be allowed to give a keyword to a unit for a battle. If you do so, treat the unit as having that keyword on its warscroll for the duration of the battle.

102

23.0 FACTION TERRAIN WARSCROLLS

The information needed to use a faction terrain feature in a battle is found on its **faction terrain warscroll**.

23.1 NAME

Every faction terrain warscroll has a **name** at the top, which corresponds to the name of the scenery piece or combination of scenery pieces that represent the terrain feature.

23.2 SET-UP

All faction terrain warscrolls include **set-up** instructions. These will tell you if the terrain feature consists of a single scenery piece or multiple scenery pieces, and how to set them up on the battlefield. The set-up instructions may also contain other important information that tells you how to use the faction terrain feature in a game.

23.3 SCENERY RULES

Faction terrain warscrolls include a list of **scenery rules** that the terrain feature has in addition to any other scenery rules that it may have. The effect of a scenery rule is treated in the same way as the effect of an ability for rules purposes (see 1.6).

24.0 ENDLESS SPELL AND INVOCATION WARSCROLLS

The information needed to use an endless spell in a battle is found on its **endless spell warscroll**. Similarly, the information needed to use an invocation in a battle is found on its **invocation warscroll**.

24.1 NAME

Every endless spell warscroll and invocation warscroll has a **name** at the top, which corresponds to the name of the miniature or combination of miniatures that represent the endless spell or invocation.

24.2 PARTS

This will tell you if the endless spell or invocation is made up of more than one **part**. Each part will have its own base and all of the parts together are considered to be a single endless spell or invocation. The warscroll will explain how the different parts must be set up.

24.3 SUMMONING

This entry on the warscroll lists the spell or prayer that is used to summon that endless spell or invocation.

24.4 ABILITIES

Endless spell and invocation warscrolls include **abilities** that apply to that endless spell or invocation.

1. Name
2. Set-up
3. Scenery Rules

1. Name
2. Parts
3. Summoning
4. Abilities

The effects of endless spell and invocation abilities are not the same as the effects of spells or prayers. Therefore, abilities that allow a unit to ignore the effects of spells or prayers will not work on them. For example, an artefact of power that allows the bearer to ignore the effects of spells will not allow them to ignore the effects of endless spell abilities.

When we republish a set of Pitched Battle profiles, the new version takes precedence over versions with an earlier publication date or no publication date.

1. Faction
2. Type
3. Unit Size
4. Points
5. Battlefield Role
6. Notes

The Pitched Battle profile for Liberators can be found in the table for the Stormcast Eternals faction.

During a battle, if a unit is at its maximum unit size, no further models can be added to it and any that would be added to it are removed from play.

25.0 PITCHED BATTLE PROFILES

Every unit in Warhammer Age of Sigmar has a **Pitched Battle profile**. Pitched battle profiles can be found in the latest 'Pitched Battle Profiles' book, and each battletome has the Pitched Battle profiles for all of the units found in it. You will need the Pitched Battle profiles when you pick your army (see 1.4).

① STORMCAST ETERNALS					
WARSCROLL	UNIT SIZE	POINTS	BATTLEFIELD ROLE	**⑥**	NOTES
Vindictors	5	140	Battleline		
Yndrasta, the Celestial Spear	1	300	Leader		Single, Unique
Knight-Arcanum	1	150	Leader		Single
Knight-Vexillor with Banner of Apotheosis	1	125	Leader		Single
Lord-Imperatant	1	160	Leader		Single
Annihilators	3	190			
Praetors	3	155			

(Diagram callouts: ② by WARSCROLL column, ③ by UNIT SIZE column, ④ by POINTS column, ⑤ by BATTLEFIELD ROLE column)

25.1 FACTION

Pitched battle profiles are organised into tables, each of which contains the Pitched Battle profiles for one **faction** (see 1.1).

25.2 TYPE

The first entry in a Pitched Battle profile lists the **type** of unit that the Pitched Battle profile is for (see 22.1).

25.3 UNIT SIZE

These entries list the minimum number of models a unit must have. When you select a unit to be part of your army, you must take it at the minimum unit size unless it can be taken as an **understrength** unit or a **reinforced** unit (see below).

25.3.1 UNDERSTRENGTH UNITS

An **understrength** unit is one that has fewer models than its minimum unit size.

25.3.2 REINFORCED UNITS

A **reinforced** unit has twice as many models as its minimum unit size. If you can include reinforced units in your army, you can reinforce units with the Battleline battlefield role twice. A unit that is **reinforced twice** has 3 times as many models as its minimum unit size and counts as 2 units towards the number of reinforced units you can include in your army. If the description for a unit says that it is a single model, it cannot be reinforced.

25.4 POINTS VALUE

This entry lists the **points value** of a unit with this Pitched Battle profile. Points are used in some battlepacks when picking an army. For example, a battlepack may say you can take units in your army with a combined value of 1,000 points.

When this is the case, spending the appropriate number of points on a unit allows you to take 1 unit of that type, with any of the optional upgrades to which it is entitled and that you wish to take. If you take a reinforced unit, double the points value of the unit. If you take a unit that has been reinforced twice, triple the points value of the unit. If you take an understrength unit, you still have to pay the points value of a unit that has the minimum number of models.

25.5 BATTLEFIELD ROLES

Some units are assigned one or more **battlefield roles**, which appear in this entry on their Pitched Battle profile. Sometimes a battlepack or battleplan will limit the number of units with a specific battlefield role that you can take or require you to take a unit with a specific battlefield role. For example, a battlepack might say you must have at least 1 unit with the Leader battlefield role and cannot have more than 3 units with the Behemoth battlefield role.

25.5.1 CONDITIONAL BATTLEFIELD ROLES

Sometimes, the Notes column on a Pitched Battle profile will tell you to change the battlefield role of units of that type if certain conditions are met. For example, choosing a certain model to be your general can mean the battlefield role of certain units changes to Battleline. Where this is the case, unless noted otherwise, the unit loses all of the battlefield roles in the Battlefield Role column of its Pitched Battle profile and just has the battlefield role specified in the Notes column instead.

A unit that has a conditional battlefield role keeps it for the entire battle, even if the conditions that required it to have that battlefield role in the first place change during the battle (your general is slain, for example).

25.6 NOTES

This entry contains any special rules that apply if you want to take a unit that uses this Pitched Battle profile in your army.

25.6.1 UNIQUE AND SINGLE

If the Pitched Battle profile for a unit says '**Unique**' in the Notes column, it means that you cannot include more than 1 unit of that type in your army. If it says '**Single**', then units of that type cannot be reinforced.

25.7 TERRAIN, ENDLESS SPELLS AND INVOCATIONS

The Pitched Battle profiles table for a faction also includes the faction terrain, endless spells and invocations that are part of that faction (if there are any).

25.8 ALLIES

Below a faction's Pitched Battle profiles table, you will find a list of **allies** that can be taken in an army from that faction (see 27.1). The allies list will detail which factions you can take allied units from and any restrictions that apply to their use. Allied units cannot be generals.

Example: Royal Terrorgheists in a Flesh-eater Courts army from the Gristlegore subfaction become Battleline units. They are no longer Behemoth units as noted in the Battlefield Role column on their Pitched Battle profile.

26.0 BATTALIONS

Battalions are formations of specific units that give you access to additional abilities. There are two types of battalion: **warscroll battalions** and **core battalions**. The battlepack you are using will say whether you can use battalions and which types of battalion you can use. Battalions are picked after you have picked the units for your army.

1. Name
2. Organisation
3. Unit Icon
4. Ability
5. Ability Icon

Warscroll Battalion   Core Battalion

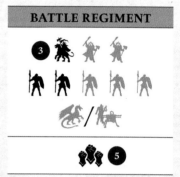

26.1 ORGANISATION

Usually, a unit can only belong to one battalion. However, some very large battalions include other, smaller battalions. In this case, it is possible for a unit to belong to two different battalions at the same time.

Each battalion is made up of units from your army and can only be taken if the appropriate units from your army are available. The **organisation** section lists the units that can or must be included in the battalion.

In a warscroll battalion, the units are listed by unit type or keyword. For example, '1 Liberators unit' means a unit that uses the Liberators warscroll, while '1 **PALADIN** unit' means a unit that has the **PALADIN** keyword on its warscroll.

In a core battalion, the units are listed by **unit icon**. Refer to the key on the right to see which units are indicated by which unit icons. Units that must be included are indicated by **mandatory** unit icons, while units that can be taken are indicated by **optional** unit icons.

26.2 BATTALION ABILITIES

Each battalion has one or more **battalion abilities**. Battalion abilities are used in the same way as abilities on a warscroll (see 1.6).

The abilities for a warscroll battalion appear on the battalion's warscroll. The abilities for a core battalion are listed by **battalion ability icon**. Refer to the key on the right to see which battalion abilities are indicated by which battalion ability icon. If several battalion ability icons are separated by a '/', you must pick which of those abilities the battalion has when you take the battalion for your army.

26.2.1 ONE-DROP DEPLOYMENT

The only battalions that can use the one-drop deployment rule are core battalions that have the Unified battalion ability icon.

If a core battalion has the **Unified** icon (see right), then after you set up a unit from the battalion, you must set up **_all_** of the other units from the battalion, one after the other, and you are not allowed to set up units that are not part of the battalion until all of the units in the battalion have been set up. In addition, if the set-up instructions for a battle say that the players must alternate setting up units one at a time, then after you set up a unit from the battalion, you must set up **_all_** of the other units from the battalion, one after the other, before your opponent is allowed to set up another unit.

26.3 CORE BATTALIONS

You can include any of the following core battalions in your army if the battlepack you are using says that you can use core battalions.

WARLORD	BATTLE REGIMENT	GRAND BATTERY

VANGUARD	LINEBREAKER	COMMAND ENTOURAGE

UNIT ICONS
(Mandatory/Optional)

 Commander: Leader

 Sub-commander: Leader with a Wounds characteristic of less than 10

Troops: Unit that is not Leader, Artillery or Behemoth

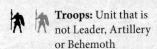 **Artillery:** Artillery

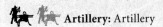 **Monster:** Behemoth that is not Leader

BATTALION ABILITY ICONS

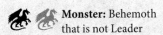 **Unified:** One-drop Deployment (see 26.2.1).

Expert: Once per battle, 1 unit from this battalion can receive the All-out Attack or All-out Defence command without the command being issued and without a command point being spent.

Magnificent: When you pick enhancements for your army (see 27.3), you can pick 1 extra enhancement.

Slayers: Once per battle, 1 unit from this battalion can receive the All-out Attack or Unleash Hell command without the command being issued and without a command point being spent.

Strategists: Once per battle, when you receive command points at the start of your hero phase, you can receive 1 extra command point.

Swift: Once per battle, 1 unit from this battalion can receive the At the Double or Forward to Victory command without the command being issued and without a command point being spent.

An army that is made up of two or more factions (not including allies) cannot use allegiance abilities, unless noted otherwise.

If all of the units in your army are from the Stormcast Eternals faction, then your army is known as a 'Stormcast Eternals' army. Likewise, if all of the units in your army are from the Ossiarch Bonereapers faction, your army is known as an 'Ossiarch Bonereapers army', and so on.

If you pick a subfaction for your army, your army is still considered to be an army from the faction that the subfaction is part of. For example, if you pick the Hammers of Sigmar subfaction for your army, your army is both a Stormcast Eternals army and a Hammers of Sigmar army.

If a rule forces you to give an enhancement to a Unique unit, the unit cannot use it during the battle and it has no effect.

27.0 ALLEGIANCE ABILITIES

If all of the units in your army are from a single faction, then you can use that faction's **allegiance abilities**. Allegiance abilities are split into two types: **battle traits** and **enhancements**. Sets of allegiance abilities are included in the battletomes published for Warhammer Age of Sigmar, and a set of **universal enhancements** that can be used by any army are included in section 27.5.

27.1 ALLIED UNITS

1 in 4 units in your army can be allies (see 25.8). Allied units are ignored when determining if the units in the army are from a single faction.

27.2 BATTLE TRAITS

Most **battle traits** are abilities that can be used by all or some of the units in the army. However, many battle traits have other effects, such as changing the way the player picks their army or allowing the player to summon new units mid-battle.

27.2.1 SUBFACTIONS

Some factions contain one or more **subfactions**. The battle traits for the faction will tell you how or if you can pick a subfaction for your army.

27.3 ENHANCEMENTS

Each set of allegiance abilities includes a number of **enhancements** that are given to specific units in an army. Enhancements are divided into **command traits**, **artefacts of power**, **spell lores**, **prayer scriptures**, **mount traits**, **triumphs** and one or more sets of **unique enhancements**.

Enhancements are picked after you have chosen the battalions for your army (see 26.0). You can always take 1 enhancement of each type for your army, and the battalions or battlepack you are using may allow you to take additional enhancements for your army.

27.3.1 ENHANCEMENT RESTRICTIONS

Enhancements cannot be given to Unique units (see 25.6.1) or allied units, unless noted otherwise. In addition, artefacts of power and command traits that affect attacks made by friendly models do not affect attacks made by their mounts, unless noted otherwise.

27.3.2 COMMAND TRAITS

Each time you take a **command trait** enhancement, you can pick 1 command trait and give it to your general. You can never pick more than 1 command trait for your army, and command traits can only be given to a general that is a **Hero**.

27.3.3 ARTEFACTS OF POWER
Each time you take an **artefact of power** enhancement, you can pick 1 artefact of power and give it to a HERO in your army. A HERO cannot have more than 1 artefact of power.

27.3.4 SPELL LORES
Each time you take a **spell lore** enhancement, you can pick 1 spell for each WIZARD in your army from any of the spell lores available to that WIZARD (you can pick different spells from different spell lores for different WIZARDS). Each WIZARD knows the spell that you picked for them in addition to the other spells they know.

27.3.5 PRAYER SCRIPTURES
Each time you take a **prayer scripture** enhancement, you can pick 1 prayer for each PRIEST in your army from any of the prayer scriptures available to that PRIEST (you can pick different prayers from different prayer scriptures for different PRIESTS). Each PRIEST knows the prayer that you picked for them in addition to the other prayers they know.

27.3.6 TRIUMPHS
Each time you take a **triumph** enhancement, you can pick 1 triumph for your army. Each triumph you pick can be used only once per battle, and can only be used if the points total of your army is less than that of your opponent's army.

27.3.7 UNIQUE ENHANCEMENTS
Some sets of allegiance abilities include **unique enhancements**. Each set of unique enhancements will explain how they are used if you take one or more of them for your army.

27.4 SUBFACTION ALLEGIANCE ABILITIES
Sometimes the rules for a subfaction will give you access to a further set of allegiance abilities. If the allegiance abilities for a subfaction include a command trait and the general of your army has the keyword for that subfaction, then that command trait must be the one you give to your general. If the allegiance abilities for a subfaction include an artefact of power and any HEROES in your army have the keyword for that subfaction, then that artefact of power must be the first artefact of power given to one of those HEROES.

*Most rules for artefacts of power refer to the **bearer**. The bearer is the model to which an artefact of power has been given (see section 27.5.2 for some examples).*

Taking a spell lore enhancement allows <u>every</u> WIZARD in the army to know 1 spell from a spell lore.

Taking a prayer scripture enhancement allows <u>every</u> PRIEST in the army to know 1 prayer from a prayer scripture.

If you are allowed to take more than 1 triumph, you can pick the same triumph more than once if you wish.

Many factions in Warhammer Age of Sigmar are very large and diverse. For example, the Ossiarch Bonereapers are organised into different 'Legions', each with their own fighting styles, relics and idiosyncrasies. Subfaction allegiance abilities allow you to theme your army even further, should you wish, and to reflect these differences in your battles.

27.5 UNIVERSAL ENHANCEMENTS
The following enhancements can be used by any army.

27.5.1 UNIVERSAL COMMAND TRAITS
Battle-lust: *This general is always eager for combat.*

You can re-roll run rolls and charge rolls for this general.

Skilled Leader: *This general directs their forces with consummate skill.*

If this general is on the battlefield at the start of your hero phase, roll a dice. On a 5+, you receive 1 extra command point.

High Priest: *This general is a wise and experienced cleric.*

You can re-roll chanting rolls for this general.

Heroic Stature: *This mighty general towers over those under their command.*

Add 1 to this general's Wounds characteristic.

Master of Magic: *This general's knowledge of the arcane is unsurpassed.*

Once per hero phase, you can re-roll 1 casting roll, dispelling roll or unbinding roll for this general.

27.5.2 UNIVERSAL ARTEFACTS OF POWER
Amulet of Destiny: *This amulet subtly influences the fate of the one who bears it.*

The bearer has a ward of 5+.

Vial of Manticore Venom: *This potent venom can be applied to a weapon's edge, rendering it even deadlier.*

Pick 1 of the bearer's melee weapons. Add 1 to wound rolls for attacks made with that weapon.

Arcane Tome: *The pages of this ancient grimoire grant the bearer arcane power.*

The bearer becomes a **WIZARD** that knows the Arcane Bolt and Mystic Shield spells. They can attempt to cast 1 spell in your hero phase and attempt to unbind 1 spell in the enemy hero phase. If the bearer is already a **WIZARD**, they can attempt to cast 1 additional spell instead.

Seed of Rebirth: *This seed-shaped gem hails from Ghyran, the Realm of Life.*

You can re-roll heroic recovery rolls for the bearer.

27.5.3 UNIVERSAL SPELL LORE
Flaming Weapon: *One of the caster's weapons is engulfed by arcane fire.*

Flaming Weapon is a spell that has a casting value of 4. If successfully cast, pick 1 of the caster's melee weapons. Add 1 to Damage characteristic of that weapon until your next hero phase.

Levitate: *The spellcaster makes themselves or an ally lighter than air.*

Levitate is a spell that has a casting value of 8 and a range of 18". If successfully cast, pick 1 friendly unit wholly within range and visible to the caster. That unit can fly until your next hero phase.

Ghost-mist: *At the wizard's command, a thick pall of mist descends over a nearby area of the battlefield.*

Ghost-mist is a spell that has a casting value of 5 and a range of 6". If successfully cast, pick 1 terrain feature within range and visible to the caster. Until your next hero phase, visibility between 2 models is blocked if a straight line 1mm wide drawn between the closest points of the 2 models passes across more than 3" of that terrain feature. This effect does not block visibility to or from models with a Wounds characteristic of 10 or more.

27.5.4 UNIVERSAL PRAYER SCRIPTURE

Guidance: *The gods speak to their faithful, guiding them towards victory.*

Guidance is a prayer that has an answer value of 5. If answered, you receive 1 command point.

Heal: *The gods listen to the prayers of their followers, healing the wounds they have suffered.*

Heal is a prayer that has an answer value of 3 and a range of 12". If answered, pick 1 friendly model within range and visible to the chanter. You can heal up to D3 wounds allocated to that model.

Curse: *The priest calls upon the gods to render their enemies helpless before the battle zeal of the faithful.*

Curse is a prayer that has an answer value of 4 and a range of 9". If answered, pick 1 enemy unit within range and visible to the chanter. Until your next hero phase, if the unmodified hit roll for an attack that targets that unit is 6, that unit suffers 1 mortal wound in addition to any normal damage.

27.5.5 UNIVERSAL TRIUMPHS

Bloodthirsty: *Victory has made this army eager for the fight.*

Once per battle, after you make a charge roll for a friendly unit, you can say that it is bloodthirsty. If you do so, you can re-roll that charge roll.

Inspired: *The warriors of this army are filled with such conviction that they cut down their foes without pause or mercy.*

Once per battle, after you pick a friendly unit to shoot or fight, you can say that it is inspired. If you do so, add 1 to wound rolls for attacks made by that unit until the end of that phase.

Indomitable: *The dauntless warriors that make up this army will stand fast even in the face of overwhelming odds.*

Once per battle, after you take a battleshock test for a friendly unit, you can say it is indomitable. If you do so, no models from that unit will flee in that battleshock phase.

Sometimes a battleplan will require you to pick the location in the Mortal Realms where the battle is taking place. Depending on the location you pick, one or more realm rules will apply in the battle. These rules will be included in the battlepack that is being used.

28.0 BATTLEPACKS

Before you can wage war in a game of Warhammer Age of Sigmar, you must select a battlepack.

28.1 BATTLEPACK INSTRUCTIONS

All battlepacks include sections that explain how to select the units in your army and what **special rules** apply when fighting battles using the battlepack. These sections are followed by the **battleplans** that are used when fighting battles using that battlepack.

28.1.1 ARMY SELECTION

This section of the battlepack explains how to pick an army when you fight a battle using the battlepack.

28.1.2 SPECIAL RULES

This section of the battlepack will tell you which optional core rules, such as allegiance abilities and battalion abilities, you must use. It may also include additional special rules that are used when you fight a battle using that battlepack.

28.1.3 MYSTERIOUS TERRAIN

Some battlepacks will instruct one or both of the players to roll on the **Mysterious Terrain table**, below, to determine additional scenery rules that apply to certain terrain features. If this is the case, the rules for the battlepack will specify who rolls on the table and for which terrain features.

D6	Scenery Rule
1	**Damned:** In your hero phase, you can pick 1 friendly unit within 1" of any terrain features with this rule. That unit suffers D3 mortal wounds but you can add 1 to hit rolls for attacks made by that unit until your next hero phase.
2	**Arcane:** Add 1 to casting, dispelling and unbinding rolls for models while they are within 1" of any terrain features with this rule.
3	**Inspiring:** Add 1 to the Bravery characteristic of units while they are wholly within 1" of any terrain features with this rule.
4	**Deadly:** Each time a unit is set up or finishes a normal move, run, retreat or charge move within 1" of any terrain features with this rule, roll a dice. On a 1, that unit suffers D3 mortal wounds.
5	**Mystical:** Add 1 to chanting and banishment rolls for models while they are within 1" of any terrain features with this rule. In addition, models have a 6+ ward while they are within 1" of any terrain features with this rule.
6	**Sinister:** Subtract 1 from the Bravery characteristic of units while they are wholly within 1" of any terrain features with this rule.